The Unconscious: Invention or Discovery?

The Unconscious:
Invention or Discovery?
A Historico-Critical Inquiry

D. B. Klein

If science is not to degenerate into a medley of ad hoc *hypotheses, it must become philosophical and must enter upon a thorough criticism of its own foundations.*

Alfred North Whitehead

The gift of professional maturity comes only to the psychologist who knows the history of his science.

Edward G. Boring

Goodyear Publishing Company, Inc.
Santa Monica, California

Library of Congress Cataloging in Publication Data

Klein, David Ballin, 1897–
The unconscious–invention or discovery?

Includes index.
1. Subconsciousness. 2. Psychology--History.
I. Title.
BF315.K56 154.2 76-28872
ISBN 0-87620-922-3

ISBN: 0-87620-922-3
Y-9223-2

Interior design: Jacki Thibodeau
Permissions: Jane Hellesoe-Henon and Stacey Maxwell
Manuscript editor: David Dexter

Current printing (last digit):
10 9 8 7 6 5 4 3 2 1

Printed in the United States of America

Acknowledgments

Our thanks to the following copyright holders for permission to use material:

Excerpt from G. W. Allport, *Pattern and Growth in Personality* (New York: Holt, Rinehart and Winston, Inc., 1961). Reprinted by permission.

Excerpts from Edwin G. Boring, *A History of Experimental Psychology*, 2nd ed., © 1950, pp. 38, 168, 309–10, 743. Reprinted by permission of Prentice-Hall, Inc., Englewood Cliffs, New Jersey.

Excerpts from K. Bühler, "On Thought Connections," in *Organization and Pathology of Thought: Selected Sources*, Translation and Commentary by David Rapaport (New York: Columbia University Press, 1951).

Excerpt from T. Dobzhansky, "Of Flies and Men," *American Psychologist* 22 (1967): 41–48. Reprinted by permission of the publisher.

Excerpts from Henri F. Ellenberger, *The Discovery of the Unconscious: The History and Evolution of Dynamic Psychiatry*, © 1970 by Henri F. Ellenberger, Basic Books, Inc., Publishers, New York. Reprinted by permission of Basic Books, Inc., and Penguin Books Ltd.

Portions of Letters 228 and 272 from *The Letters of Sigmund Freud–1873-1939*, Selected and Edited by Ernst L. Freud, Translated by James and Tania Stern, © 1960 by Sigmund Freud Copyrights Ltd., London, Basic Books, Inc., Publishers, New York, and The Hogarth Press. Reprinted by permission of the publishers.

Excerpts from Sigmund Freud, *A General Introduction to Psychoanalysis*. Authorized English Translation of the Revised Edition, by Joan Riviere. Reprinted by permission of Liveright Publishing Corporation. Copyright © 1920, 1935 by Edward L. Bernays. Copyright renewed 1948. British edition published by George Allen & Unwin Ltd.

Excerpts from Sigmund Freud, *The Interpretation of Dreams*, translated from the German and edited by James Strachey, published in the United States by Basic Books, Inc., by arrangement with George Allen & Unwin Ltd. and The Hogarth Press Ltd.

Excerpts from *The Collected Papers of Sigmund Freud,* Volumes III, IV, and V, edited by Ernest Jones, M.D. Authorized translation by Alix and James Strachey for Volume III; authorized translations by Joan Riviere for Volume IV; edited by James Strachey for Volume V: published by Basic Books, Inc., by arrangement with The Hogarth Press Ltd. and The Institute of Psycho-Analysis, London, and Sigmund Freud Copyrights Ltd. Reprinted by permission of Basic Books, Inc., and The Hogarth Press Ltd.

Excerpts from *The Life and Work of Sigmund Freud,* Volumes I, II, and III, by Ernest Jones, M.D. © 1953 by Ernest Jones, Basic Books, Inc., Publishers, New York and The Hogarth Press, London. Reprinted by permission of the publishers.

Excerpt from E. R. Hilgard, *Theories of Learning*, 2nd ed., (New York: Appleton-Century-Crofts, Inc., 1956). Reprinted by permission of Prentice-Hall, Inc., Englewood Cliffs, New Jersey.

Excerpt from H. S. Liddel, "Conditioning and Emotions," *Scientific American* 190 (1954): 48–56. Reprinted by permission of the publisher.

Table from D. B. Lindsley, "Psychological Phenomena and the Electroencephalogram," *Electroencephalography and Clinical Neurophysiology* 4 (1952): 443–456.

Excerpt from J. Marmor, *Psychiatry in Transition* (New York: Brunner/Mazel, 1974). Reprinted by permission of the publisher.

Excerpts from G. Murphy and R. O. Ballou, *William James on Psychical Research* (New York: Viking Press, Inc., 1960). Reprinted by permission.

Portion of letter from Ralph Barton Perry, *The Thought and Character of William James* (Boston: Little, Brown and Company, 1935). Reprinted by permission of Alexander R. James, Literary Executor.

Portions of letters from R. B. Perry, *The Thought and Character of William James,* Vol. II (Boston: Little, Brown and Company, 1935). By permission of Alexander R. James, Literary Executor.

Excerpt from R. Rabkin, "Is The Unconscious Necessary?" *International Journal of Psychiatry* 8 (1969): 570–578. Reprinted by permission of the publisher.

Excerpts from J. P. Seward, "The Structure of Functional Autonomy," *American Psychologist* 18 (1963): 702–710. Reprinted by permission of the publisher.

Excerpts from E. von Hartmann, *Philosophy of the Unconscious–Speculative Results According to the Inductive Method of Physical Science*, translated by W. C. Coupland (New York: Harcourt, Brace and World, 1931; London: Routledge & Kegan Paul Ltd.). Reprinted by permission of the publisher.

Excerpts from R. M. Warren and R. P. Warren, *Helmholtz on Perception: Its Physiology and Development* (New York: John Wiley & Sons, Inc., 1968). Reprinted by permission of the publisher.

Excerpts from Lancelot Law Whyte, *The Unconscious before Freud*, © 1960 by Basic Books, Inc., Publishers, New York.

To Elizabeth Isaacs
and
To the Memory of M. Legis Isaacs

Contents

Foreword

It is an unfortunate truism, particularly in the study of human behavior, that most of what has previously been written by eminent scientists and philosophers is forgotten or unknown to modern workers in the field. Indeed the contemporary explosion of scientific periodicals and publications makes this almost inevitable. Nevertheless, one of the consequences of this phenomenon is that old truths are constantly being rediscovered and fallacies long disproven continue to be put forth anew.

One of the extraordinary talents of Professor Klein, superbly demonstrated in his monumental *History of Scientific Psychology* (Basic Books, 1970) and again in the present volume, is that he has not only read extensively, but that he *remembers* what he has read. More than anyone I have ever met, he "knows the history of his science," and thus is able to bring a rare and precious perspective to bear on current concepts and percepts.

One such formulation that has gained widespread acceptance in Western thought, because of the influence of Freud's persuasive writings, is that of "the unconscious" as a separate compartment of the human mind. As such it is frequently and glibly referred to by literary authors, art critics, and psychohistorians no less than by psychoanalysts and other students of human behavior. Professor Klein subjects this concept to a searching and scholarly historical analysis and does so with uncommon perspicacity, logic, and elegance.

One of the problems that one encounters in evaluating some of Freud's concepts is not only that he employed and expounded them in diverse ways as his ideas evolved over half a century, but also that he so often used them loosely and without bothering to define his terms. Thus when subjected to the kind of rigorous evaluative thinking that Professor Klein employs, they are often found wanting.

Yet Dr. Klein would be the first to admit that there is a kernel of correctness in Freud's views on the importance of what he called the unconscious that cannot be ignored. Although many of Freud's more conservative followers would probably reject the statement as too simplistic, Ernest Jones, dean of British psychoanalysts and Freud's official biographer, considered "Freud's own definition" of psychoanalysis to be "simply the study of mental processes of which we are unaware, *of what for the sake of brevity we call the unconscious*" (italics mine). The psychoanalytic method, then, to paraphrase Professor Klein, is aimed at "making the unobserved observable, the implicit explicit, the unknown known, the concealed exposed, and the latent manifest."

What Dr. Klein objects to, however, is the reification of "the unconscious," and the fragmentation of mind into two minds—a conscious one and an unconscious one. He insists, quite properly, on the unity of mental life, and in the end suggests an approach whereby the essential elements of what Freud was describing are retained without breaching that essential unity. One might wish only that Professor Klein had elaborated to a greater extent on information theory and the concept of the brain as a processor and storer of data.

What makes this volume particularly fascinating is the orderly, logical, tightly reasoned process by which Professor Klein arrives at his final conclusions. He writes cogently and with rare lucidity, and illustrates his thesis throughout with insightful and delightful examples. No one will come away from reading this book without a vastly enriched historical, scientific, and philosophic understanding of the complex elements that have gone into the evolution of our current ideas about conscious and unconscious mental processes in human beings.

JUDD MARMOR, M.D.

Franz Alexander Professor of Psychiatry
University of Southern California
and
Former President
American Psychiatric Association

Preface

Preparation for writing this book encompasses more than forty years of active identification with the fields of general, systematic, philosophical, and historical psychology on the one hand and those of mental hygiene, psychopathology, and clinical psychology on the other. Predictably, the concept of mental life as unconscious was found to play a more prominent role in the latter than in the former fields. As a consequence, I kept being reminded of a divergence in outlook between those who approached the study of mental life from the standpoint of classical psychology as contrasted with those who approached the study from the standpoint of psychodiagnosis and psychotherapy. In other words, in the course of my reading, teaching, clinical consulting, and research supervision I was never altogether unmindful of an implicit but persistent problem whose nature and implications I might one day subject to explicit formulation and analysis.

All through the years, at least intermittently, I kept noting and often recording such evidence as chanced to be cited in support of belief in the operation of unobservable or hidden processes presumed to be mental. This evidence was rather heterogeneous. It included alleged unconscious instigators of posthypnotic behavior, ad hoc psychoanalytic interpretations of case histories, laboratory studies of verbal associations attributable to unconscious determinants, and allusions to quasi-mystical unconscious forces to be found in the older journals of psychical research as well as in the newer ones concerned with parapsychology.

It should thus be obvious that in undertaking to write this book I was not starting from scratch; I had a welter of both clear and vague ideas along with a collection of assorted notes when I started to write. Initially there was recurrent concentration upon the implications of what I had come to regard as the crucial question of the unconscious as fact or fiction. A few of these implications are introduced in Chapter 1 in the course of an initial orienting survey of the broad scope of the problem. As noted there, the many meanings of the word *unconscious* proved to be a stumbling block right from the start–it was manifestly impossible to do justice to all these many and often contradictory meanings in a single comprehensive definition. At the same time I realized that just as getting to understand the meaning of words like *unloved, unemployed,* and *undemanding* is contingent upon prior understanding of their antitheses, so understanding of the word *unconscious* presupposes prior familiarity with the concept of consciousness. This made the unconscious a derivative of the conscious and called for a hasty review of some topics directly related to the concept of consciousness, including the question of consciousness in differing animal phyla, shifts in levels of consciousness from alertness to drowsiness, and man's capacity for empathic identification with the consciousness of others.

As stressed in my opening chapter, William James had taken a dim view of the concept of mind as unconscious, finding it incompatible with his hopes for a *science* of psychology. This dim view was also shared by other founding fathers of scientific psychology, who with James had given expression to such negative views prior to 1890, some years before the rise of psychoanalysis. They were thus rejecting pre-Freudian versions of the unconscious. In particular, as discussed in Chapter 2, they were concerned with nineteenth-century views of the unconscious, especially those presented in the successive editions of von Hartmann's *Philosophy of the Unconscious.* Interest in this pre-Freudian unconscious was persistent, since there were twelve editions of his book, with the first appearing in 1868 and the twelfth in 1923. There was even a critical monograph concerned with his views published as recently as 1967. Thus von Hartmann's endorsement of belief in mind as unconscious had lasted for close to a century, which is a chief reason for devoting a whole chapter to his views.

It should be noted that von Hartmann had predecessors and contemporaries–men like Leibnitz, Schopenhauer, and Herbart–who shared many of his views. In fact, by the 1880s belief in the existence of mental states as unconscious had become so widespread that, as considered in some detail in Chapter 3, William James deemed it necessary to subject this belief to a critical examination in his *Principles* of 1890. As just mentioned, he was unable to support this belief in mind as unconscious.

James was not the only pioneer scientific psychologist to repudiate belief in the unconscious. By the 1890s he along with Wundt and Brentano had voiced objections to the unconscious as an explanatory principle in their respective psychological systems. Despite differing psychological standpoints and even though working independently of one another, these three–James,

Wundt, and Brentano—were as one in eliminating the unconscious from what they envisaged as the foundations of a scientific psychology. The name of Ebbinghaus is to be added to these three, for he had come to grips with this issue in his doctoral dissertation which had been based upon a critical analysis of von Hartmann's defense of the unconscious. This was in 1873. Thus, in general, by the time of Freud academic psychology had already examined and evaluated the concept of unconscious mind and had found it unacceptable.

Some twenty years later, when Freud was writing his *Interpretation of Dreams* during the 1890s, he was mindful of this rejection of the unconscious by academic psychology. He referred to it as a conflict between academic and medical psychology. It can also be regarded as a clash between the scientific psychology of the laboratory and the psychoanalytic psychology of the consulting room. The nature and implications of this clash constitute the subject matter of Chapter 4.

Upon reading and re-reading much of what Freud and others had written in defense of the concept of mental states as unconscious, I was struck by the frequency with which the defense centered upon references to hidden motives, repressed wishes, and sublimated desires. Drives to action were thus presumed to be buried in the unconscious, making psychoanalysis a motivational psychology. At the same time and independently of Freud academic psychology was also fostering a dynamic psychology in theories of motivation sponsored by McDougall, Woodworth, and others. Under the circumstances, the subject of unconscious motivation as related to the latter theories called for a separate chapter. As developed in Chapter 5, the subject entails discussion of evidence in support of the latter theories as well as in support of such concepts as instinctive behavior, causation, repression, sublimation, and functional autonomy. In particular, I deemed it important to elaborate upon such distinctions as the one between motivation and causation, another between desires and the causes of desire, and a third between endogenous and exogenous motives.

It was also important to call attention to the many ways the word *unconscious* has come to be used in different psychological contexts. Some of these ways are more factual whereas others are definitely more hypothetical. These ambiguous and hypothetical aspects of the unconscious, as presented in Chapter 6, have to do with the possible testing of some of Freud's hypotheses as well as with the more immediately pertinent issue of the unconscious as a scientific concept.

In Chapter 7, the closing chapter, this issue of the status of the unconscious as a scientific concept is subjected to a retrospective survey against the background of the earlier chapters. Accordingly, in terms of this background I reverted to consideration of the conflict between those who, like James, view the unconscious as fiction and those who, like Freud, acknowledge it as fact. In doing so I hoped to resolve the conflict and thus bring about a rapprochement between academic psychology on the one hand and medical phychology on the other. To accomplish this, as indicated by the title of this chapter, I revived and elaborated upon a somewhat neglected distinction between sensory and non-sensory ideation. In terms of this distinction, so it seemed to me, it is possible to provide for a scientific account of unconscious thinking without having to invoke a *deus ex machina* in the form of a mythical entity called *The Unconscious.*

In the course of working on these chapters I had often to deal with topics of seeming relevance and importance, but whose precise bearing on the central inquiry kept eluding me. On such occasions I found that talking over the difficulty with my wife facilitated clarification. As I talked, hitherto unsuspected implications of a given topic would be disclosed. Often she would call my attention to the obscure and repetitious; sometimes she supplied an apt and illuminating commonsense illustration. In this kind of setting I would continue my monologue until clarification was achieved. As a patient captive audience of one, and far more than she ever suspected, she was of immeasurable help. For this as well as for her constant encouragement I am profoundly grateful.

March, 1976 D. B. K.

I

Introductory Survey

The concept of unconscious mental life has many implications often overlooked in casual, everyday allusions. If taken to mean unconscious consciousness, it is either manifestly contradictory or mysteriously paradoxical. On the other hand it may connote a separate psychic entity presumed to function autonomously as if independent of control by the waking self. Many other functions have been attributed to the unconscious by students of the subject; the more significant ones will be discussed in subsequent chapters. By way of preparation for these later chapters this chapter surveys those aspects of the unconscious having a direct bearing on psychological theory in general, as opposed to those aspects related to rival schools of medical psychology. In other words, this preliminary survey says nothing about an unconscious id, a racial unconscious, unconscious sibling rivalry, or kindred notions belonging to the realm of dynamic psychiatry. It is more concerned with the relevance of the unconscious for normal psychology, rather than abnormal psychology.

In particular, this introductory survey will lead up to this question: Does the concept of mind as unconscious promote human understanding and the interests of psychology as science? This, of course, suggests that the concept might militate against efforts to foster the scientific understanding of mind and personality. William James (1842–1910) recognized this contingency and warned against it in a famous statement to the effect that belief in states of mind as unconscious can become "the sovereign means for believing what one likes in psychology, and of turning what might become a science into a tumbling-ground for whimsies" (James, 1890, Vol. I, p. 163). E. B. Titchener (1867-1927) was equally emphatic in his recognition of such a threat to scientific psychology. He wrote that "we voluntarily leave the sphere of fact for the sphere of fiction" when we "invent an unconscious mind to give coherence and continuity to the conscious" (Titchener, 1917, p. 40). This statement has provocative implications which ought to be explored.

THE UNCONSCIOUS: FACT OR FICTION?

By referring to the unconscious mind as invented, Titchener was evidently thinking of it as improvised rather than discovered. To ask whether an unconscious mind has been discovered or invented is akin to asking whether God has been discovered or invented. Both queries involve such common antitheses as fact versus fiction, the perceptual versus the conceptual, the real versus the imaginary, and the actual versus the hypothetical. Furthermore, just as those convinced of God's existence differ among themselves about the nature of God, so those persuaded of the reality of the unconscious differ among themselves about the nature of the unconscious. In fact, it is impossible to formulate a comprehensive definition broad enough to do justice to what the term has come to mean for the many students of mental life convinced of the real existence of an unconscous mind. There are too many meanings to render this possible. In their psychological dictionary English and English (1958, p. 569), after alluding to *unconscious* as "one of the most troublesome terms in the psychological disciplines," added this comment:

> It is said that there are no less than 39 distinct meanings of *unconscious;* it is certain that no author limits himself consistently to one. And nearly all meanings are closely linked to debatable theories. Any user of the term therefore risks suggesting agreement with theories he may deplore.

Debatable theories are also implicit in the numerous meanings of the word *God.* They include naive, anthropomorphic beliefs; highly abstract, nonanthropomorphic Hegelian Absolutes; trinitarian as contrasted with unitarian beliefs; deistic as opposed to theistic beliefs; parochial versus universal beliefs; and, more recently, debates about God being dead or alive. As a consequence, merely to know that several people confess to a belief in God is not to know whether they share a common belief. Some of them may be harboring a conviction of God's readiness to promote their welfare and to protect them from danger by magical intervention—the kind of conviction which prompts chaplains of rival armies to invoke God's blessings on *their* troops and, by implication, His curses on the troops of the enemy. For those who identify God with Aristotle's unmoved mover or with Spinoza's pantheistic concept, this kind of conviction is childish nonsense. Their God is not to be confused with the personal God of the military chaplains. Although both they and the chaplains profess to believe in God, were they to elaborate upon what their respective beliefs mean in detail, they would find it impossible to endorse one another's beliefs. Analogously, those who entertain convictions about an unconscious mind might find themselves in sharp disagreement were they to dilate upon just what these convictions mean to each of them. Without such clarifying elaboration it is impossible to know what interpretation to place on allusions to man's unconscious mind. For example, in line with the analogy under consideration, one student of the unconscious, Lancelot Whyte (1960, pp. 9-10), is evidently convinced of a relationship between religious faith and the unconscious:

> For today *faith, if it bears any relation to the natural world, implies faith in the unconscious.* If there is a God, he must speak there; if there is a healing power, it must operate there; if there is a principle of ordering in the organic realm, its most powerful manifestation must be found there. The unconscious mind is the expression of the organic in the individual.

Since Whyte fails to supply evidence in support of what he thus attributes to the unconscious, there is no way of evaluating the soundness of whatever reasons prompted the foregoing conclusions. Just why a God, if He does exist, must communicate *via* the unconscious is never explained. It may be that other students of the unconscious also entertain notions of God's nearness to the unconscious. Maybe this accounts for the fact that some of them have recourse to a capitalized designation for the concept—by writing the *U*nconscious.

Comparable allusions to conscious processes do not appear to have elicited capitalized references to the *conscious.* Seemingly, conscious phenomena are too diverse for such a unifying label. On the other hand, processes attributed to the Unconscious seem to be regarded as less heterogeneous and thus amenable to the unifying designation of the capital letter. Similar considerations in the realm of religion are shown in the lower-case designation for the gods of polytheism as contrasted with the upper-case designation for the God of monotheism.

THE UNCONSCIOUS A DERIVATIVE OF THE CONSCIOUS

Neither gods nor God are ever perceived in the course of everyday experience in the way common objects like chairs, birds, and stones are perceived. The existence of such common objects can be demonstrated by direct inspection once they become objects of consciousness or awareness. Those who entertain convictions regarding the existence of divine beings lack this kind of demonstration. As invisible forces, benign powers, omniscient agencies, or however else divine beings may be described, their existence cannot be confirmed by direct inspection. Their invisibility renders them nonperceptible and consequently incapable of becoming objects of consciousness like chairs, birds, and stones. Whatever the believer attributes to them in the way of power, benevolence, interests, or other characteristics is abstracted or derived from his consciousness of such characteristics. His belief or conviction is thus a concept rather than a percept—something he has inferred from his experience rather than something he has actually experienced.

In fact, virtually all statements regarding unconscious mental processes are also inferences or conceptual derivatives from the realm of consciousness. To ascribe some action to an unconscious wish implies knowledge of wishing as a conscious process. This applies to the person interpreting the action and not to the one indulging in the action. In a clinical setting, it applies to the therapist and not to his patient. Unless the therapist were aware of the nature of wishing as it is ordinarily experienced he would not know enough to attribute the operation of an unconscious wish to his patient. In doing so he is maintaining that the action was instigated by a wish even though the patient failed to realize being influenced by a wish. This amounts to an *as if* interpretation: despite his lack of realization the patient acted *as if* he were wishing for something.

By way of illustration, let it be assumed that the action in question concerns the patient's troubles with his son. They clash over the son's vocational choice—the father urging a professional goal entailing a university education and the son, bored by high school studies but fascinated by automobile engines, wanting to enroll at a trade school in order to become a garage mechanic. In discussing the conflict with the therapist the father presents himself as having nothing but the son's welfare at heart. As he sees it, the boy's poor grades at high school are due not to lack of ability but to laziness and his wasting time tinkering with cars. Looking into the future, he foresees the boy as a grown man feeling regret at being a garage mechanic, since many of his current friends will have become lawyers, engineers, bankers, and men of affairs. He sees himself as protecting the boy from such regret. However, what the therapist sees is an unconscious desire for the enhancement of family prestige rather than an unselfish interest in having the boy find a congenial vocational niche for himself. Unwittingly, the father is subordinating the boy's welfare to his own interests. In his clinical notes the therapist might list the father's efforts to justify himself as rationalization, meaning that spurious reasons have displaced the real reasons. As such it would be a self-deceptive maneuver—obvious to the therapist, but of which the father is unaware, or unconscious.

Does this mean that rationalization is always an unconscious process? If it were, then nobody could ever have recognized it. Somebody had to be conscious of it before it could be assumed to be operative as an unconscious process. Emerson was conscious of it when, as Gordon Allport (1897–1967) pointed out, he said, "That which we call sin in others is experiment for us," and other authors, as Allport noted, had also been aware of it under different names, such as *fiction, myth, hypocrisy* (Allport, 1961, pp. 158–159). Not until 1908 did Ernest Jones (1879–1958) introduce the term *rationalization* as a technical designation for the process. Once a process of this kind has been called to our attention by being described and labeled, we can then more readily be aware of it in ourselves.

This holds true for all the mechanisms or dynamisms frequently regarded as unconscious mental processes—projection, introjection, reaction formation, undoing, conversion, and so on. As quirks of the human mind their occurrence has been noted long before technical terms had been coined for them. For example, Epictetus, the Stoic philosopher, seems to have been aware of the mechanism of conversion when he asked, "Why, then, do you walk as if you had swallowed a ramrod?" Shakespeare was an especially acute observer. The mechanism of undoing is revealed by Lady Macbeth as she rubs her hands and cries, "Out, damned spot! out, I say!" Recognition of projection is clearly evident in this quotation from Henry VI: "Suspicion always haunts the guilty mind; the thief doth fear each bush an officer." In Hamlet there is recognition of reaction formation when the Queen says, "The lady doth protest too much, methinks." There is no need to add more examples. The ones cited suffice to show initial awareness of conscious processes before equivalent processes can be assumed to be functioning unconsciously. In this sense the unconscious is a derivative of the conscious. Knowledge of the conscious is thus prior to what is attributed to the unconscious. To stress what has already been mentioned: the attribution is *inferred* from this prior knowledge. Consequently, unless the nature of the conscious processes is understood, there can be no adequate understanding of the inferred unconscious ones. In syllogistic terms this is tantamount to saying that judgment of an inferred conclusion's validity depends upon understanding of the underlying premises.

A CONTINUUM FROM CONSCIOUSNESS TO COMA

In a general sense everybody may be presumed to know something about the nature of consciousness. Even young children soon learn the difference between being asleep and being awake. When a little older they learn the difference between being wide awake and being drowsy, and they may still be in their nursery years when they understand everyday expressions like "I had a dream," "This *really* happened," and "Let's pretend." Later they come to know the meaning of sentences like "He seemed dazed," "The lady fainted," and "The boxer is still unconscious." Of course this last sentence may leave some of them uncertain as to whether the unconscious boxer is just asleep, but the more sophisticated youngsters are likely to suspect that there must be some difference between being knocked unconscious and lapsing into normal sleep.

A very, very sophisticated prodigy may even be prepared to argue that, aside from the word *unconscious,* there is little in common between an unconscious boxer and an unconscious sleeper. As he sees it, the only reason both are said to be unconscious is because neither one is awake, but lack of wakefulness does not necessarily mean suspension of consciousness. A sleeper is conscious of his dreams and, should he be receiving training as a psychoanalyst, will tell his analyst about them, since the analyst regards dreams as revelatory of the sleeper's unconscious. However, this is not to be confused with the meaning of the word *unconscious* as employed with reference to the victim of a knockout. Unlike the sleeper, the knockout victim may remain unconscious for days and have to be hospitalized and fed intravenously. His condition would call for the services of a neurologist rather than a psychoanalyst. Instead of regarding this condition as a form of sleep, the neurologist would describe it as a *coma.*

Whoever first introduced the word *coma* as a medical term must have viewed the comatose patient as being profoundly asleep, since the word comes from the Greek *koma*, meaning "deep sleep." Nevertheless, the condition is to be distinguished from deep sleep.[1] Although both coma and deep sleep are characterized by no vestige of consciousness, electroencephalographic recordings indicate a difference in these states of unconsciousness. In fact, such EEG or brain wave recordings have been used to differentiate various levels of sleep from various levels of wakefulness. D. B. Lindsley, who is both a psychologist and an EEG specialist, has conceived of these levels as a continuum ranging from the inertness of death at one extreme to the most intense degree of consciousness at the other.

The accompanying table gives a clear summary of Lindsley's discussion of this continuum. The table is taken from his paper on psychological phenomena and the the EEG (Lindsley, 1952[2]) and shows how given levels of the continuum are related to EEG changes, to degrees of consciousness, and to control of behavior. It is to be noted that the most extreme level of consciousness or awareness is associated with violent emotional upheaval. Acute anxiety, uncontrollable rage, and disorganized states of panic exemplify this level. Under these conditions one is vividly aware of being aware, but there is reduced capacity to think more clearly and to act efficiently. Emotional excitement and cogent reasoning do not go together and one may be paralyzed by terror and immobilized by rage.

To be left speechless when terrified or enraged is a well-known phenomenon. The victim of stage fright may have trouble controlling his speech muscles. At the time, he is intensely conscious of his distressing visceral commotion and this consciousness of inner turmoil may render it difficult or impossible for him to recall the lines of the speech he had memorized. In the language of Lindsley's table, he is too confused for effective management of the "serial responses" he intended to make. To dissipate the confusion he

---

[1]Deep sleep need not be drugged or anesthetized sleep; for the deep sleep of exhaustion is not indicative of brain pathology. Coma, on the other hand, presupposes such pathology. In addition to brain damage attributable to concussion, coma may also be due to diabetes, liver disease, uremia, low blood sugar, and other disturbances of brain metabolism. An account of such disturbances is supplied by J. F. Fazekas and R. W. Alman in their volume on *Coma* (1962).

[2]In a personal communication dated 1975 Professor Lindsley reported that he saw no reason to introduce any changes in his 1952 table.

Psychological States and Their EEG, Conscious, and Behavioral Correlates

Behavioral Continuum	*Electro-Encephalogram*	*State of Awareness*	*Behavioral Efficiency*
Strong, excited emotion (Fear) (Rage) (Anxiety)	Desynchronized: Low to moderate amplitude; fast, mixed frequencies.	Restricted awareness; divided attention; diffuse, hazy; "Confusion."	Poor (lack of control, freezing-up, disorganized).
Alert attentiveness	Partially synchronized: Mainly fast, low amplitude waves.	Selective attention but may vary or shift. "Concentration" anticipation, "set."	Good (efficient, selective, quick, reactions). Organized for serial responses.
Relaxed wakefulness	Synchronized: Optimal alpha rhythm.	Attention wanders —not forced. Favors free association.	Good (routine reactions & creative thought).
Drowsiness	Reduced alpha & occasional low amplitude slow waves.	Borderline, partial awareness. Imagery & reverie. "Dream-like states."	Poor (uncoordinated, sporadic, lacking sequential timing).
Light sleep	Spindle bursts & slow waves (larger). Loss of alphas.	Markedly reduced consciousness (loss of consciousness). Dream state.	Absent
Deep sleep	Large & very slow waves (synchrony but on slow time base). Random, irregular pattern.	Complete loss of awareness (no memory for stimulation or for dreams).	Absent
Coma	Isoelectric to irregular large slow waves.	Complete loss of consciousness, little or no response to stimulation; amnesia.	Absent
Death	Isoelectric: Gradual and permanent disappearance of all electrical activity.	Complete loss of awareness as death ensues.	Absent

would have to be less conscious of himself. This amounts to saying that by attending to his inner turmoil his attention is diverted from the business at hand; hence the confusion. With attention divided, and the concomitant distraction, he is overwhelmed by too many concurrent impressions. To be overwhelmed by sensory impressions in this way is to be too conscious for integrated control of the situation.

Panic behavior is disintegrated behavior. The victim of panic is overwhelmed by a superabundance of intense sensory impressions; hence his lack of control. On the other hand drowsiness or apathy also militate against effective control. These states are marked by diminished consciousness as contrasted with the excess characteristic of the panic state. For optimal efficiency an Aristotelian golden mean between excess and deficiency appears to be a prerequisite. This is one conclusion to be drawn from consideration of the continuum of awareness outlined in the third column of Lindsley's table. It illustrates one meaning of the concept of consciousness; namely, the capacity to notice or be aware of the entire gamut of external and internal sensations along with imagery based upon these sensations. In accordance with this meaning people talk about being aware of sights, sounds, and other external or exteroceptive sources of stimulation as well as being conscious of hungers, thirsts, and other kinds of internal or interoceptive sources of stimulation.

Another meaning of consciousness, also suggested by the table, refers to the continuum from wakefulness, to sleep, to coma. In terms of this meaning the rested, wide-awake person is said to be fully conscious and is regarded as less conscious when weary and still less conscious when he falls asleep. Should his sleep be the deep sleep of exhaustion, he may be judged to be unconscious. Although he fails to respond to the sound of the alarm clock or when subjected to a mild push, he can be aroused by a loud call or vigorous prodding. In this respect his unconsciousness is different from the unconsciousness of the comatose patient. Although still alive in terms of respiration and heart action, the victim of coma is unresponsive even to forceful means of arousal. He fails to react when his name is shouted or when jabbed by a pin or drenched with ice water. Unlike the exhausted sleeper, he appears to be devoid of sensation and feeling and gives the impression of being a mindless, vegetative organism–unless he can be aroused to wakefulness this impression will persist. Thus it seems that to be mindful means to be awake and to be awake means to be conscious. If this is so, then mind, wakefulness, and consciousness may be synonymous concepts.

CONSCIOUSNESS AND THE EGOCENTRIC PREDICAMENT

The concept of awareness can also be added to these three synonymous concepts, for to be conscious means to be aware of something. It is in this sense that the comatose patient is held to be unconscious, or lacking awareness. He ceases to be unconscious once he gives evidence of being sensitive to sounds or sights or pains or any other provocative source of stimulation. If this be so, then, as a minimal criterion, sensitivity becomes the *sine qua non* of consciousness. However, although we can be directly and immediately aware of our own sensitivity, this is not true of our recognition of the sensitivity of animals or of other persons. Their pains are not our pains in terms of sensory immediacy. In the case of a wounded dog we *infer* its pain from its behavior and in the case of a wounded man we also *infer* his pain even though he, unlike the dog, is able to tell us about it.

Verbal report serves to increase our confidence in the validity of such an inference, but this is not the same as the man's awareness of pain. He *has* the pain and we are now confident that he has it without having it ourselves. Even though we sympathize with him or have an empathic identification with his suffering, nevertheless such sympathy or empathy still leaves us free of his pain. Our conscious content continues to be different from his conscious content. Under the circumstances, our verbal report of what we are experiencing will not be a precise duplicate of his verbal report. He will report being in pain and we will report knowing about his pain. His will be direct knowledge of existing pain while ours will be *inferred* or indirect knowledge about his pain.

The distinction in question is the familiar one William James referred to as the difference between *knowledge of acquaintance* as contrasted with *knowledge-about.* The difference, he noted, is reflected in some languages other than English (1890, Vol. I, p. 221). In Latin the infinitive for "to know" is either *noscere* or *scire*; in French the corresponding terms are *connaître* and *savoir*; and in German they are *kennen* and *wissen.*[3] By way of clarification James declared that he knows the color blue when he sees it and the flavor of a pear when he tastes it—this is knowledge of acquaintance. However, he then added:

> I cannot impart acquaintance with them to any one who has not already made it himself. I cannot describe them, make a blind man guess what blue is like, define to a child a syllogism, or tell a philosopher in just what respect distance is just what it is, and differs from other forms of relation. At most, I can say to my friends, Go to certain places and act in certain ways, and these objects will probably come.

At the risk of mentioning the obvious it might be of some interest to ask whether following James's suggestions would have enabled any two of his friends to have precisely identical knowledge of given color or taste experiences. Supposing each of them had savored fragments of the same pear, would the resulting acquaintance with the pear's "flavor" be the same for the two friends? An affirmative answer has to be based upon inference and cannot be in terms of a reciprocal exchange of sensory impressions. There is no way for them to invade one another's gustatory or olfactory privacy. At best they can compare notes by means of detailed verbal description of their respective "flavors," but this will merely serve to enhance confidence in the validity of the inference. It will not transform the inference into direct ac-

---

[3]There is a suggestion of these German words in the differing connotation of the English words *knowledge* and *wisdom.*

quaintance with the friend's awareness of the pear's taste. The impossibility of effecting such transformation has long been recognized as an insoluble predicament and is commonly referred to as the *egocentric predicament.*

For present purposes it suffices to think of the egocentric predicament as having to do with the inherent privacy of one's thoughts, feelings, perceptions, images, memories, cravings, worries, and related phenomena of consciousness. Because of this privacy such phenomena can never be shared directly with others. This holds true for our observations of surrounding events as well as for our observations of events of our inner life—for the sunsets we look at as well as the ambitions we cherish. It holds true for casual observations of everyday affairs and for the deliberate, controlled observations of the laboratory scientist. As the physicist P. W. Bridgman once noted, "simple inspection of what one does in any scientific enterprise will show that the most important part of science is private" (1945, p. 281).

When the scientist ventures to make his "private" observations and reasonings public by giving lectures and writing technical articles, he still fails to circumvent the egocentric predicament. His hearers and readers have to content themselves with *their* private understanding of what he observed and thought. Their understanding is a function of inferences drawn from what he had to say. If he, as a chemist, describes a new compound as smelling like rancid butter, they infer this to mean a smell akin to or identical with their own experience of such a smell. Lacking such experience they would have to locate some rancid butter and sniff it. Only then could they infer something about the chemist's olfactory experience; but being an inference this would not be the equivalent of a direct personal awareness of the olfactory experience as experienced by the chemist. Moreover, should one of them lack sensitivity to odors there would be no way for him as the victim of anosmia to obtain the experience upon which the inference is based. Consequently, he would be deprived of adequate understanding of the chemist's description.

Our understanding of the experiences of others is thus based upon our own experiences. The more people are like us in the sense of belonging to our social class and sharing our cultural heritage, the more easily we can understand one another. Furthermore, the more highly specialized professional classes become, the less easily can we as outsiders understand what they have to report. Truisms of this sort account for the readiness with which Annapolis graduates identify with naval traditions, the ease with which veteran accountants peruse financial reports, and the facility with which veteran detectives understand the argot of a criminal gang. To outsiders the specialized vocabulary of such groups, being largely incomprehensible to them, may be stigmatized as jargon. Technical words, the esoteric use of familiar words, and the occasional interpolation of foreign words leave them mystified and frustrated; hence their recourse to a derogatory term like *jargon.*

Listening to jargon leaves the uninitiated outsider mystified. He is in the position of a visitor to Madrid who, though ignorant of Spanish, is nevertheless trying to follow the conversation of some natives in the lobby of his hotel. Although he hears their words, he cannot know what they are saying nor what it is they seem to find so amusing. From their laughter he infers the amusement, but he can infer nothing from their talk. In telling about this upon his return home he might not employ the word *infer* in describing the incident. Instead he might say, "I judged one of them had told a joke because they were all laughing, but I couldn't even guess what the joke was about. It must have been some kind of Spanish joke."

Thus our impressions of other people's minds and personalities are matters of judgment, guesswork, and belief–in contrast with affairs of direct, self-validating perception, illustrated by our immediate recognition of familiar objects such as apples, dogs, telephones, and shoes. When other people refer to the latter objects we assume or take it for granted or infer or judge that their awareness of them resembles or may be precisely like our awareness. However, the egocentric predicament renders it impossible to get at their awareness by direct inspection. When they speak of being hungry or tired we can only *judge* their experiences to be more or less the same as when we feel famished or fatigued. Our judgment is influenced not only by their words, but also by their actions and appearance. We can observe the tremors, retarded gait, and sunken cheeks of the starving man just as we perceive the stooped posture, shuffling walk, and drooping eyelids of the exhausted man. These are all indications of conscious states symbolized by simple sentences like "I am hungry" and "I am tired." As indications they enable us to make judgments of the man's trouble.

CONCERNING JUDGMENT OF HUMAN AND ANIMAL CONSCIOUSNESS

In dealing with his patient's troubles the physician makes judgments in terms of complaints made by the patient as well as in terms of what is evident to him in the course of a routine physical examination. The final judgment or diagnosis is the resultant of both sets of indications: the patient's complaints *and* the physician's observations. A medical diagnosis in many instances thus depends on the consciousness of the patient and the consciousness of the examining physician. Complaints in the way of pains, blurred vision, loss of appetite, and ringing in the ears pertain to the consciousness of the patient. As such they are not open to the physician's inspection. For him they are *symptoms* of the illness, just as his findings are *signs* of the illness. Of course, often there are indications of injury or illness which can be observed by both patient and physician. They both can see the swollen joint or the dislocated shoulder or the rash of which the patient complains. In these instances the complaints may be classified as signs as well as symptoms, and the precise term employed becomes a matter of descriptive preference.

A veterinarian does not consider such a preference. His animals have no verbal complaints to make–no symptoms to reveal. All his diagnostic conclusions are the results of signs observable immediately or after having been elicited by routine maneuvers and laboratory reports. This might suggest that, unlike the physician, the veterinarian does his medical work without regard to the consciousness of his patients; but such is not the case. Before undertaking surgery on a sick animal he renders it unconscious by means of an anesthetic. He obviously acts as if his dog and cat patients can experience pain. Moreover, since he sometimes decides that a particular animal is blind or deaf, he is also acting as if his patient is no longer conscious of visual and auditory sensations. Nor does he hesitate to endow his animals with organic sensations in the way of hunger and thirst. Were he to be asked how he knows that animals are conscious of sensations of pain, light, sound, hunger, and thirst he would call attention to the ways their anatomic equipment resembles human anatomy and the ways their reactions to specific modes of stimulation are similar to human reactions. The closer the animal's anatomy resembles human anatomy the more confident he would be of what he attributes to the animal's consciousness. For this reason he would be less hesitant to ascribe consciousness to a chimpanzee than to a frog, and more uncertain about an oyster's consciousness than a frog's. He might even be quite certain that paramecia and other protozoa are incapable of being conscious of anything.

Actually this last issue is not likely to confront him in the course of his practice as a veterinarian. Sick or injured paramecia are not apt to be listed among his patients, so any convictions he might entertain about the consciousness of protozoa would not be founded on intensive and detailed experience with such organisms. One man who did have such experience, however, was the biologist H. S. Jennings (1868–1947), whose 1906 book *Behavior of the Lower Organisms* is replete with experimental reports of their behavior. Neither experiment nor observation, Jennings acknowledged, can serve to confirm or refute any opinion regarding an animal's consciousness. Nevertheless he believed it is often useful to attribute consciousness to an animal as we customarily do in dealing with the dog, since this gives us better understanding and control of the dog's actions. With reference to the question of the consciousness of an amoeba, a protozoan whose nature had become as familiar to him as the nature of dogs becomes familiar to a veterinarian, he had this to say (1965, p. 481):

> If Amoeba were so large as to come within our everyday ken, I believe it beyond question that we should find similar attribution to it of certain states of consciousness a practical assistance in foreseeing and controlling its behavior. Amoeba is a beast of prey, and gives the impression of being controlled by the same elemental impulses as higher beasts of prey. If it were as large as a whale, it is quite conceivable that occasions might arise when the attribution to it of the elemental states of consciousness might save the unsophisticated human being from the destruction that would result from the lack of such attribution. In such a case, then, the attribution of consciousness would be satisfactory and

useful. In a small way this is still true for the investigator who wishes to appreciate and predict the behavior of Amoeba under his microscope.

In thus attributing "elemental states of consciousness" to protozoa Jennings was opposing those biologists who advocated purely mechanistic interpretations of unicellular behavior. The leading proponent of such interpretations at the time was Jacques Loeb (1859-1924). According to his *tropistic theory* the organism's reactions are automatic, forced movements toward or away from given sources of stimulation. Its movement toward a source of light was called *heliotropism* and toward the ground *geotropism.* The upward growth of the stem of a plant is indicative of a heliotropic orientation, just as the downward growth of the roots reveals a geotropic orientation. Similarly, thermotropisms were mentioned in connection with movements induced by changes in temperature. An amoeba or paramecium moving toward a warm object was governed by a positive thermotropism and its retreat from a hot object was attributed to a negative thermotropism. As Loeb regarded it, there was no need to assume any awareness of warmth and cold in order to account for these reactions. They are forced movements just as the movements of the pointer on a compass are forced movements. It can point north without having to be conscious of north, or of north as the opposite of south. This *reductio ad absurdum* may suffice to show the implications of Loeb's tropistic theory as applied to what he called the *mechanistic concept of life* (Loeb, 1912).

Endorsement of this concept is tantamount to holding that principles of physics and chemistry are enough to account for the activities of living creatures. Their chemical constitution and anatomic structure determine their behavior. Consciousness as a supposititious concomitant of behavior is taken to be a mere by-product or epiphenomenon devoid of causal efficacy—akin to the smoke pouring from the furnace of a busy factory. W. K. Clifford (1845-1879), the famous British mathematician and philosopher, introduced a now oft-cited simile to explain this standpoint. He pointed out that, from the standpoint of epiphenomenalism, attributing causal efficacy to consciousness is like arguing that the friendship between the locomotive engineer and the conductor, rather than the metal coupling, accounts for the linkage between the locomotive and the train it is pulling.

Loeb's mechanistic concept, it should be evident, does not require any judgment of a living creature's consciousness. There is no need to ask whether a heliotropism involves awareness of light. It is enough to note how the creature reacts to light as a stimulus, just as it is enough for a student of photography to note that his film is affected by light without having to judge whether or not the film "sees" the light. In terms of Loeb's concept, scientific investigations in psychology can proceed without getting involved in debates about the nature of consciousness or the possible existence of unconscious mental influences. His concept is congruent with the outlook of those psychologists whose behavioristic commitment entails disparagement of mentalistic interpretations. For them mentalism, as contrasted with mechanism, appears to have an unscientific connotation. They prefer to conceive of psychological issues in terms of the language of physics.

There are, however, innumerable psychological issues whose understanding would not be facilitated by exclusive dependence on the physicist's technical vocabulary. How, for example, would talk about cathode rays or Ohm's law enable one to understand the despondency of a jobless man, the terror of a lost child, or a philatelist's interest in old postage stamps? Nor would the language of physics be of much help when trying to understand a monk's asceticism, a sadist's cruelty, a philanthropist's generosity, or a profligate's extravagance.

THE PSYCHOLOGY OF UNDERSTANDING

The list of issues could be extended to include the entire gamut of human interests, values, foibles, eccentricities, aspirations, and whatever else falls within the scope of the psychology of desire and motivation. Consequently, the quest for this kind of understanding becomes a psychological one involving appreciation of the feelings and emotions of other people. It calls for a knowledge of human nature such as that exhibited in the writings of Shakespeare, Dickens, Dostoevski, and Ibsen. Their literary creations reflect an empathic insight into the inner life of their characters. They understood man's hopes, lusts, ideals, frustrations, prejudices, loyalties, triumphs, conflicts, anxieties, and similar emotional ups and downs incident to the pursuit of personal goals.

Viewed in the abstract, the psychology of understanding under consideration is manifestly more conscious than unconscious. Because it calls for self-knowledge and empathy it is a prerequisite for insightful growth in our knowledge of human nature. In fact, Margaret Mead, the anthropologist, regards this as indispensable for understanding alien cultures. As she sees it, "disciplined introspection and empathy are essential to the study of the unique characteristics of human kind" (1976, p. 905). Moreover, this kind of *empathic* understanding is not to be confused with understanding based upon feelings of sympathy.

In the case of sympathy we identify with another person's emotional experience to the extent of at least minimal arousal of the same kind of emotion we attribute to him. Thus his indignation becomes our anger, his terror our fear, and his grief our sadness. By this process of emotional identification an exciting scene on the stage induces excitement in the audience. There is actual emotional arousal, as indicated by changes in breathing, heart action, posture, and facial expression.

Empathy, on the other hand, need not involve such emotional identification. There is appreciation of another individual's joys or sorrows without sympathetic arousal of kindred emotional states. Thus we can understand or appreciate the frustration of the golfer who has missed an important putt even though we do not feel frustrated. A teacher can appreciate the elation of the succesful student and the despondency of the unsuccessful one without having to experience corresponding feelings of triumph and defeat. This makes empathy a more mature and sophisticated response than sympathy. This is so in the sense that empathy is more cognitive than sympathy, calling for greater insight into the nature of the provocative situation. Of course, frequently the empathic reaction also involves sympathy with another person's plight. The two concepts are not mutually exclusive. However, as suggested by the previous examples, they can occur independently of one another.

Furthermore, developmentally considered, it seems safe to say that sympathy comes before empathy. A crying baby in a hospital nursery often seems to provoke crying in the other babies, just as the startled reaction of one animal may initiate a stampede of the herd. Sometimes after an isolated cough a series of coughs may come from an audience, yawns often precipitate other yawns, and laughter engenders laughter. All such familiar reactions are manifestations of sympathy on the part of the infants, animals, and adults—they are different from empathic reactions. In fact, the difference is important enough to merit more than incidental attention.

THE NATURE OF EMPATHIC UNDERSTANDING

Empathy, as already implied, is a distinctively human process. It calls for a certain level of maturity—infants as well as animals are incapable of empathic reactions—and as a reaction it is less spontaneous than behavior attributable to arousal of sympathy. Unlike reactions of sympathy, empathic reactions are initiated for the purpose of better understanding of others. This objective makes empathy more cognitive and more deliberate than sympathy. To play a dramatic role effectively the actor has to empathize rather than sympathize with the character to be portrayed. To accomplish this he has to identify with the kind of personality the role calls for in terms of the play's action. This means interpreting his lines as symbolic of the personality in question. His facial expression, gestures, accent, and tone of voice must also be included in his interpretation. Taken all together it is as if, while on the stage, he were projecting himself into the inner life of another person. In doing so, it might also be said that it is as if he were *feeling himself into* what he has come to understand as the correct interpretation of the playwright's intention. This italicized phrase comes close to the original or root meaning of empathy as a derivative of the German word *Einfühlung.* A literal English translation of the German would be "feeling into." Titchener (1917, p. 417) made this clear by stating that "Empathy . . . is the name given to that process of humanising objects, of reading or feeling ourselves into them."

The "objects" in question were objects of aesthetic interest, since the concept of *Einfühlung* was first employed to account for differences in aesthetic appeal. According to Thomas Munro (1970, p. 222), the art historian, the theory of *Einfühlung* was introduced by F. T. Vischer (1807–1887) in a volume on aesthetics. This was in 1846 so that, as a new German word, the term is not very old. It is even younger as a psychological term, for it was not until the psychologist Theodor Lipps (1851–1914) developed the psychological implications of Vischer's theory that the notion of empathy was given currency in psychological circles. This was started around the year 1903 with the publication of the first volume of a two-volume work by Lipps called *Ästhetik.*

As indicated by the title, Lipps was primarily concerned with an analysis of the nature of aesthetic judgments. For him these judgments involved *Einfühlung,* or empathy, which E. F. Carritt, the Oxford aesthetician and student of the writings of Lipps, interpreted to mean that "Aesthetic pleasure is an enjoyment of *our own* activity *in* an object" (1923, p. 273). As translated by Carritt, Lipps gave his central doctrine this succinct formulation: "All consciousness that there is a psychical existence outside me originates in *Einfühlung,* in the objectification of a feeling of my own aroused in me by another's expression of life" (1923, p. 277).

This amounts to saying that without empathy there can be no understanding or appreciation of the thoughts, feelings, and motives of others. However, it seems that Lipps did not regard his theory of *Einfühlung* as applicable to the notion of an unconscious mind; for, according to James, Lipps had subjected "the notion of unconscious thought . . . to the clearest and most searching criticism which it has yet received" (1890, p. 175).

The "objectification of a feeling" to which Lipps referred indicates that the empathic reaction is a form of projection. As applied to aesthetics, this phase of the Lipps theory may be illustrated by the way people are affected by disturbances of balance and proportion. The sight of a slanting picture often impels us to straighten it. This common impulse, according to Lipps, is due to our projection of the muscular imbalance induced by the sight of the slant to the frame. Similarly, the sight of a very heavy frame suspended by a fragile-looking cord may arouse feelings of uneasiness as the observer projects muscular tensions into the frame as if the frame were getting set for a sudden crash. To revert to what Lipps had said about aesthetic enjoyment: in these instances the displeasure is also a consequence "of *our own* activity *in* an object." This is not to say that Lipps was attributing a feeling of tension to an inanimate object. The feeling is recognized as "our own" and not the object's feeling, just as we can appreciate the potential energy of a coiled spring without endowing the spring with consciousness of energy.

However, should we find ourselves comparing the coiled spring to the tensed muscles of a tiger about to jump and wondering whether the spring is feeling the strain, then we would be on the verge of endowing the spring with incipient consciousness, or what Lipps called "a psychical existence." To treat inanimate objects in this way is to be guilty of the *pathetic fallacy* of attributing human characteristics to objects. Instances of the pathetic fallacy are revealed by literary allusions to "angry clouds," "challenging mountains," "inviting food," "tired machines," and the "cruel storm." Whether descriptive phrases like these are actually indicative of fallacious thinking is open to question. Often they are intended as purely figurative expressions, as if to say: this object reminds me of what it is like to be feeling like this. Only when they are interpreted as literally endowing the inanimate object with distinctively human attributes is the thinking to be stigmatized as fallacious.

The pathetic fallacy is a variant of anthropomorphic thinking in the sense that like anthropomorphism it involves reading human nature into nonhuman objects or events. As a mode of empathic understanding it thus serves as a reminder of the need to guard against error in one's quest for this kind of understanding. We may be mistaken in our judgments of the feelings not only of animals, but also of people. Since the word *pathetic* in the present context has to do with the life of feeling and emotion, such mistaken judgments might also be considered instances of the pathetic fallacy. For example, are we mistaken in attributing pride to the peacock and stubbornness to the mule? If so, the erroneous judgments would serve as instances of the pathetic fallacy. Actually we have no way of knowing what, if anything, like pride and stubbornness these animals are capable of experiencing. We may be reading more into the situation than the facts justify.

A clarifying example of this is supplied by interpretations that have been made of the agitated behavior of cats deprived of their kittens before they are weaned. The signs of distress are understandably judged to be indications of maternal "grief" for the lost kittens, especially since maternal "joy" returns if just a single lost kitten comes back to the mother. However, to attribute grief to the animal would involve the pathetic or anthropomorphic fallacy. As brought out by G. S. Gates many years ago (1928, pp. 174-177), the cat's distress is not the animal equivalent of human mourning. Instead, it is occasioned by painful distention of the mammary glands and is eliminated by the return of a single kitten. It would thus be possible to comfort the 'grieving' cat by means of a "mechanical kitten" in the form of a breast pump.

The feelings and intentions we attribute to people may be as mistaken as those we ascribe to animals. Judgments of character are notoriously fallible and it is not at all unusual for people to be disillusioned in one another. Getting to know the minds of other people—to understand them as they really are—is not easy. Even psychiatrists may require many days of observation before being able to settle questions of the sanity of some of their patients. This entire issue is a venerable one dating back to the early stages of psychology's history in the time of Aristotle (384-322). In fact, Aristotle called attention to it on the very first page of his psychological treatise entitled *De Anima,* meaning *On the Soul.* As employed by Aristotle the word *soul* was not a designation for a ghostly apparition or disembodied specter. Instead it came close to the ordinary connotation of the word *mind;* hence Aristotle had reference to the problem of understanding mind when he wrote: "To attain any assured knowledge about the soul is one of the most difficult things in the world."

FROM MIND AS CONSCIOUS TO MIND AS UNCONSCIOUS

The basic question embodied in the title of this book might justify the following paraphrase of Aristotle's dictum: to attain any assured knowledge or understanding of the unconscious mind is one of the most difficult things in the world. Furthermore, as noted early in this chapter, since the concept of an unconscious mind is a derivative of the concept of a conscious mind, there can be no understanding of the former concept without prior understanding of the latter concept. This is so obvious as to be called a truism. Paradoxically, however, as will be brought out in a later chapter, this was not obvious to Freud; for he ventured to derive the conscious from the unconscious. There is no need to elaborate upon this now. By way of preparation for later chapters the more immediate need is to consider some implications of this truism.

In light of the truism it appears imperative to introduce an account of the psychology of consciousness before saying anything about the psychology of the unconscious. To supply a detailed account would call for a separate volume. As a matter of fact, years ago when psychology was defined as the science of consciousness or experience all introductory textbooks were dealing with the psychology of consciousness. This was during a period following the first official establishment of a psychological laboratory as an integral part of university organization. The place was the University of Leipzig and the year was 1879. Consequently, within the very near future psychology as a self-conscious laboratory science will have been in existence for a hundred years. In terms of historical perspective this is a short span of years; hence the accomplishments of scientific psychology in the family of other science should be judged accordingly. But this is an incidental issue.

A more important issue has to do with the fact that the early pioneer laboratory studies were focused on phenomena of consciousness. The crux of each study called for introspective reports of impressions perceived or judged or discriminated and, if possible, subjected to some kind of measurement. In thus launching psychology as a *science* the founding fathers by their use of techniques of controlled introspection in reality were disregarding and actually rejecting the etymologically literal meaning of psychology as the science of the soul. In effect, for them psychology as science was the study of mind as consciously experienced. This continued, in general, to be the outlook of most academic psychologists until the early decades of the present century. By the 1920s, with the rise of behaviorism under the aegis of John B. Watson (1878–1958), a drastic change took place. Introspective observation was stigmatized as unscientific and thus reports based upon it were held to be suspect. In fact, as a behaviorist Watson was prepared to deny the existence of mind and consciousness. He did this quite bluntly in the following sentence during the course of an address delivered at a symposium concerned with *The Unconscious* (1927, p. 96): "If the behaviorists are right in their contention that there is no observable mind-body problem and no separate entity called mind—then there can be no such thing as consciousness and its subdivision."

The preceding sequence of changes gave rise to a quasi-humorous comment to the effect that psychology had first lost its soul, then it became mindless, and finally lost consciousness and was left with unconscious or nonconscious behavior. Of course, not all psychologists became followers of Watson, so there was no complete cessation of interest in phenomena of consciousness; but there was widespread distrust of introspection and increasing stress on the importance of operational definitions. Textbooks no longer defined psychology as the study of consciousness. Instead it became the study of experience as dependent on the experiencing person or the study of human and animal nature or the science that studies the behavior of human beings and animals. Most of them acknowledged the difficulty of providing a satisfactory definition. Indeed this continues to bother writers of introductory textbooks. For example, within the very recent past Brown and Herrnstein faced the difficulty quite candidly by starting their introductory textbook with this opening sentence (1975, p. 3): "We may as well have the scandal out at once and get it over with: 'psychology' cannot be defined."

What makes psychology as science refractory to a simple clarifying definition is its broad scope and the imprecision of some of its key terms. Its enhanced scope has become evident in recent years by a revival of interest in and study of conscious phenomena—reflected in a burgeoning literature[4] dealing with such varied phases of consciousness as meditation, dreaming, relaxed wakefulness, daydreaming, biofeedback, and awareness of visceral and glandular changes. Were the founding fathers cognizant of this literature, it seems safe to say, they would welcome the studies in question as elaboration of their pioneer studies of the nature of conscious content.

It is important to bear in mind that the founding fathers were engaged in their studies of conscious content in order to safeguard the status of psychology as science. It was as if they were effecting its transformation from a mental philosophy into a genuine science. At the time—during the last third of the nineteenth century—there were some philosophers who had espoused the doctrine of unconscious mental processes. This was years before Freud

---

[4]By this time the relevant bibliography would call for a list of hundreds of books and articles. With reference to the phases just listed the following might be consulted: Ornstein on consciousness (1972), Wallace and Benson on meditation (1972), the Woods and Greenhouse anthology on dreams and dreaming (1974), Foulkes and Fleisher on relaxed wakefulness (1975), Singer on daydreaming (1975), Wickramaskera on biofeedback (1974), and Miller on awareness of visceral and glandular changes (1969). A summary review of some of these and related topics is to be found in a special section of the *Saturday Review* of February 22, 1975, entitled "Mind and Supermind—Expanding the Limits of Consciousness." It introduces both factual and decidedly speculative data pertaining to parapsychology, biofeedback, meditation, and mystical and quasi-religious experiences. The section also provides a list of close to thirty organizations engaged in what is described as consciousness research.

had come out in its support. In their view this doctrine with its advocacy of belief in unconscious consciousness could not be endorsed. It constituted a threat to psychology's scientific aspirations and hence had to be rejected. In other words, this nineteenth-century rejection of the unconscious was not occasioned by the rise of psychoanalysis. Instead, as explained in the next chapter, it was precipitated by and directed against pre-Freudian versions of the unconscious, especially as reflected in a widely circulated book, Eduard von Hartmann's *Philosophy of the Unconscious.*

REFERENCES

Allport, G. W. 1961. *Pattern and Growth in Personality.* New York: Holt, Rinehart and Winston.

Bridgman, P. W. 1945. "Rejoinders and Second Thoughts." *Psychological Review* 52: 281–284.

Brown, R., and Herrnstein, R. J. 1975. *Psychology.* Boston: Little, Brown and Company.

Carritt, E. F. 1923. *The Theory of Beauty.* London: Methuen & Co.

English, H. B., and English, A. C. 1958. *A Comprehensive Dictionary of Psychological and Psychoanalytical Terms.* New York: Longmans, Green and Company.

Fazekas, J. F., and Alman, R. W. 1962. *Coma–Biochemistry, Physiology, and Therapeutic Principles.* Springfield, Illinois: Charles C. Thomas.

Foulkes, D., and Fleisher, S. 1975. "Mental Activity in Relaxed Wakefulness." *Journal of Abnormal Psychology* 84: 66–75.

Gates, G. S. 1928. *The Modern Cat: Her Mind and Manners.* New York: The Macmillan Company.

James, W. 1890. *Principles of Psychology,* Vol. I. New York: Henry Holt and Company.

Jennings, H. S. 1965. "On the Continuity of Psychological Processes." *A Source Book in the History of Psychology,* edited by R. J. Herrnstein and E. G. Boring, pp. 472–481. Cambridge: Harvard University Press.

Jones, E. 1908. "Rationalisation in Every-Day Life." *Journal of Abnormal Psychology* 3: 161–169.

Lindsley, D. B. 1952. "Psychological Phenomena and the Electroencephalogram." *Electroencephalography and Clinical Neurophysiology* 4: 443–456.

Loeb, J. 1912. *The Mechanistic Concept of Life.* Chicago: University of Chicago Press.

Mead, M. 1976. "Towards a Human Science." *Science* 191: 903–909.

Miller, N. E. 1969. "Learning of Visceral and Glandular Responses." *Science* 163: 434–445.

Munro, T. 1970. "Aesthetics." In *Encyclopaedia Britannica,* Vol. 1, pp. 221–224.

Ornstein, R. E. 1972. *The Psychology of Consciousness.* San Francisco: W. H. Freeman and Company.

Singer, J. L. 1975. "Navigating the Stream of Consciousness–Research in Daydreaming and Related Inner Experience." *American Psychologist* 30: 727–738.

Titchener, E. B. 1917. *A Text-Book of Psychology.* New York: The Macmillan Company.

Wallace, R. K., and Benson, H. 1972. "The Physiology of Meditation." *Scientific American* 226: 84–90.

Watson, J. B. 1927. "The Unconscious of the Behaviorist." In *The Unconscious—A Symposium,* pp. 91–113. New York: A. H. Knopf.

Whyte, L. L. 1960. *The Unconscious before Freud.* New York: Basic Books, Inc.

Wickramaskera, I. 1974. "Heart Rate Feedback and the Management of Cardiac Neurosis." *Journal of Abnormal Psychology* 83: 578–580.

Woods, R. L., and Greenhouse, H. B., eds. 1974. *The New World of Dreams—An Anthology.* New York: Macmillan Publishing Co.

2

Von Hartmann's Pre-Freudian Unconscious

As noted at the close of the preceding chapter, the concept of mind as unconscious had aroused opposition even before the rise of psychoanalysis. The concept had already ceased to be a novelty by the 1870s, many years before Freud had given it currency. In fact, in his survey of pre-Freudian references to it Lancelot Whyte has written that "it cannot be disputed that by 1870–1880 the general conception of the unconscious mind was a European commonplace, and that many special applications of this general idea had been vigorously discussed for several decades" (1960, pp. 169–170). Moreover, as noted by Whyte, the latter vigorous discussion was the culmination of allusions to the concept stemming from a few incidental ones in the seventeenth and eighteenth centuries and the more frequent and increasingly deliberate ones of the nineteenth century. More than forty writers are listed by Whyte as having preceded Freud in "the successive discovery of the . . . unconscious mind in post-Cartesian Europe."

Whyte seems to have taken the existence of unconscious mental states for granted. This is suggested by the fact that his post-Cartesian writers all contributed to the "discovery" of such states, just as post-medieval explorers can be said to have contributed to the discovery of new lands across the Atlantic. In terms of this analogy it is as if Whyte were thinking of the unconscious mind not as a hypothetical construct, but as an inferred reality indicative of hitherto unknown realms of mental existence. This was evident from his opening chapter in which he gave italicized emphasis to being "concerned with the developing awareness . . . of *the need to infer* from the facts of immediate conscious experience *the existence of unconscious mental* processes" and also to being concerned with the European tradition "that first gave this inference clear conceptual formulation" (p. 11). He was not at all "concerned" with writers who had entertained misgivings about such an inference. At all events he failed to draw up a list of writers who had questioned the conclusions reached by those mentioned in his list of those who had contributed to the "discovery" of the unconscious mind. This failure is understandable in view of his own unquestioned acceptance of the reality of mind as unconscious.

In this connection it is especially interesting to note that Whyte failed to consider the critical stand taken by James in the *Principles* of 1890. There is just incidental reference to James in two places and neither one has to do with the *Principles.* That a man of his erudition was unacquainted with this classic is hard to believe, as is that in his survey of "the unconscious before Freud" he had overlooked the stand taken by James. What makes such possible oversight of particular interest is that James had anticipated Whyte with reference to the importance of the 1870s for studies of the unconscious. They both mention some of the same writings on the unconscious published during this decade, in view of which James had asked, "Can states of mind be unconscious?" In his answer, as mentioned in the introductory chapter, James found belief in mental states as unconscious to be "the sovereign means for believing what one likes in Psychology, and of turning what might become a science into a tumbling-ground for whimsies" (Vol. I, p. 163).

More than ten closely printed pages are devoted to a critical examination of evidence that had been cited in support of a belief in unconscious mental states. As is brought out in Chapter 3, James found this evidence unconvincing. Whyte's failure to consider the negative evaluation of this evidence is to be regretted; otherwise he might have been on the alert for the "whimsies" James found in these writings of the 1870s.

WHYTE'S RECOGNITION OF VON HARTMANN

In particular he might have been more critical of one work in which James found the concept of unconscious mental states to have been "most systematically urged" (Vol. I, p. 164). Whyte refers to this work at some length and by way of implicit commendation writes, "its influence throughout Europe has sometimes been underestimated" (1960, p. 163). This was Eduard von Hartmann's *Philosophy of the Unconscious.* James and Whyte reacted differently to the evidence "urged" by von Hartmann in support of the unconscious, with James questioning its cogency and Whyte seeing it as preparation for later endorsement of Freudian teachings. It must be realized that James read von Hartmann long before the emergence of the latter teachings, so his was a pre-Freudian critique. On the other hand, Whyte before reading von Hartmann had already been convinced of the cogency of Freud's evidence in support of belief in the unconscious. For this reason, as suggested by the following quotation, although not unmindful of shortcomings in von Hartmann's work, he could nevertheless admire it as setting the stage for Freud's later handling of these shortcomings (1960, pp. 164–165):

> His work is an extraordinary achievement in 1868, and it proves that when Freud was twelve years of age, twenty-six aspects of unconscious mental activity in man had already been considered in detail in a famous work. But it is neither good philosophy nor good science. It does not state what is known and what is not known; what are the real problems; how they should be solved; or what effect their solution might have on man.

Whyte then presents several passages from von Hartmann's "extraordinary achievement" by way of showing "that von Hartmann could see far in 1868." To understand what Whyte believed von Hartmann "could see," and what James believed he had so "systematically urged," it is necessary to become more familiar with the concept of the unconscious as envisaged by von Hartmann. His treatment was so detailed and complex that a full account of his views is out of the question. Fortunately, though, for present purposes there is no need for such full treatment; consideration of some of his key ideas will suffice. But before turning to these key ideas a few facts about von Hartmann's life and work ought to be introduced.

BIOGRAPHICAL SKETCH

Eduard von Hartmann was born in 1842 and died in 1906—his life spanned the period marked by the emergence of the founders of modern psychology. This means he was a contemporary of men like Wundt, Brentano, James, Bain, Fechner, Helmholtz, Ribot, Galton, and others who had directly or indirectly given direction to the new psychology of the laboratory by the decade of the 1890s. He was not actively associated with the experimental investigations being prosecuted by its sponsors; instead his influence on the developing psychology of the time was almost entirely a function of his ardent advocacy of the unconscious. Whether this served to enhance psychology's efforts to become increasingly scientific is subject to debate. His advocacy was enthusiastically welcomed by some and vehemently spurned by others.

Current historians of psychology do not list him among the founding fathers of scientific psychology. However, one of his contemporaries, G. Stanley Hall (1844-1924), included von Hartmann as one of the six men selected for his 1912 book entitled *Founders of Modern Psychology.* In short, he seemed to regard von Hartmann as much a "founder" as Fechner, Helmholtz, and Wundt. At least this is suggested by the title of the book; but it is hardly supported by the chapter devoted to von Hartmann's specific teachings and many writings. Nevertheless, probably the most detailed account in English of von Hartmann's life and work is to be found in this chapter. It contains some personal reminiscences of Hall's visits with von Hartmann during his student days in Germany, and at the close of the chapter there is a list of more than forty of von Hartmann's publications (1912, pp. 241-243).

His publications ranged over many fields and kept him occupied throughout his adult life. From the year 1867 when he obtained his doctorate at the University of Rostock until many decades later there was a steady output of publications, some of them appearing posthumously. He was not distracted by any academic responsibilities since he never held a teaching post. In fact, as a semi-invalid afflicted with a rheumatic impairment of his knees, he was forced to lead a quiet, sheltered life free from the distractions of travel and engagements away from home. But he compensated for these restrictions by extensive and varied intellectual journeys as revealed by his bibliography. Thus he wrote on metaphysics, on politics, on drama, on religion, on ethics, on aesthetics, on Darwinism, on psychology, on Romeo and Juliet, and even on spiritualism. He even wrote a compendium or *Grundriss* of systems of philosophy that required eight volumes for its completion.

This staggering productivity was in addition to his best known work, his *Philosophy of the Unconscious.* Even this kept him busy revising successive editions after the first one in 1868, ending with the posthumous appearance of the twelfth in 1923. The first English translation was based on the ninth German edition and was published in 1884 and reprinted in 1931 in New York. In addition to this translation, Darnoi's study is an excellent source of information in English: *The Unconscious and Eduard von Hartmann–A Historico-Critical Monograph.* The appearance of this study in 1967 indicates that interest in von Hartmann's unconscious of 1868 has persisted for almost a century. What follows, unless otherwise noted, will be based upon Darnoi's study and the 1884 English translation of the original.

Von Hartmann's book has this revealing subtitle: "Speculative Results According to the Inductive Method of Physical Science." This suggests the prospect of conclusions based upon more or less plausible conjectures as determined by inductive reasoning about relevant data. The relevant data and the conjectures, it soon become evident, had to do with Hegel's dialectics, for early in Volume I von Hartmann declared, "It may be said . . . that the theme of the present book is mainly the elevation of Hegel's unconscious philosophy of the Unconscious into a conscious one" (1884, p. 22). Such endorsement of Hegelianism, as might be expected, set the stage for adventurous ideational exploration over vast areas.

The scope of these exploratory ventures does not lend itself to easy description. Nevertheless, it can at least be hinted at by noting the general organization of the book. The book actually consists of three books or volumes. In Volume I the reader is introduced to two long accounts dealing with (*a*) "the manifestations of the unconscious in bodily life" and then (*b*) "the unconscious in the human mind." Volume II is devoted to the "metaphysics of the unconscious" and Volume III is concerned with "the irrationality of volition and the misery of existence." At the end of the latter volume "the physiology of the nerve-centres" is treated in a concluding Appendix.

THREE LEVELS OF THE UNCONSCIOUS

The three volumes reflect von Hartmann's recognition of three layers or levels of the unconscious and they also reflect his indebtedness to earlier writers, particularly Hegel and Schopenhauer. In general, like Schopenhauer, he is pessimistic in his philosophic outlook, as already suggested by his reference to "the misery of existence." The philosophic outlook of Hegel is clearly suggested by the first of the three layers of the unconscious, which von Hartmann called the *absolute* unconscious and regarded as the matrix or spiritual foundation of the universe from which the other layers originate. One of these, the *physiological* unconscious, was assumed to be the dynamic source of evolutionary processes involved in the creation of all forms of life from the simplest organism to man. The third layer was the *psychological* unconscious, deemed to be the source of all experienced phenomena or of every kind of awareness or state of consciousness. This made consciousness dependent upon or a function of the psychological unconscious. From this viewpoint von Hartmann was revealing the influence of Kant, to the extent that the unconscious was identified with Kant's noumenal world and the conscious with Kant's phenomenal world. Another way to put this is to equate the unconscious with Kant's *Ding an sich,* "thing-in-itself," and the conscious with the objectively experienced Kantian phenomenal world. Moreover, in relating the unconscious to the "irrationality of volition" von Hartmann was borrowing from Schopenhauer's interpretation of Kant's thing-in-itself, since Schopenhauer had explicitly identified volition or will with the thing-in-itself.[1]

In addition to Kant, Hegel, and Schopenhauer there are many other writers mentioned by von Hartmann as having influenced his thinking about the unconscious. Among these are Leibnitz, Hume, Fichte, Herbart, Fechner, Carus, and even Wundt. The more than a thousand pages of the book are thus the outcome of the confluence of many streams of ideation stemming from a diversity of philosophic origins. The result is a miscellany of fact and fancy, of realism and idealism, of physics and psychophysics, of physiology and psychology, of the abstract and the concrete, of induction and deduction, of the a priori and the empirical, and—in general—of the known and unknown or unknowable. To reduce such a miscellany to a comprehensive summary is out of the question. However, a few examples from different parts of the book may help to get a general impression of its variegated contents. Specifically, these examples may accomplish two objectives: first, to reveal a few of the vivid examples said to account for the popular success of the book, and second, to reveal a few of the "whimsies" James associated with the hypothesis of unconscious mental life.

---

[1] Schopenhauer's discussion of "the world as will" is characterized by repeated references to this identification with the Kantian distinction. The following sentence illustrates (Edman, p. 75): "The *will* as a thing-in-itself is quite different from its phenomenal appearance, and entirely free from all the forms of the phenomenal, into which it first passes when it manifests itself, and which therefore only concerns its *objectivity,* and are foreign to the will itself."

SOME SPECIFIC EXAMPLES

By way of introduction to specific examples of von Hartmann's speculations it may be of interest to note what he has to say about "consciousness in plants." After describing how the hinged blades of the leaves of the Venus flytrap close in on the ensnared insect, he wrote that the leaf "*feels* the struggling of the insect." In this connection he declared, "we have thus found consciousness in the plant."

Von Hartmann also found volition to be operative in the spinal segments[2] of a headless frog. In his own words:

> But now, if the ganglia of lower animals have their independent wills, if the spinal cord of a decapitated frog has its will, why should not the so much more highly organized ganglia and spinal cord of the higher animals and man also have their will?

As a matter of fact von Hartmann was emphatic in giving the latter question an affirmative answer. In this glorification of will as an unconscious process he was following Schopenhauer. Moreover, this process of willing was conceived of as the goal-directed execution of an intention. The following quotation will suffice as illustration: "The *dog* will not separate itself from its master; it *wills* to save the child who has fallen into the water; the bird *will* not let its young be injured . . ." (italics added).

From the foregoing it appears that von Hartmann was ready to endow animals with purposive action. Furthermore, as already suggested, he was also ready to interpret reflex behavior as purposive. This extreme endorsement of teleology is clearly indicated in this sentence taken from Volume III and thus a product of material cited in the first two volumes: "The most certain proof of the inner psychical side of the reflex process is the *teleological* character of this reaction, which is expressed in the thoroughgoing purposiveness of the physiological . . . reflexes." As might be expected, instincts as well as reflexes were interpreted teleologically, with the concept of instinct being defined as "purposive action without consciousness of the purpose." Instinctive behavior was thus regarded as being regulated by un-

---

[2]Actually, von Hartmann was not the first to attribute volitional consciousness to spinal reflexes. In a monograph of 1853 dealing with "the sensory functions of the vertebrate spinal cord" the physiologist Eduard Pflüger had already arrived at this conclusion. Pflüger's stand was criticized by E. B. Holt in his 1914 volume on *The Concept of Consciousness* (p. 204), and years later Boring considered the issue in his *History* and suggested that the question of consciousness at the spinal level is a "pseudoproblem" and "insoluble because the answer to it depends on the definition of consciousness." By way of explaining Pflüger's stand Boring had this to say (1950, p. 38):

> Pflüger argued that consciousness is a function of all nervous action, that you cannot distinguish between the action of the brain and the cord, and that spinal reflexes must therefore be regarded as conscious. He pointed out that these reflexes are purposive in the sense that they are specifically localized and useful to the organism. The frog's leg scratches the exact point where its skin has been irritated by the application of acid.

conscious mental forces rather than by nonconscious bodily mechanisms. Such a force, he held, accounts for the hexagonal precision of the honeycomb's cell, since the "bee . . . carries in itself the unconscious representation of the hexagonal cell, accurate to half an angular minute."[3] A similar force, he indicated, enables the herbivorous animal to be sensitive to the presence of a carnivorous beast; as illustration he reported that horses become terrified when first confronted with the sight or smell of carnivores.

To account for the horse's terror von Hartmann had recourse to what James would doubtless have classified as a striking "whimsey," since the horse's reaction was attributed to "unconscious clairvoyance"[4] or clairvoyant intuition. Nor was the magic of clairvoyance limited to horses, as indicated by the following example:

> . . . when pigeons and dogs, after having been turned around twenty times in a sack and carried off to an unknown region, nevertheless run home in a straight line, no one can say anything more than that their instinct has guided them, *i.e.*, the clairvoyance of the unconscious has enabled them to divine the right path.

The preceding quotation is taken from Volume I and was introduced as one of "the manifestations of the unconscious in bodily life." However, it exemplifies relatively restrained speculation when compared with this tribute to God's clairvoyance in Volume II and is thus revelatory of the "metaphysics of the unconscious" (p. 247):

> Of this unconscious clairvoyant intelligence we have come to perceive that in its infallible purposive activity, embracing out of time all ends and means in one, and always including all necessary data within its ken, it infinitely transcends the halting, stilted gait of the discursive reflection of consciousness, ever limited to a single point, dependent on sense-perception, memory, and inspirations of the Unconscious. We shall thus be compelled to designate this intelligence, which is superior to all consciousness, at once unconscious and *super*-conscious.

ON DEPARTURES FROM THE INDUCTIVE METHOD

The foregoing excursion into the "metaphysics of the unconscious" culminating in the paradox of a "*super*-conscious" unconsciousness illustrates von Hartmann's speculative daring. By identifying the latter unconsciousness with God's intelligence he was evidently disregarding his announced intention

---

[3] Cited by Whyte (p. 165).

[4] As pointed out by Darnoi (p. 33), this is a literal translation of the German word *Hellsehen* employed by von Hartmann and meaning "to see by means of clairvoyance."

of arriving at "speculative results according to the inductive method of physical science." Dogmatism had replaced the empiricism of induction. Having conceived of the unconscious as the metaphysical equivalent of Kant's noumenal realm there was no way of either proving or disproving whatever one's fancy attributed to this realm; hence fancy might triumph over fact.

Incidentally, he had such confidence in the validity of the Kantian metaphysics that he did not hesitate to write as if Kant had already discovered the unconscious. At all events, even though von Hartmann wrote his philosophy of the unconscious long before the rise of psychoanalysis, he introduced what might be construed as a Kantian anticipation of a Freudian tenet when he wrote, "Kant was the first who sought in the unconscious for the essence of sexual love" (Vol. I, p. 22). Whether this meant a Kantian quest for sexual love in the Kantian noumenal world or in the Kantian transcendental realm of apperception[5] was not made clear.

What was made clear, though, by this confident appeal to a Kantian unconscious so early in his very long book, was von Hartmann's unquestioning endorsement of the concept of mind as unconscious. Uncertainty or skepticism regarding the scientific justification for the concept was conspicuous by its absence. It was almost as if his "inductive method" were not so much for the purpose of bringing something hitherto unknown to light as for the purpose of winning support for an a priori conviction. Accordingly, from this viewpoint his method may have been more deductive than inductive.

In reality his method is difficult if not impossible to classify in terms of this last dichotomy. For example, how shall findings attributed to "clairvoyant intuition" be classified? Is the attribution of "feelings" to plants a product of inductive or deductive reasoning, or is it a consequence of empathic dogmatism or projection? As must be obvious, von Hartmann failed to limit himself to "the inductive method of physical science" as announced in his subtitle. It seems that he used a variety of approaches rather than a single one and that some of them were too unsystematic to be called *methods*; hence their designation as *approaches* may be less misleading. In some respects this is a minor issue reducible to the problem of finding appropriate descriptive vocabulary.

A more momentous and challenging issue involved evaluation of his work as a whole. In other words, how did critics judge his work? One way to approach this is to ask whether the successive editions of his book aroused a preponderance of favorable or unfavorable critical comment.

---

[5]Kant's *Critique of Pure Reason*, among many other psychological distinctions, makes a distinction between empirical apperception and transcendental apperception. The former involves direct experience, but the latter eludes direct observation. Being transcendental, it is unconscious in one of the meanings of unconsciousness. As a concept it was presumed to account for the unity of consciousness; hence the famous Kantian phrase "transcendental unity of apperception." According to Kant, this kind of apperception, although not perceptible, is nevertheless "thinkable" and given in "intuition" as "pure *a priori* knowledge."

HOW THE BOOK WAS JUDGED BY HALL

The fact that the book, as indicated by the twelve editions from 1868 to 1923, was a publishing success is of course not necessarily indicative of its endorsement by the scientific community. This fact does indicate continuing interest in von Hartmann's speculations by different groups of readers over a span of five or more decades, however. Some of these readers had occasion to register their opinions of the book in various printed media. According to Hall, such printed reactions to his book were noted and collected by von Hartmann. These he published in a prospectus containing "scores of excerpts from the daily and periodical press from Russia to California commenting upon his system" and from which Hall culled some representative of dispraise and others representative of acclaim as shown in these two paragraphs (pp. 189–190):

> Professor Michelet . . . expressed "honest pity" for an author who brings such "miserable nonsense" into the philosophical mart. J. C. Fischer pronounced it a "pyramid of absurdity," fit to excite "universal laughter." One writer averred that von Hartmann had "shamefully duped the world"; another called his book a "snarl of idiotic stupidity"; "reason run mad"; "the odor of death pervading the whole volume"; "purely pathological"; "frivolity and pretense"; "the jugglery of logic"; "a plea for moral bankruptcy"; "a philosophic Dunciad"; "an apotheosis of ignorance and old Mother Night"; and similar verdicts almost by the score have been pronounced by adversaries. Dr. Hausermann feared that the doctrine of the infallibility of the Unconscious would tend to the notion of a potential infallibility of the pope.
>
> On the other hand, Dr. Lasson considered it one of the best expressions of the tendency of modern times, admirably calculated to reconcile not only Hegel and Schopenhauer, but the classic works of German philosophy with the methods and results of modern science. Prof. Kapp called it the inauguration of a "new way of regarding the universe." Other writers too numerous to mention have acknowledged his system to be "brilliant," "genial," of a "thoroughly pure and noble moral tone," "a remarkable bit of culture history which will survive the next century," "suggestive to an unparalleled degree," etc., etc., and a writer in the *Journal of Speculative Philosophy* even called it "encouraging," elevating and ennobling. It is probably not too much to say with Dr. Kirchmann that its reception not only among scholars but throughout the reading world was unprecedented in the previous history of philosophy, and that on the whole von Hartmann is treated with increasing respect even by his enemies.

Hall failed to supply evidence for the "increasing respect" allegedly being accorded von Hartmann by his enemies. In fact, after a page or two of rather hyperbolic tribute to the effect that von Hartmann has "vindicated the ideal against materialism" and has "erected a new altar to the unknown God," Hall seemed to register decreasing respect for von Hartmann by the following comment (p. 192):

> On the other hand, that both in personal intercourse and in the tone of most and especially the later of his writings he was often arrogant, arbitrary, and dogmatic cannot be denied. His constructions were often painfully forced, his analyses fanciful, and he was probably more than suspected of the vanity of the neologist which inclined him to express views and to form paradoxes whose strongest commendation to his own mind was that no one before him had uttered or even seen them. He was not seldom more ingenious in supporting or defending his positions than philosophical in choosing them, but the event showed no reason to believe the predictions of some of his opponents that . . . he would end . . . as an unmitigated quack and fanatic.

NEGATIVE JUDGMENTS BY EBBINGHAUS AND BY JAMES

Had it occurred to Hall, he might have added that if the charge of quackery had been widespread and valid, von Hartmann's views would have been ignored in university circles—yet by the 1870s they had become a subject for doctoral dissertations. In fact, it was in 1873 that a young man who was to make his mark as one of the pioneer experimental psychologists was awarded his doctor's degree by the Bonn University after successful defense of a dissertation concerned with von Hartmann's *Philosophy of the Unconscious.*[6]

This was Hermann Ebbinghaus (1850–1909), whose name is likely to remind psychologists of nonsense syllables, the saving method, curves of forgetting, and the completion test. All these are to be listed among his contributions to laboratory psychology and serve to establish him as one of the founding fathers of scientific psychology.[7] His interest in the methodology of science as applied to psychology was already manifest in his reaction to von Hartmann's work on the unconscious, as Woodworth made clear in a memorial tribute to Ebbinghaus. After noting that Ebbinghaus had treated von Hartmann's work "in severely critical fashion," Woodworth had this to say about the dissertation's implications for psychology as science (1909, pp. 253–254):

> . . . we have evidence that Ebbinghaus already had advanced ideas regarding the proper scope of psychology—the evidence being contained in two of the "theses" which he undertook to defend in his doctor's examination. These were that "psychology, in the widest sense, belongs under philosophy in no more intimate way than natural philosophy belongs there"; and that "existing psychology consists more of logical abstractions and verbal classification than of knowledge of the real elements of mind."

[6]The German title of the dissertation, as cited by Boring, was *Ueber die Hartmannsche Philosophie des Unbewussten* (1950, p. 431).

[7]For an older appreciative survey of these contributions see the section on Ebbinghaus in Boring's history (1950, pp. 386–392). A more recent survey along with an outline of changes in the way of "sophisticated methodology" that have come to characterize modern investigations of the experimental territory first explored by Ebbinghaus is to be found in a 1968 article by Postman.

Many years later David Shakow had occasion to examine the dissertation; as had Woodworth, he too found it to be very critical of von Hartmann's array of arguments. He cites Ebbinghaus as having written, "Wherever the structure is touched, it falls apart," and, "What is true is alas not new; the new is not true" (1930, p. 510).

There can thus be no question about how Ebbinghaus viewed the treatment of the philosophy of the unconscious at the time. This was at the beginning of his career; however, there does not seem to have been any change in his negative attitude later on in his career. His last book, the famous[8] *Abriss der Psychologie* or *Compendium of Psychology,* was published in 1908, the year before his death. In it he has an introductory chapter dealing with the history of psychology from the time of the Greeks to the early years of the twentieth century, or from the time of Aristotle to the days of Titchener and Thorndike. When he reaches the decade of the 1870s there is no mention of von Hartmann either in the body of the chapter or in the fairly detailed bibliography at the end (pp. 22-23). There is no reference to his doctoral dissertation in any of the chapters. Although he alludes to the voluntarism of Kant, Fichte, and Schopenhauer, he does not associate this with the concept of the unconscious. In fact, any allusion to such a concept, in view of his early interest in it, is conspicuous by its absence.[9] What he had found unacceptable in 1873 was still unacceptable in 1908.

Independently of the Ebbinghaus dissertation, William James also found von Hartmann's pleas in behalf of the unconscious unacceptable. He was even more devastating in his criticism of von Hartmann's arguments. He refused to give them serious consideration and dismissed them with this withering comment (Vol. I, p. 169):

---

[8]This is the book that contains this famous frequently quoted opening sentence: "Psychology has a long past, but only a short history." In the original German: "Die Psychologie hat eine lange Vergangenheit, doch nur eine kurze Geschichte."

[9]This finding may not apply to an earlier text by Ebbinghaus, namely, the 1905 publication of his *Grundzüge der Psychologie.* In this book, according to Brett, Ebbinghaus "accepts the Unconscious as explanatory principle" (1921, p. 188) but suggests that clarification of the use of the term *Unconscious* is to be found on a later page where Brett seems to be equating this use of the term as the equivalent of a subliminal process. At all events, this is what he has to say about it (p. 196):

> Consciousness is equivalent to a certain "height" attained by a process; below that level the process exists as unconscious sensation or idea. This, we are told, must not be read as though there could be an unconscious consciousness; what is unconscious is the process. The relation between the process and the consciousness is analogous to the relation between heat and light; if the vibrations of the luminiferous ether increase in rapidity, radiant heat passes into light. We cannot say the heat causes the light; nor must we say the process causes the consciousness.

There does not appear to be a comparable reference to the unconscious in the *Abriss*; hence it may be that he was no longer accepting it even as an "explanatory principle."

Hartmann fairly boxes the compass of the universe with the principle of unconscious thought. For him there is no namable thing that does not exemplify it. But his logic is so lax and his failure to consider the most obvious alternatives so complete that it would, on the whole, be a waste of time to look at his arguments in detail.

SOME CONTEMPORARY JUDGMENTS

Despite such adverse judgments, von Hartmann's book continued to find readers. It was translated into English in 1931, some forty years after the scathing indictment by James, and interest in the book continued well into the 1960s. For example, as previously noted, in 1960 Whyte called the book "an extraordinary achievement" even though "it is neither good philosophy nor good science." Then, more recently, Darnoi published his critique of the book in 1967. In general, he was just as severe as James in his indictment of the book; but, unlike James, he did examine von Hartmann's arguments in some detail.

In particular he pointed out that, contrary to the book's subtitle, von Hartmann's "discovery" of the unconscious was not an exclusive product of *inductive* reasoning. He felt that von Hartmann was already convinced of the existence and preponderant influence of the unconscious when he embarked upon his search for evidence. This made his mode of procedure more *deductive* than inductive, or more a matter of finding proof for a preconceived conviction by being on the alert for supporting data and blind to negative evidence.

Nor should von Hartmann's excursion into Kantian metaphysics be overlooked in this connection. In fact, Darnoi called specific attention to this affiliation with Kant's philosophy by referring to von Hartmann's mode of procedure as being that of a "criticist," or one whose thinking reflects the orientation of the famous Kantian critiques. However, this did not suffice as an adequate account of the methodology involved. Instead of being a single mode of procedure it involved a heterogeneous assortment of procedures. This was the conclusion arrived at by Darnoi upon completion of his critical analysis of von Hartmann's book (p. 168):

> It is an amalgamate of empiricism, speculative inductivism, and *probabilism,* and it is designed to bring forth von Hartmann's preconceived claim concerning the nature of his metaphysical noumenon. In the description of von Hartmann's criticistic method there is a deceivingly insignificant and almost unnoticeable adjective, viz., "speculative"; yet it is the key to the enigma of von Hartmann's philosophy. To the question as to how can von Hartmann expect to gain speculative results from exclusively empirical data the answer is to be found in the "speculative" aspect of his criticistic method. The term in its actual usage and employment means "clairvoyant intuition," which in turn means that the analysis of the phenomena is undertaken according to a predetermined view in mind leading inevitably to the discovery of the unconscious.

Von Hartmann is accorded more sympathetic treatment in Henri Ellenberger's *The Discovery of the Unconscious.* This monumental survey of the history and development of the subject is more recent than the study by Darnoi and far more extensive in its coverage. It was published in 1970 and, among other topics, devotes considerable space to the contributions of those writers Lancelot Whyte had included among the pre-Freudian "discoverers" of the unconscious. Among those listed by Ellenberger as having had a direct influence on the philosophy of von Hartmann are Carus, Schopenhauer, and Nietzsche. He holds that "the closest approach to psychoanalysis is to be found in the philosophies" of these four (p. 542). In particular he notes that von Hartmann had preceded Freud by having regarded slips of pen and tongue "as manifestations of the unconscious" (p. 495). He also sees him as one of "Jung's predecessors" (p. 729). In general, Ellenberger is more impressed by the nature and scope of von Hartmann's illustrative material than by his theorizing. In this connection he writes (p. 210):

> The main interest of the *Philosophy of the Unconscious* lies not so much in its philosophical theories as in its wealth of supporting material. Von Hartmann collected numerous and relevant facts concerning perception, the association of ideas, wit, emotional life, instinct, personality traits, individual destiny, as well as the role of the unconscious in language, religion, history, and social life.

From this it is evident that Ellenberger judged von Hartmann's "facts" as being "relevant" to individual and social psychology as well as to some of the humanities. By implication this relevance was presumed to be "supporting" belief in the unconscious, not as a hypothetical construct, but as a genuine mental reality existing separate from or in independence of the reality of consciousness as ordinarily experienced. Complete endorsement of such a belief paves the way for *discovery* of the unconscious. It is equivalent to what Darnoi recognized as "a predetermined view," in light of which such discovery is inevitable. It may be that being on guard against this kind of view made Darnoi especially sensitive to von Hartmann's "clairvoyant intuition" and more skeptical than Ellenberger about the relevance of the wealth of factual material cited by von Hartmann.

In fairness to Ellenberger it is important to note that his orientation with reference to von Hartmann's book is different from Darnoi's orientation. Darnoi was exclusively concerned with a critical analysis of von Hartmann's work from the viewpoint of scientific method. Ellenberger, on the other hand, was concerned with von Hartmann in incidental rather than exclusive fashion. His interest in the work was centered on its role in the "evolution of dynamic psychiatry," along with similar roles of many other writers; hence von Hartmann's shortcomings as a critical thinker were played down.

Actually, Ellenberger was not unmindful of the importance of critical thinking for the accomplishment of his gigantic undertaking. He makes this evident in the introduction to his book by declaring that it "is intended to be a history of dynamic psychiatry based on a scientific methodology" in which he plans never to "take anything for granted" and also to maintain "a sharp line of distinction between the facts and interpretation of facts" (p. v). Apparently he had the latter distinction in mind when he subordinated von Hartmann's "philosophical theories" to the vast collection of "relevant facts." Nevertheless, in many instances, what struck him as factual seems to have impressed Darnoi as speculative. Moreover, to revert to an earlier point, some of these facts must have struck William James as "whimsies."

CONCERNING THE DETERMINANTS OF BELIEF

How are these differing interpretations or divergent perceptions to be explained? In other words, for more than a century–from 1868 to 1970–through successive editions and in successive generations, the same work has been welcomed by some and rejected by others. As in any debate about a controversial topic the same group of relevant facts has elicited contradictory evaluations as evidence for or against a given conclusion, with those upholding the affirmative set to interpret the facts in one way and proponents of the negative set to interpret them differently.

The "set" is the equivalent of a predisposition or hope or desire to have one side prevail. It entails the kind of wishful thinking incident to taking sides in connection with any contest. When this happens, as in any competitive confrontation, strong feelings are aroused and calm, impersonal evaluation of evidence is hardly to be expected. To a greater extent than is commonly realized our beliefs and convictions tend to be fathered by our feelings and desires with critical evaluation of the "relevant facts" being relegated to a subordinate role in the process.

Many years ago this commonplace observation was subjected to experimental study by investigation of the relationship between belief and evidence as contrasted with the relationship between belief and desire. With reference to the latter the investigator, F. H. Lund, found the correlation to be .88, or more than twice the correlation of .42 between belief and evidence.

In metaphoric language this suggests that the heart is more influential than the brain in winning support for given beliefs. Wishful thinking may prevail over logical thinking. When this occurs there often is a reluctance to consider evidence or opinions at variance with our convictions. In the present context, for example, neither Whyte nor Ellenberger had anything to say about the results of the Ebbinghaus analysis and rejection of von Hartmann's arguments in support of the unconscious. But this neglect may have been due to the difficulty of locating this 1873 doctoral thesis. The same explanation does not apply, however, to their failure to say anything about James's negative attitude toward the general drift of von Hartmann's arguments. In fact, there is no mention of the entire section of the *Principles* of 1890 (Vol. I, pp. 164–176) in which James in addition to registering his rejection of von

Hartmann's arguments also presented and evaluated some ten arguments advanced by others.

A CONCLUDING COMMENT

These ten arguments were treated by James in disregard of their possible bearing on von Hartmann's philosophy of the unconscious. In other words, no attempt was made to relate any of them to von Hartmann's three levels of the unconscious or his notion of clairvoyant intuition or his belief that plants have feelings. Instead, each one was presented as a separate line of evidence to be evaluated in terms of arguments offered pro and con. This made for ten more or less independent lines of evidence, whose nature and cogency, as just implied, are in general different from that introduced in the present chapter. Consequently, further discussion is put off until the next chapter.

The evidence introduced in the present chapter, it should now be realized, had to do with arguments cited in support of belief in mind as unconscious during the last century—in the 1870s, when Ebbinghaus was writing his doctoral dissertation on von Hartmann's *Philosophy of the Unconscious.* This was at a time when thoughts about psychology *as science* were just beginning to receive serious consideration. In this connection it is well to recall that Ebbinghaus was a pioneer experimental psychologist and is thus to be listed with the founding fathers of scientific psychology. This lends added significance to his critique of von Hartmann's arguments in support of the dogma of mind as unconscious. It indicates rejection of the unconscious by scientific psychology. Moreover, this was in the very decade when the first psychological laboratory was being established. In large measure such rejection was the chief focal point of the present chapter and, as will soon be evident, is altogether congruent with the central thesis of the next chapter.

REFERENCES

Boring, E. G. 1950. *A History of Experimental Psychology.* New York: Appleton-Century-Crofts.

Brett, G. S. 1921. *A History of Psychology,* Vol. III. London: George Allen & Unwin, Ltd.

Darnoi, D. N. E. 1967. *The Unconscious and Eduard von Hartmann—A Historico-Critical Monograph.* The Hague: Martinus Nijkoff.

Ebbinghaus, H. 1909. *Abriss der Psychologie,* 2nd Edition. Leipzig: Veit & Comp.

Edman, I., ed. 1928. *The Philosophy of Schopenhauer.* New York: Random House, The Modern Library.

Ellenberger, H. F. 1970. *The Discovery of the Unconscious—The History and Evolution of Dynamic Psychiatry.* New York: Basic Books, Inc.

Hall, G. S. 1912. *Founders of Modern Psychology.* New York: D. Appleton and Company.

Hartmann, E. von. 1931. *Philosophy of the Unconscious–Speculative Results According to the Inductive Method of Physical Science.* Translated by W. C. Coupland. New York: Harcourt, Bruce and Company. (Translation based upon the 9th German edition of 1884.)

Holt, E. E. 1914. *The Concept of Consciousness.* London: George Allen and Company, Ltd.

James, W. 1890. *The Principles of Psychology,* Vol. I. New York: Henry Holt and Company.

Lund, F. H. 1925. "The Psychology of Belief." *Journal of Abnormal and Social Psychology* 20: 174–196.

Postman, L. 1968. "Hermann Ebbinghaus." *American Psychologist* 23: 149–157.

Shakow, D. 1930. "Hermann Ebbinghaus." *American Journal of Psychology* 42: 505–518.

Woodworth, R. S. 1909. "Hermann Ebbinghaus." *Journal of Philosophy, Psychology and Scientific Methods* 6: 253–256.

Whyte, L. L. 1960. *The Unconscious beforè Freud.* New York: Basic Books, Inc.

3

James on Mind as Unconscious

That James had misgivings about mind as unconscious was indicated at the very beginning of Chapter 1 by the quoting of his famous warning that the distinction between the conscious and the unconscious being of a mental state "is the sovereign means for believing what one likes in psychology, and of turning what might become a science into a tumbling-ground for whimsies." He then added that the distinction "has numerous champions, and elaborate reasons to give for itself." This statement occurs in the early part of the *Principles* (Vol. 1, p. 163) and, since the writing took twelve years, was probably written in the late 1870s or early 1880s. In other words, long before Freud the concept of mind as unconscious had numerous defenders. The circulation of the successive editions of von Hartmann's book indicates persistent popular endorsement of the concept. Consequently, James held, reasons advanced in its support ought to be subjected to critical analysis in order to determine whether such endorsement is justified. As formulated by James, the basic issue calls for consideration of this question:

DO UNCONSCIOUS MENTAL STATES EXIST?

For expository purposes James treated this question as a proposition to be debated between those prepared to answer in the affirmative and those taking the negative. In his survey of the relevant literature he found ten arguments advanced by different champions and presented each of these in the form of a *Proof* for the existence of unconscious mental states followed by a

Reply as it might have been advanced by an upholder of the negative. The pages devoted to the resulting debate (Vol. I, pp. 164-176) contain ten *Proofs* along with correlated replies. Taken as a whole they serve to summarize the general drift of the controversy in the pre-Freudian decades. As might be expected, after the lapse of so many years some of these arguments would no longer be advanced by contemporary "discoverers" of the unconscious. However, a few of them, sometimes slightly modified, are still current and thus merit examination in terms of both their original consideration by James and their later modifications.

PETITES PERCEPTIONS AND THE UNCONSCIOUS

In his review of evidence cited in support of a belief in the existence of unconscious mental states James began with a famous argument first introduced by Leibnitz (1646-1716). This involved recognition of the difference between readily perceptible sensory impressions and those too faint to be perceived. In the terminology of Leibnitz the former would be *apperceived* and the latter would be composed of *petites perceptions.* The roar of the ocean waves, Leibnitz indicated, is apperceived and yet each separate wave would not be heard were it to occur in isolation. Nevertheless, unless each wave had some influence, the totality of waves constituting the roar could never be heard. In the words of Leibnitz, if each little wave has zero influence, "one would not hear 100,000 waves, for of 100,000 zeros one can never make a quantity."

Even though this argument had often been cited in support of the doctrine of the unconscious,[1] James questioned its cogency. As he saw it, there is a fallacy in concluding that what is true of an organization of things must also be true of its component parts. This, of course, is the fallacy of division and can be illustrated by reference to the composition of carbon monoxide as a poisonous gas. To conclude that its components carbon and oxygen as independent elements must also be poisonous to some degree would obviously be contrary to fact. Similarly, it would be contrary to fact to argue that round marbles cannot be arranged to form a triangle or a square or any other nonspherical pattern. With specific reference to the petites perceptions it would also be contrary to fact to argue that a minute fragment of a cause must to some degree exercise the same effect as the entire causal agent. For example,

---

[1]For example, in the following passage Boring alludes to this argument in citing Leibnitz as a sponsor of the unconscious (1950, p. 168):

> Leibnitz also gave us a doctrine of degrees of consciousness and thus also of the *unconscious.* The *petite perception* of the monad is unconscious. The sound of the single falling drop of water may be regarded as an unconscious perception. This continuum passes through perception to apperception. There are many echoes of this view. The negative sensations of Fechner were *petites perceptions.* There is the apperception of Herbart and Wundt. There is the whole doctrine of the unconscious . . . often related to apperception and the degrees of consciousness.

a certain degree of force is needed to depress the key of a typewriter, but the weight of a speck of dust falling on the key does not result in an infinitesimally small depression of the key. A minimum amount of force is needed to move the key and any lesser amount does not move it at all. In this connection James quoted John Stuart Mill's formulation of the underlying principle: "A certain *quantity* of the cause may be a necessary condition to the production of *any* of the effect." This, James indicated, applies particularly when the effect "is a mental state."

Somewhat related to the petites perceptions of Leibnitz was an argument to the effect that to experience the harmony of musical chords it is necessary for the individual vibrations to be counted so as to reveal the simple ratios involved. Since there is no direct awareness of such counting, it was argued that the counting must take place unconsciously. In his reply James argued that the effect of the chords on the brain may be such as to give rise to an immediate and direct awareness of a pleasing sound. Consequently, there would be no need to assume any antecedent counting either conscious or unconscious. After all, one can detect the difference between a very high note and a very low one without first having to count the individual vibrations.

HYPNOSIS AND THE UNCONSCIOUS

In connection with a different kind of *Proof* for the unconscious James had occasion to refer to hypnosis in his *Reply*. Sponsors of the unconscious had called attention to the fact that somnambulists may execute rather complex activities while asleep and be unable to recall any of their activities upon awakening. Because of such amnesia, it was argued, the activities must have been guided or controlled by unconscious mental operations. In his *Reply* James wrote, "Consciousness is forgotten, as in the hypnotic trance." He also noted the similarity between the forgetting of dreams upon awakening[2] and the phenomenon of posthypnotic amnesia. As he saw it, neither somnambulism nor hypnosis involves the operation of unconscious mental forces. Incidentally, he was familiar with hypnotic phenomena not only in terms of published accounts, but also in terms of firsthand experience as a hypnotist. This is evident from a letter he wrote to Professor Carl Stumpf (1848–1936) in 1886 in which, among other reports of his laboratory engagements, he had this to report (Perry, Vol. II, p. 65): "I am *hypnotizing,* on a large scale, the students, and have hit upon one or two rather pretty unpublished things of which some day I hope I may send you an account."

James's appeal to hypnosis as a means of disproving the contention of those who attributed somnambulism to unconscious mental control is particularly interesting when it is recalled that by the time of Freud the same appeal

---

[2]This topic, as might be expected, was not overlooked by Freud in his classic *Interpretation of Dreams.* He discussed it in a section having this caption: "Why Dreams Are Forgotten after Waking."

was introduced in support of belief in such control. Posthypnotic behavior came to be mentioned as especially cogent evidence indicative of the unconscious at work. Freud cited it as evidence as early as 1900 in his *Interpretation of Dreams* in connection with his analysis of the dream of one of his patients. In the course of her associations to the dream she reported a peculiar remark she had made to her husband. Upon being asked to account for the remark she was unable to supply any plausible or satisfactory reasons for having made it. This reminded Freud that when a person "carries out a posthypnotic suggestion and is asked why he is acting in this way, instead of saying that he has no idea, he feels compelled to invent some obviously unsatisfactory reason" (1938, p. 285). He did not introduce a concrete instance of posthypnotic behavior at the time, but limited his comment to being reminded of "one of Bernheim's hypnotized patients." This was an allusion to Hippolyte Bernheim (1837–1919), a physician at Nancy in France and a pioneer student of hypnotic phenomena.

Freud was again reminded of one of Bernheim's patients years later when he was writing his paper "Some Elementary Lessons in Psycho-Analysis." This was in 1938 just a year before his death—the paper was never finished. It was intended for the "lay public" and consequently the "lessons" are unencumbered by technical terms. One of Freud's chief objectives was to demonstrate that "mental acts which are unconscious do exist," and he pointed out the relevance of hypnotic experiments for such demonstration. In his own words, any person "who has witnessed such an experiment will receive an unforgettable impression and a conviction that can never be shaken." He then proceeded to supply an example of posthypnotic behavior. In a footnote he explained, "I am describing experiments made by Bernheim at Nancy in 1889 at which I myself assisted" (1938, p. 285).

In Freud's example Bernheim, having placed his umbrella in a corner of the hospital ward, gave instructions to a hypnotized patient to the following effect: I am going to leave the ward and when I return you will greet me by placing the opened umbrella over my head. After arousing the patient Bernheim departed. Upon his return the patient met him with the open umbrella in compliance with the instructions. When questioned about the meaning of his act the patient seemed embarrassed as he explained that he thought the doctor would open his umbrella inside the room before going out into the rain. This explanation, Freud noted, "is obviously quite inadequate and made up on the spur of the moment to offer some sort of motive for his senseless behaviour. It is clear to us spectators that he is in ignorance of his real motive." However, the spectators, having been present when the suggestions were introduced, know what it is that "is at work" in the patient's unconscious.

Just as Freud regarded this as convincing proof for the unconscious, so have many others, who believe that a demonstration of posthypnotic suggestibility will make for "conviction that can never be shaken." Furthermore, this continues to be a contemporary belief. For example, as recently as 1972 a psychoanalyst, Michael Beldoch, in the course of a critique of behavioristic neglect of man's "feelings, dreams, art, and ideas" had this to say (p. 13): "As for the unconscious (*so easy to demonstrate with a simple ten-minute posthypnotic suggestion*), the behaviorists have nothing to say whatever, despite the ample evidence that it plays a significant role in human affairs" (italics added).

As a student of hypnosis James was, of course, very familiar with posthypnotic suggestibility. He mentioned it in a brief passage concerned with hysteria and automatic writing (Vol. I, pp. 208-209) and at greater length in his chapter on hypnotism (Vol. II, ch. 28) in which the closing paragraphs (pp. 613-615) are devoted to a detailed description of the phenomenon. Moreover, even though he alluded to the "mystery" of delayed response to the hypnotist's command, he did not solve the mystery by reference to an unconscious mind. Instead, as indicated by the following, he believed it to be a function of consciousness as *dissociated* from the main current of experienced events (Vol. II, p. 614):

> The mechanism by which the command is retained until the moment for its execution arrives is a mystery which has given rise to much discussion. The experiments of Gurney and the observations of M. Pierre Janet and others on certain hysterical somnambulists seem to prove that it is stored up in consciousness; not simply organically registered, but that *the consciousness which thus retains it is split off, dissociated from the rest of the subject's mind.*

THE CONCEPT OF DISSOCIATION

James was thus accounting for posthypnotic or delayed suggestibility in terms of the concept of *dissociated* as opposed to unconscious mental states. Dissociation refers to the segregation of groups of experiences brought together because of some unifying interest. The resulting groups sometimes make for a *compartmentalization* of thought and outlook. A familiar instance of this is the student who objects to having his grammar corrected by the chemistry professor, as if the subject of grammar belongs to a different cognitive compartment from the subject of chemistry. Clergymen on occasion are confronted with compartmentalized or dissociated thinking in parishioners who protest if a sermon touches upon the ethics of rugged individualism, high interest rates, or any exploitative business practice. Those who protest believe sermons should deal with religious ritual and the abstractions of theology and not with the domain of commerce and industry. For them it is as if there is a mutually exclusive dichotomy between the appropriate affairs of the church on the one hand and those of the counting house on the other. Moreover, such dichotomous or dissociated thinking is not always ego-defensive as in the preceding instances. Those of us who do our "scientific" thinking in terms of atomic physics continue to harbor the commonsense view of matter in our "nonscientific" pursuits. In reading the paper or biting into an apple we do not think of ourselves as reacting to invisible patterns of whirling electrons.

In brief, our scientific view of matter is dissociated from our commonsense view of matter.

Compartmentalized or dissociated thinking is thus different from thinking attributed to the dynamics of the unconscious. As already indicated, James was mindful of this distinction when he referred to the "split off, dissociated" consciousness of somnambulists and hypnotized subjects. In particular he accounted for posthypnotic compliance with an ostensibly "forgotten" command by its dissociated retention.

Until shortly after the turn of the century the concept of dissociation continued to receive attention and acceptance in psychological discussions.[3] In later decades interest in the concept waned and often it was not even mentioned in introductory textbooks. As a result it has ceased to have wide currency. However, in connection with his many studies of hypnotic phenomena over a span of more than twenty years Hilgard, like James, has found the concept useful and especially applicable to the phenomenon of posthypnotic behavior. In his own words (1971, p. 576):

> I am inclined to believe that the notion of dissociation ought to be revived, and it may turn out to be more useful than the concept of state or trance. The same applies to post-hypnotic behavior carried out to a signal, after the subject feels himself "out of hypnosis." It was sometimes argued in the past that hypnosis was reinstated when the signal for the post-hypnotic behavior was given; . . . this, however, seems to force the notion that hypnotic responses occur only within a hypnotic state, and there is little supporting evidence for this.

---

[3]As a concept it was often introduced in accounts of multiple personality, coconsciousness, and automatic writing. William James, for example, considered these topics in his chapter on the "consciousness of self" (Vol. I, pp. 379–400). Coconsciousness as related to multiple personality was stressed by Morton Prince (1854–1929) in his study of the famous Beauchamp case as reported in his 1906 volume entitled *The Dissociation of a Personality.* The subject of automatic writing was given separate consideration in a small volume by Anita Mühl containing a bibliography of 273 references (1930, pp. 204–214). James Miller discussed dissociation as related to the unconscious (1942, pp. 220–230). As brought out by Gardner Murphy (1947, pp. 435–440), the concept of dissociation was a key issue for Pierre Janet (1859–1947) in his studies of psychopathology.

Finally, dissociation may also have some relevance for contemporary studies of neuropathology involving so-called split-brain surgery. These studies–especially those developed by R. W. Sperry and his associates–have been concerned with modifications of consciousness following transection of the corpus callosum or the neural linkage between right and left hemispheres. This results in dissociation or severance of right brain awareness from left brain awareness and vice versa. As Sperry expressed it in one of his papers (1969, p. 532): "In the surgically separated state, the two hemispheres appear to be independently and often simultaneously conscious, each quite oblivious of the mental experiences of the opposite hemisphere and also of the incompleteness of its own awareness."

This paper was directly concerned with the concept of consciousness. Relevant bibliographic references are supplied at the end of this paper as well as in a later (1970) paper dealing with an elaboration and clarification of issues raised in the earlier one.

Even if the concept of dissociation be deemed worthy of revival especially to account for compartmentalized thinking in general and posthypnotic behavior in particular, it might nevertheless be argued that the concept fails to account for the motivation of posthypnotic behavior. Freud, it will be recalled, found Bernheim's patient to be ignorant of the "real motive" for his posthypnotic maneuver with the umbrella. The patient made no mention of Bernheim's return to the ward as the occasion for the maneuver, as if he failed to recognize the return as the cue or signal for the execution of the instruction given him when hypnotized. Instead, upon being questioned, he justified the maneuver by mentioning the rain outside. As frequently interpreted, such justification would be classified as a rationalized or spurious motive, as contrasted with the real motive, namely, the command given by the hypnotist. In other words, the real motive is a function of this command–inability or failure to recall the command, it has been argued, indicates its unconscious activation.

Accordingly, as already indicated, the foregoing kind of interpretation has come to make posthypnotic behavior virtually the equivalent of an objective demonstration of unconscious motivation. To repeat Freud's words: as a demonstration it will make for "a conviction that can never be shaken." However, the conviction depends on acceptance of the interpretation as valid; before endorsing its validity, the possibility of alternative interpretations ought to be explored.

DETERMINING TENDENCIES AND DELAYED REACTIONS

One alternative interpretation involves a reconsideration of the motivational implications of the subject's apparent inability to perceive any relationship between his posthypnotic act and the experimenter's command to delay the act until he returns to the ward. Is it correct to regard the command as a motive? After all, the command states what should take place and not why it should take place. The "why" or motive for the act has to do with factors antecedent to the command. This amounts to asking what prompts the apparently blind obedience to the hypnotist's instructions–even bizarre or ridiculous ones. In turn, this is the equivalent of asking what motivates people to participate as subjects in demonstrations of hypnosis whether in hospitals, dental clinics, psychology laboratories, or in the privacy of home or office. This, of course, will differ from subject to subject and even from setting to setting. For one it might be curiosity concerning the experience, for another it might be desire to please the experimenter, for a third it might be fear of the dentist's drill, while for the college student it might be the prospect of special academic credit or even financial reward offered for serving as a subject. Sometimes a combination of these and other motives might be operative. Any combination or any single motive accounts for readiness to listen to and comply with suggestions.

It is also well to note that induction of hypnosis involves simple commands to fixate a bright object, to relax particular muscle groups, to breathe slowly, to observe sensations of strain around the fixated eyes, to listen carefully to whatever is being said by the operator, and so on and on. Unless there is compliance with these simple suggestions hypnosis cannot be induced. In other words, the ritual of induction in and of itself initiates a set to carry out whatever is being suggested.

As a matter of fact, under given conditions, it is possible to induce people to comply with instructions–even ridiculous and arbitrary ones–without induction of hypnosis. This has sometimes been demonstrated by professors of psychology as an introduction to later study of hypnosis as a separate topic. Being accustomed to classroom demonstrations of psychological phenomena, the students do not find it unusual for the professor at one meeting to tell them to get ready for a different kind of experiment. He then tells them to open their notebooks to a blank page and write "Mary had a little lamb." Under these words they are then told to draw four squares, one triangle, and to print their last names as spelled backwards. Now the notebooks are to be closed and they are to sit with eyes closed, the right arm extended upward and the left arm extended horizontally. With the entire class exhibiting this rather bizarre posture the professor now says, "Why are you carrying out all these suggestions?" This request for a report of the instigating motive or motives leaves the students both startled and perplexed. Their compliance with the instructions had taken place in the absence of deliberate analysis of reasons for or against such compliance. In their failure to note this they might be said to have been *unconscious* or ignorant of what prompted or motivated their compliance; but this is different from saying the motives were buried in some mysterious realm called the unconscious. Nor would it be correct to call the professor's instructions the motives for the sequence of acts, and hence neither are the hypnotist's instructions to be called motives. They function as cues or signals for the acts in question and both the students and the hypnotized subjects get *set* to respond to the signals.

This reference to the term *set* has to do with motor sets and with mental sets or *Aufgaben.* They designate attitudes of preparation for intended reactions. For example, our taut muscles as we are driving on an icy highway constitute a motor set or readiness to respond to the threat of a skid. Technically, such readiness is called a *determining tendency.* Moreover, in the traditional reaction-time experiment such a tendency was ascribed to the alert subject set to respond to the anticipated signal. Similarly, in word association experiments the subjects prepare for the stimulus words in accordance with instructions to respond with synonyms, antonyms, rhymes, or French equivalents as the case may be. Each separate preparation for a given kind of response exemplifies introduction of a distinctive mental set or *Aufgabe*. In the course of reading these sentences we experience a medley of conscious shifts in attitude depending on ease or difficulty of understanding, interest or boredom in ideas aroused, focused or wandering attention, and other concomitants of the thought process. As constituents of the thought process such ideational shifts are called *conscious attitudes.*

As technical terms *Aufgaben,* determining tendencies, and conscious attitudes were introduced into psychology early in the present century by investigators at the University of Würzburg. Under the leadership of Oswald Külpe (1862–1915) these investigators had been studying what came to be called *imageless* thinking. A detailed account of the nature and scope of these studies is not essential at this point but will be introduced in a more relevant context to be developed in Chapter 7 in connection with a discussion of imageless or non-sensory thinking. Here it will be sufficient to call attention to the central teaching of the Würzburg investigators, namely, that *Aufgaben* and determining tendencies and conscious attitudes can function effectively in the absence of any sensory or imaginal representation. For this reason they were called imageless in the sense of being devoid of any characteristic subject to observation or description. In referring to them as imageless they were being designated as "unconscious" in the sense of lacking any specifiable or describable sensory or imaginal impression. In other words, they lacked the slightest vestige of any olfactory, visual, kinesthetic, cutaneous, or any other possible sensory or imaginal characteristic. In metaphoric language, they were naked cognitive activities. As activities, even though impalpable and invisible, they controlled and regulated thought and action. Whether two numbers like 7 and 9 are to be added, multiplied, or squared will be determined by controls in the form of definite *Aufgaben* or mental sets. Analogously, whether a track athlete is going to jog or sprint or hurdle or vault will be a function of controls in the form of specific determining tendencies.

Both mental sets and determining tendencies, it is important to realize, are introduced by way of preparation for a given undertaking. Thus, with reference to arithmetic, even before the numbers are encountered the mental set for dealing with them will have been introduced. Similarly, the track athlete's determining tendency is brought into play before the contest starts. The runner's determining tendency to sprint is initiated while crouching at the starting mark. As a postural attitude it prepares him for instant reaction to the sound of the starter's pistol. This, of course, is an automatic reaction as contrasted with a volitional reaction.

As applied to the Würzburg reaction-time experiments this example from track athletics illustrates an important finding revealed by these experiments, namely, that initiation of the determining tendency occurs in the fore-period by way of preparation for instant reaction to the stimulus. In other words, as a voluntary act or deliberate intention it precedes execution of the act. As applied to Freud's example of posthypnotic behavior, this means that the act of opening the umbrella upon Bernheim's return to the ward was automatic rather than volitional. The volitional resolve took place upon hearing, understanding, and accepting the instructions. Motivation for such acceptance, as already indicated, is a function of factors antecedent to the instructions.

Consequently, the posthypnotic act is not a product of some underlying motive so much as it is a result of the determining tendency or volitional set incident to acceptance of the instructions. Subsequent execution of the intended act is no more mysterious than any ordinary delayed execution of some planned action, such as getting a book from the library on the way home from work or attending a meeting next week. Securing the book or attending the meeting are instances of what Hunter (1913) called delayed reactions. He found that even animals are capable of delayed reaction to some degree, with the duration of the tolerated delay being longer the more advanced the animal. If posthypnotic responsiveness be recognized as a variant of Hunter's delayed reactions, it may cease to be viewed as a quasi-abnormal phenomenon revelatory of hidden motives in operation.

HIDDEN MOTIVES AND THE FALLACY OF SENSATIONALISM

The subject of hidden motives is directly related to the subject of mind as unconscious. Indeed, for some psychologists the concept of mind as unconscious is virtually synonymous with the concept of unconscious motivation. As they understand it, the unconscious will not reflect psychological phenomena unrelated to motivation as the central issue. Because of this emphasis on motivation they may think of themselves as dynamic psychologists or dynamic psychiatrists. As is well known, such descriptive self-characterizations are largely post-Freudian or twentieth-century developments.

However, the question of unconscious motivation had already become a subject of controversy in pre-Freudian nineteenth-century decades. In fact, William James devoted several pages to the topic (Vol. I, pp. 170–176) along with related topics attributed to unconscious mental states. With specific reference to the topic of unconscious motivation as presented by its defenders he had this to say about the kind of evidence they introduced as "proof" for their contention (pp. 170–171):

> There is a great class of experiences in our mental life which may be described as discoveries that a subjective condition which we have been having is really something different from what we had supposed. We suddenly find ourselves bored by a thing which we thought we were enjoying well enough; or in love with a person whom we imagined we only liked. *Or else we deliberately analyze our motives, and find that at bottom they contain jealousies and cupidities which we little suspected to be there.* Our feelings towards people are perfect wells of motivation, *unconscious* of itself, which introspection brings to light [italics added]. And our sensations likewise: we constantly discover new elements in sensations which we have been in the habit of receiving all our days, elements, too, which have been there from the first, since otherwise we should have been unable to distinguish the sensations containing them from others nearly allied. The elements must exist, for we use them to discriminate by; but they must exist in an unconscious state, since we so completely fail to single them out. . . . Consider, too, the difference

> between a sensation which we simply *have* and one which we *attend to.* Attention gives results that seem like fresh creations; and yet the feelings and elements of feeling which it reveals must have been already there—in an unconscious state.

James found the reasoning leading to the foregoing kind of "proof" for unconscious motivation to be a "tissue of confusion." The confused thinking, he indicated, is not limited to the analysis of motivation, but includes other instances of psychological analysis. What he had in mind might be illustrated by an argument to this effect: since words can be analyzed into syllables and isolated letters, therefore a child acquires its mother tongue by first learning to sound the single syllables and letters and later putting them together to form words and sentences.

This sort of conclusion is obviously contrary to fact. As an argument it resembles the outmoded basis for tracing the origins of mind to initial apprehension of sensations in the abstract. Sensations were taken to be the building blocks of mind and the psychological equivalent of the atoms of physics; hence this kind of thinking about mind came to be characterized as "atomistic analysis."[4] James was most explicit in his expression of objections to psychological atomism. On the first page of his famous chapter "The Stream of Thought" (Vol. I, p. 224) he declared that nobody "ever had a simple sensation by itself" and that "what we call simple sensations are results of discriminative attention, pushed often to a very high degree." As a consequence he regarded it as making for "havoc" in psychology to assume that sensations "are the first things to take up in psychology." This Jamesian criticism of atomistic analysis was echoed by Brett in this trenchant sentence (1912, p. 85): "The fallacy of sensationalism lies in its persistent habit of constructing the history of mind backward; it finds in sensation the last product of analysis, and then makes it the first element of construction."

The "tissue of confusion" mentioned by James, it should now be evident, was a product of this fallacy of sensationalism. As just suggested, it can be exemplified in terms of the atomistic analysis involved in a theory to the effect that speech development proceeds from initial mastery of the sensa-

---

[4]Atomistic analysis reduced conscious content to mental "elements" as units of sensation. These units turned out to be artifacts. However, "elements" of sensation in terms of colors, tones, and other modalities are not artifacts in this sense. This is made clear in Charles Hartshorne's *Philosophy and Psychology of Sensation,* in which he supplies a critical survey of the "immediate data of consciousness" experienced as "sensory qualities" and examined from these five viewpoints (p. 6):

1. Mathematical *continuity*
2. Aesthetic meaning or *affective tone*
3. The fundamentally *social* character of experience
4. Biological *adaptiveness*
5. *Evolution* from a common origin

tions aroused by isolated letters to their subsequent linkage into words and then into phrases and sentences expressive of different thoughts. Actually, of course, we may have different thoughts or ideas aroused by a given word or combination of words.

Failure to discriminate among such different thoughts may serve to illustrate another kind of fallacy, or what James called a fallacy. This, as he pointed out, is the fallacy of believing "that two thoughts about one thing are virtually the same thought, and that this same thought may in subsequent reflections become more and more *conscious* of what it really *was* all along from the first." The meaning of a word constitutes one thought, its etymology is another thought, its spelling a third thought, and its foreign language equivalents still additional thoughts. To fuse all these thoughts into a single thought is bound to result in "confusion."

James was especially critical of those who found evidence for the reality of unconscious mental states in such a fused thought. This happened when it was assumed that the later "parts" of the fused thought had emerged from some unconscious or implicit stratum of the earlier fragments. Consider the word *facetious.* It is altogether likely to be a familiar word to readers of this chapter. In general, they may be presumed to know what the word means; if not, any dictionary will supply its meaning. However, the dictionary will not reveal an interesting fact about the sequence of vowels in the word, namely, that they include all the vowels in their alphabetical sequence. Under the circumstances, had James used this illustration, he would have called perception of *aeiou* in the word different from the earlier perception of its meaning. Moreover, he would have been explicit in denying that the sequence must have been buried in the unconscious upon initial exposure to the word. The fallacy involved, as expressed in symbols, takes this form: If we first have idea *A* about object *X* and later entertain idea *B* about object *X,* then *B* must already have been rooted in *A*.

CAN THE *SAME* IDEA BE BOTH CONSCIOUS AND UNCONSCIOUS?

James gave less symbolic expression to the same fallacy when he attributed it to failure to note the difference "between simply *having an idea* at the moment of its presence and subsequently knowing all sorts of things about it." Existence of the idea in this sense of *having* it is thus restricted to the instant of its actual occurrence. This is the same as saying that there is only one way in which to *have* an idea and that is to be conscious of it; when replaced by another idea the first idea *qua* idea ceases to exist. To believe otherwise by relegating it to some unconscious phase of existence struck James as meaningless and absurd. In fact, after noting that it is "unintelligible and fantastical" to allocate the *same* idea to conscious and unconscious phases of existence, he added this clarifying comment (Vol. I, p. 173):

> There is only one 'phase' in which an idea can be, and that is a fully conscious condition. If it is not in that condition, then it is not at all. Something else is, in its place. The something else may be a merely physical brain-process,[5] or it may be another conscious idea. Either of these things may perform much the same function as the first idea, refer to the same object, and roughly stand in the same relations to the upshot of our thought.[6] But that is no reason why we should throw away the logical principle of identity in psychology, and say that, however it may fare in the outer world, the mind at any rate is a place in which a thing can be all kinds of other things without ceasing to be itself as well.[7]

In order to reveal the need for attention to the principle of identity in its bearing on unconscious motivation James reverted to the instance of "suddenly" finding ourselves "in love with a person whom we imagined we only liked." At the moment of discovery, James noted, we are giving the name of "love" to a conscious state which as a feeling for another person had not been *named* previously. But this earlier unnamed feeling had not been precisely identical with the later one of being in love. It was a less "inflamed feeling" than the later one, but this did not make it an "unconscious" feeling. In fact, in the beginning, had we named our feeling it might have been called a feeling of interest in or attraction for another person and now, in retrospect, it may appear to have been "faint" in comparison with our current love. In other words, according to James (p. 174):

> A faint feeling may be looked back upon and classified and understood in its relations to what went before or after it in the stream of thought. But it, on the one hand, and the later state of mind which knows all

---

[5] According to Ernest Jones, Freud at one time came close to equating the unconscious with a "physical" process. In the words of Jones (1953, Vol. I, p. 368):

> [Freud's] experience had taught him that the most complicated processes of thought could go on without being accompanied by consciousness, and he habitually referred to these as "unconscious mental processes." Yet how far from dogmatism he was in the matter may be seen from this quotation which follows a passage concerning the displacement of affects: "Perhaps it might be more correct to say: these processes are not of a psychical nature at all, but are physical processes the psychical consequences of which are represented as if what is expressed by the words 'detachment of the idea from its affect and false connection of the latter' had really happened."

Freud had reached this conviction concerning a physical basis for mental processes by the turn of the century. He gave expression to it in the following sentence of the opening chapter of *The Interpretation of Dreams* (pp. 41–42): "Even when investigation shows that the primary exciting cause of a phenomenon is psychical, deeper research will one day trace the path further and discover an organic basis for the mental event."

[6] This sentence might be cited to show that James had been writing a functional psychology even before the school of functional psychology had come into existence.

[7] More extensive discussion of the principle of identity was introduced by James on a later page (Vol. I, pp. 459–460) concerned with the sense of sameness. In this connection he developed the implications of this italicized text: "*the mind can always intend, and knows when it intends, to think of the Same.*"

> these things about it, on the other, are surely not two conditions, one conscious and the other 'unconscious,' of the same identical psychic fact. It is the destiny of thought that, on the whole, our early ideas are superseded by later ones, giving fuller accounts of the same realities. But none the less do the earlier and the later ideas preserve their own several substantive identities as so many several successive states of mind. To believe the contrary would make any definite science of psychology impossible. The only identity to be found among our successive ideas is their similarity of cognitive or representative function as dealing with the same objects.

To illustrate the "representative function" or "successive ideas" it might prove revealing to dwell upon the concept of *school* as it develops in the course of our dealings with the theme of school from early childhood to maturity. Through the years there are innumerable ways in which we chance to deal with, talk about, or think about school. Each of these ways when experienced as an idea, although pointing to our "representative" of school as a concept, is nevertheless *qua* idea different from all our other ideas of school. In early childhood one of our ideas of school might have been elicited or symbolized by the word *Kelly,* the name of the crossing guard who helped us across a busy traffic intersection each morning. The name of the first-grade teacher, the school janitor's torn cap, the lame boy who sat next to us, a fight on the playground, and a myriad other incidents might thus constitute ways in which we experienced ideas of school. These early incidents are followed by many others as we advance through the academic hierarchy on up to the upper levels of postgraduate studies. As a consequence our initial childish ideas about school come to be succeeded by increasingly complex and abstract notions pertaining to such topics as philosophy of education, learning theory, teaching credentials, integration, student government, faculty tenure, laboratory fees, black studies, and alumni support of college athletes.

All such notions deal with or are representative of some phase of the concept of school and, in the language of James, as "later ideas" they continue to "preserve their own several successive states of mind." For James their preservation during intervening periods, by implication, was a function not of a hypothetical unconscious, but of the neurology of memory. This means that when not being experienced as ideas they are nonexistent. Similarly, a pianist's glissandi are nonexistent when he is asleep or working in the garden, but they can be reactivated when he is once again sitting at the keyboard. Obviously, the ideas can also be reactivated when confronted with suitable reminders. The underlying principle amounts to this: any product of learning may be reinstated under appropriate conditions of stimulation.[8]

---

[8]Their reinstatement is a function of memory and memory, in the last analysis being a function of cerebral cells, is more of a neurological than a psychological issue. This means that facts learned and skills acquired are preserved not in an unconscious mind, but in tissues of the brain. This truism has long been taken for granted in connection with animal learning. Upon being returned to the home cage after mastery of a maze, rats were not credited with an unconscious memory of the maze pattern. Their retention

CONCERNING HERBART'S APPERCEPTIVE MASS

The accumulation of different kinds of the "successive ideas" mentioned by James becomes the basis for subsequent understanding and interpretation of novel items as they chance to be experienced. Every new concept develops around a core of accumulated ideas. To think of different concepts such as religion, taxation, or poetry is to have groups of different categories of ideas come to mind. At one time such a group or cluster of associated ideas was called an *apperceptive mass.* This designation had been introduced by Johan Friedrich Herbart (1776–1841), Kant's successor at Königsberg and a pioneer in the advocacy of an educational psychology, or what was also called a "scientific pedagogy." In accordance with Herbartian principles, teachers were urged to be mindful of the importance of the apperceptive mass for assimilation of new ideas. Lesson plans were to be organized in terms of prior introduction of relevant background information before the introduction of new material. The underlying principle continues to be reflected in university catalogues in which elementary courses are listed as required foundations for more advanced courses. In the language of Herbart, the prerequisite course is presumed to equip the student with the requisite apperceptive mass for coping with more advanced material.

Although the phrase *apperceptive mass* has long since been dropped from the modern psychologist's technical vocabulary, its original meaning may still be retained in some current allusions to the unconscious. At least those who identify the unconscious with the total background of experience in terms of which given events are interpreted are treating such a background more or

---

of the maze habit, as K. S. Lashley (1890–1958) demonstrated, depends on the integrity of brain tissue. In fact, at the end of a long series of experiments he came to the following conclusions, among others (pp. 175–176):

> The capacity to form maze habits is reduced by destruction of cerebral tissue.
>
> The reduction is roughly proportional to the amount of destruction.
>
> The more complex the problem to be learned, the greater the retardation produced by any given extent of lesion.
>
> The capacity to retain is reduced, as is the capacity to learn.
>
> A review of the literature on cerebral function in other mammals, including man, indicates that, in spite of the greater specialization of cerebral areas in the higher forms, the problems of cerebral function are not greatly different from those raised by experiments with the rat.

Incidentally, even though Lashley reached these conclusions about fifty years ago, they are by no means altogether outmoded. In fact, a contemporary experimentalist, Paul Pietsch, traces the origin of the latest neurological theory of memory, the *holographic theory,* to "the 1920s when psychologist Karl Lashley began a lifelong search through the brain for the vaults containing memory" (1972, p. 42). Needless to add, despite the progress suggested by the holographic theory, the search is far from over. At about the time when the article by Pietsch appeared another scientist, Victor F. Weisskopf, writing in a different periodical, acknowledged that "we still know very little . . . about the functioning of the nervous system, and we know practically nothing about what goes on in the brain when we think or when we use the memory" (1972, p. 144).

less as the equivalent of Herbart's apperceptive mass. Furthermore, in a more restricted sense the psychoanalytic concept of *preconscious* is even more definitely such an equivalent, since the concept refers to ideas no longer present in consciousness but which are readily reinstated when needed to answer questions and to dispose of difficulties. Thus, being able to recall one's place of birth or mother's maiden name or father's business or profession might serve as examples of reinstatement. Similarly, the schoolboy's preconscious supplies answers to questions having to do with his grade, his teacher's name, his school's football record, and so forth. Incidentally, the concept of preconscious has been subjected to varied interpretations by different psychoanalytic specialists in recent years,[9] but consideration of these interpretations would interfere with the central theme of the present chapter, namely, the reaction of James to arguments advanced in support of the existence of unconscious mental states.

One of these arguments has to do with what came to be called *unconscious inference.* Originally it was advanced by Wundt and Helmholtz.[10] However, it has come to be associated more closely with the name of Helmholtz, so that his treatment of the concept has been more influential than Wundt's. Accordingly, for present purposes there is no need to consider Wundt's view.

CONCERNING HELMHOLTZ AND UNCONSCIOUS INFERENCE

Hermann Helmholtz (1821-1894), although not a psychologist, nevertheless came to have a great influence on the efforts to promote psychology as a science. This, of course, was one of James's primary efforts in writing the *Principles* of 1890. Helmholtz's influence is suggested by the fact that he is mentioned in the *Principles* in connection with more than some fifteen different topics. The magnitude of this influence on the development of psychology as science can be appreciated by the additional fact that years later in Boring's *History of Experimental Psychology* of 1950, Helmholtz is listed as one of three founders of experimental psychology, the other two founders being Fechner and Wundt. In addition, at the close of his *History* (p. 743) Boring concluded "there are at least four very great men in psychology's history: Darwin, Helmholtz, James and Freud." There can thus be no ques-

[9]The preconscious was once called the foreconscious and the two terms are synonymous and interchangeable. In a section on "The Preconscious Unconscious" (1971, pp. 207–210) Samuel Abrams has reviewed the history of the concept along with differing interpretations suggested by various psychoanalysts in recent years. Some even suggested equating the preconscious with the concept of ego. It is virtually impossible to bring all the suggested interpretations into one comprehensive definition.

[10]According to Boring (1950, p. 309) "the theory belongs more to Helmholtz" than to Wundt, as Wundt himself granted. He also wrote that Helmholtz "had the theory first and kept it" whereas Wundt "took up the theory later and presently abandoned it." There may be some question about this. As will be brought out shortly, in the words of James both Helmholtz and Wundt had "modified their views" and "recanted."

tion about Helmholtz's eminence as a thinker and as a scientist. What he had to teach was bound to command respectful attention. Any student reading Boring's chapter concerned with the achievements of Helmholtz (Ch. 15) is also bound to be impressed.

Moreover, what is particularly pertinent in the present context is the fact that many academic generations of university students upon reading Boring's chapter have come to associate the name of Helmholtz with the concept of unconscious inference. This, of course, will be in addition to associating his name with a theory of color vision, with the resonance theory of hearing, with the invention of the ophthalmoscope, with the measurement of the speed of a nerve impulse, and with some classic volumes on physiological optics. Being introduced in this kind of setting, the phrase *unconscious inference* is likely to be surrounded with a halo of scientific endorsement. In the course of time, Boring's critical comments with reference to the phrase are likely to be forgotten and all that may be retained will be the impression of unconscious reasoning as a doctrine introduced into psychology long before Freud by the scientifically eminent Helmholtz.

What Helmholtz introduced into psychology was a theory of perception according to which recognition of objects and judgment of distance are products of experience rather than instinctive or intuitive reactions to sensory impressions. This made him an empiricist in opposition to the nativists. Accordingly, along with British empiricists he was sponsoring an associationistic theory of perception. To *see* sandpaper as rough involves an association between visual and cutaneous sensations. Similarly, it might be argued that we *learn* to associate a gradual increase in the size of a visual impression with nearness and its gradual decrease in size with remoteness. Having learned this relationship, a child watching father walk away does not say, "Daddy is getting smaller," but "Daddy is going to work." It is *as if* the child were drawing a conclusion regarding the significance of a change in the magnitude of visual impressions. There may be no explicit awareness of the actual diminution of visual sensations, nor of the reasoning process leading to the conclusion. This lack of awareness means that the conclusion was arrived at unconsciously.

Had Helmholtz used this example, he would have said the child had indulged in an *unbewusster Schluss,* literally "unconscious conclusion." This literal meaning is not quite duplicated, but only approximated by the phrase "unconscious inference," now the generally accepted English translation of the original. Actually, the difference in connotation is not momentous. Both phrases serve to call attention to Helmholtz's main contention, namely, that perception is a cognitive as well as a sensory operation and that in familiar or habitual perceptions there is no awareness of the cognitive aspect. As a result, such effortless habitual perceptions are commonly regarded as being exclusively sensory and noncognitive processes. However, according to Helmholtz, genetically considered, the development of such habitual perceptions is characterized by an implicit inductive process and induction is obviously more cognitive than sensory.

INDUCTION AS IMPLICIT IN SENSE-PERCEPTION

The recognition of induction as implicit in the concept of unconscious inference was already evident in Helmholtz's initial presentation. This was as early as 1866 in one of his volumes on optics. As cited by Herrnstein and Boring in their 1965 collection of historically important source material, his presentation contains the following allusion to induction as related to persistence of illusory perceptions in a variety of situations (Helmholtz, pp. 192–193):

> Even when we have learned to understand the physiological origin and connection of the senses, it is impossible to get rid of the illusion in spite of our better knowledge. This is because *inductive* reasoning is the result of an unconscious and involuntary activity of the memory. . . . Every evening apparently before our eyes the sun goes down behind the stationary horizon, although we are well aware that the sun is fixed and the horizon moves. An actor who cleverly portrays an old man is for us an old man there on the stage, so long as we let the immediate impression sway us, and do not forcibly recall that the programme states that the person moving about there is the young actor with whom we are acquainted. We consider him as being angry or in pain according as he shows us one of the other mode of countenance and demeanour. (Italics added.)

Furthermore, in an essay published in 1894 Helmholtz introduced the word *Inductionschluss* meaning inductive conclusion as a designation for what he had originally called an *unbewusster Schluss,* and he even interpreted some instances of animal behavior as illustrative of such an inductive operation. The essay as translated by Warren and Warren and included in their book on Helmholtz was entitled "The Origin of the Correct Interpretation of our Sensory Impressions" (1968, pp. 249–260). In it (p. 255) he wrote that an *Inductionschluss* enables animals to "shy back from some object which looks similar to another one on which they had burned themselves on an earlier occasion." In this interpretation he was reverting to the inductive factor he had already detected in his reference to unconscious inference (*unbewusster Schluss*) some thirty years before. In the intervening years, as will be brought out shortly, he had come to entertain misgivings about this notion of unconscious inference. However, in the essay under consideration it seemed to him that "within certain limits" there might be some justification for revival of the older "name" of *unbewusster Schluss,* or as he put it (pp. 255–256):

> I find even now that this name is admissible within certain limits since these associations of perceptions in the memory actually take place in such a manner, that at the time of their origin one is not aware of it,

> or is aware only in such a manner that one remembers to have observed the same process frequently before (in other words, it is recognized as something familiar). The memory of earlier cases with the accompanying circumstances can emerge more distinctly during the first repetitions of rarer observations of this kind, so that the mental process here acquires a greater analogy to conscious thought.

What Helmholtz was finding "admissible" in this essay of 1894 was his use of the word *unconscious* in his *Optics* of the 1860s. As an empiricist he was not using the word in the sense of mental factors that had originated independently of experience. Instead he was referring to our ignorance of some of the factors involved in *learning* from experience. He made this clear by noting that we learn to interpret facial expressions even though we may be unable to specify precisely what cues enable us to decide on the difference between an expression of worry and one of fatigue, or between rage and terror. We are conscious of the total impression but unconscious or ignorant of all the determinants of a given impression. Even the young child soon *learns* to judge Mother's mood by watching her face. He learns or comes to associate the image of a smiling face with a different set of expectations from the image of an unsmiling face. In the words of Helmholtz (p. 253): ". . . for the human child, most important visual images must be learned by him, and are not given by inherent organization without preceding experience." From smiling faces he learns to draw a different conclusion than from scowling faces even though he may not be explicitly conscious of the influence of these facial cues.

In terms of this example unconscious inference ceases to suggest elaborate reasoning. Instead it becomes a questionable way of referring to perceptual judgments based upon associative memory. To revert to another of Helmholtz's examples: association by similarity causes an animal to "shy back" from an object which resembles a previously experienced injurious object. The injury or burn was a cutaneous stimulus, but the object itself was a visual stimulus. According to Helmholtz, the subsequent sight of the object arouses "the memory of earlier cases" of having been injured and is thus "recognized as something familiar." It should be obvious that what Helmholtz attributed to associative memory a later generation of learning theorists attributed to conditioning. Had he been using the language of conditioning, he might have stated that with the "first repetitions" of the combination of conditioned and unconditioned stimuli the animal becomes "more distinctly" aware of the relation between the sight of the object and the subsequent burn. At this stage, to use his own words, "the mental process acquires a greater analogy to conscious thought." However, with the firm establishment of the conditioned reaction the animal will "shy back" from the conditioned stimulus of the similar looking object with quasi-reflex automatism and virtually no "conscious thought" of the memory of the burn. It might be said that at the time of reaction the animal is unconscious of the earlier injury; whether this should be called *unconscious inference* is open to question.

In fact, Helmholtz himself had questioned it some years before writing the essay in which, upon reconsideration, he had found endorsement of the phrase "admissible within certain limits." Aside from these restricted limits he had ceased to endorse the doctrine of unconscious inference. He no longer believed in the occurrence of unconscious reasoning or what some may have called reasoning in the unconscious.

HELMHOLTZ QUESTIONS UNCONSCIOUS REASONING

As noted earlier, both Helmholtz and Wundt had written about the concept of unconscious inference. This was in the 1860s and they were both attempting to account for certain aspects of perception. Then, as reported by James, by the 1870s they had changed their views of the concept (Vol. I, p. 169):

> It is to be remarked that Wundt and Helmholtz, who in their earlier writings did more than any one to give vogue to the notion that unconscious inference is a vital factor in sense-perception, have seen fit on later occasions to modify their views and to admit that results *like* those of reasoning may accrue without any actual reasoning process unconsciously taking place.

This was not the only time James discussed the modified views of Wundt and Helmholtz. He mentioned their views again in a later chapter in which he asked, "Is Perception Unconscious Inference?" and by way of introduction to the question he wrote as follows (Vol. II, pp. 111–112):

> A widely-spread opinion (which has been held by such men as Schopenhauer, Spencer, Hartmann, Wundt, Helmholtz, and lately . . . by M. Binet) will have it that *perception should be called a sort of reasoning operation, more or less unconsciously and automatically performed.* The question seems at first a verbal one, depending on how broadly the term reasoning is to be taken. If every time a present sign suggests an absent reality to our mind, we make an inference; and if every time we make an inference we reason; then perception is indubitably reasoning. Only one sees no room in it for any unconscious part. Both associates, the present sign and the contiguous things which it suggests, are aboveboard, and no intermediary ideas are required.

In thus rejecting the notion of perception involving unconscious reasoning James was once again expressing his doubts about any *mental* process being unconscious. Moreover, in this final statement voicing his opposition, his doubts came closer to being a conviction (p. 113):

> So far, then, from perception being a species of reasoning properly so called, both it and reasoning are co-ordinate varieties of that deeper sort of process known psychologically as the association of ideas, and physiologically as the law of habit in the brain. *To call perception*

> *unconscious reasoning is thus either a useless metaphor, or a positively misleading confusion between two different things.*

James was not presenting this italicized conclusion as an indictment of the views of Wundt and Helmholtz, even though they had been among the original supporters of the doctrine of unconscious inference. In a footnote (p. 111) he called attention to what he had written in the earlier chapter concerning their modified stand and made this explicit by noting that "*Wundt and Helmholtz have more recently 'recanted'*" (italics mine). This is worth stressing because, as will be considered later, this recantation has been overlooked by writers who continue to list Wundt and Helmholtz among the sponsors of belief in mind as unconscious. Had they consulted James (Vol. I, p. 169), from the bibliographic data supplied they would have learned that Wundt had renounced the latter belief in an 1876 publication and that Helmholtz had done so in an essay of 1879.

For present purposes there is little need to say more about Wundt's recantation, but it is quite pertinent to say more about Helmholtz's reasons for recanting. The reasons are to be found in the 1879 article. This article had been delivered as an address at the University of Berlin on August 3, 1878, and a translation under the title of "The Facts of Perception" is to be found in the volume by Warren and Warren (pp. 207-231). As shown in the following excerpt, Helmholtz had decided to avoid further reference to unconscious inference because what he meant by the term might be misinterpreted with what Schopenhauer and his followers had meant by the term (p. 220):

> In my earlier works I named the conceptual connections occurring in this process *unconscious conclusions.* Unconscious, in respect to the major premise based upon a sequence of experiences, each of which had long since disappeared from memory and entered consciousness only in the form of sensory impressions, not necessarily as sentences framed in words. New sensory impressions occurring in ongoing perception form the minor premise to which we apply the rule stamped in our mind by previous observations. Later I avoided that term, "unconscious conclusions," in order to escape from the entirely confused and unjustified concept—at any rate so it seems to me—which Schopenhauer and his disciples designate by the name. We are obviously concerned here with a basic process which underlies all that truly can be called thinking, although it lacks the critical sifting and completion of individual steps found in the scientific formulation of concepts and ideas.

James was in agreement with Helmholtz in repudiating Schopenhauer's views of the unconscious. In fact, he equated them with the "mythology" he had attributed to the views of Hartmann. To appreciate Helmholtz's reasons for wanting "to escape" from having his views confused with Schopenhauer's, it will suffice to read the following account of Schopenhauer's "mythology" as described by James (Vol. I, pp. 169-170):

> The visual perception . . . of an object in space results, according to him, from the intellect performing the following operations, all unconscious. First, it apprehends the inverted retinal image and turns it right side up, constructing *flat space* as a preliminary operation; then it computes from the angle of convergence of the eyeballs that the two retinal images must be the projection of a single *object*; thirdly, it constructs the third dimension and sees this object *solid*; fourthly, it assigns its *distance*; and fifthly, in each and all of these operations it gets the objective character of what it 'constructs' by unconsciously inferring it as the only possible *cause* of some sensation which it unconsciously feels. Comment on this seems hardly called for. It is, as I said, pure mythology.

It should now be evident why Helmholtz had characterized Schopenhauer's interpretation of the concept of unconscious inference as "confused and unjustified." Furthermore, in view of Helmholtz's empiricism a clash with the nativistic, intuitive voluntarism of Schopenhauer was to be expected. As an empiricist he would be expected to be on guard against confusing the products of learning and habit formation with those attributable to heredity. As he saw it, unconscious inference was such a product of learning and habit formation. This was suggested by the fact that in his disavowal of Schopenhauer's standpoint he referred to a "basic process" involved in what had been called unconscious inference, a process he regarded as underlying "all that truly can be called thinking." This calls for a word of explanation.

WHAT HELMHOLTZ MEANT BY "BASIC PROCESS"

In identifying the basic process with "thinking" Helmholtz was not equating it with critical reasoning. As he expressed the difference, the "thinking" in question "lacks the critical sifting and completion of individual steps found in the scientific formulation of concepts and ideas." He was using the word in the sense in which observation as a cognitive process characterizes perceptual learning. In learning the Greek alphabet, for example, a student might say, "I think I can tell the difference between gamma and rho." Similarly, if asked about the weather, he might gaze out the window and reply, "I think it might rain." In the judgment of facial expression, to revert to one of Helmholtz's examples, the basic process might give rise to a sentence like, "I think the man looks either perplexed or determined."

Whenever perception is difficult, thinking of some sort takes place. Once the difficulty is resolved perceptual recognition is immediate, spontaneous, and, in a literal sense, thoughtless. For instance, for readers of this book words like *reaction, association,* and *brain* would be recognized immediately. On the other hand words like *dinoflagellate, phthisical,* and *arrendamento* would probably prove to be refractory to such spontaneous perceptual recognition. Neither pronunciation nor meaning would be obvious and their mastery would entail attention to the syllables and search through dictionaries in the quest for understanding.

The perceptual challenge involved is akin to the challenge of learning a foreign language. As students of Latin or French or some other language we may recall that in the beginning as we were learning new vocabulary we kept thinking of their English equivalents. In effect we were conscious of the fact that *stella* means *star* or *penser* means *to think* and *lachen* means *to laugh.* In reading the foreign language text we would be translating each word into our native tongue. However, once we advance to the stage of being able to think in the new language the foreign text no longer seems "foreign" as we understand the words of the text without having to translate them into English equivalents.

This means that we are now *unconscious* of these equivalents as we read or converse in what had once been an alien tongue for us, *as if* we know the English meaning without being conscious of the English words. This may come close to what Helmholtz once meant by *unconscious inference.* Moreover, what he later called a *basic process* is exemplified by this shift from initial consciousness of the English equivalents to the later disappearance of such consciousness once we have reached the stage of reading the new language easily without dependence on dictionaries.

It ought to be evident that this example of the shift from initial reading efforts to later effortless reading habits holds true for comparable shifts from initial learning of any task to its later habitual execution. In other words, Helmholtz's basic process has to do with the shift from consciousness to the automatism of habit. It is the same as the kind of shift given special prominence by sponsors of functional psychology.

Advocates of functional psychology were especially concerned with accounting for the function of mind or consciousness in the biological scheme of things. They saw this as a problem-solving function as the organism is confronted with the novel, the threatening, or the perplexing. Once such a problem situation had been handled successfully, the organism was prepared to deal with any recurrence with greater dispatch as habitual control displaced conscious control.

Helmholtz, with his recognition of the basic process as intrinsic to the concept of unconscious inference, was thus really anticipating a central teaching of functional psychology. Like the functionalists he was arguing that with the establishment of autonomous control of habit there is virtual elimination of conscious control. In this sense well entrenched habitual actions may be said to take place unconsciously. As ingrained habits they may function as mechanically and as unconsciously as reflexes—no unconscious mind need be posited to account for the automatism of reflexes or the automatism of habit.

This interpretation of what Helmholtz meant by unconscious inference as related to the basic process is neither new nor original. As shown in the following quotation, it is merely an elaboration of what Boring once wrote with reference to the role of experience in the formation of unconscious inferences (1950, p. 310):

> These inferences, Helmholtz thought, are at first conscious . . . and develop by *association* and *repetition* into unconscious inferences. . . . It is the commonplace of introspective psychology that a conscious state, by repetition and under the law of habit, is telescoped and reduced until the given process is largely or entirely unconscious, as far as introspection can reveal, and as against what at first seemed to be the logically necessary essentials. Helmholtz's view is merely the principle of conscious decay under habituation.

In the light of this last principle it should be obvious that the concept of unconscious inference as understood by Helmholtz has to do with habit-formation and not with reasoning in some unconscious realm. This has failed to be noted by some modern writers who continue to include Helmholtz among those who have endorsed the concept of mind as unconscious. As previously mentioned, they evidently had overlooked James's 1890 statement to the effect that by the 1870s both Wundt and Helmholtz had "recanted" with reference to the stand taken in the 1860s. Now in the 1970s it is time to set the record straight by more explicit attention to this oversight. Helmholtz and Wundt may continue to be listed as "discoverers" of the unconscious if this error is not corrected.

CORRECTION OF AN ERROR

Among recent books dealing with the "discovery" of the unconscious in which the concept of unconscious inference is listed as part of the supporting evidence there are the 1960 volume by Lancelot Whyte and the 1970 volume by Henri Ellenberger. It so happens that the former merely lists Helmholtz as having endorsed the concept and then quotes from Wundt at greater length. However, in Ellenberger's book the treatment is different: only Helmholtz is quoted and Wundt is not even mentioned in this connection.

In the case of Whyte, Helmholtz is disposed of in a single sentence (p. 158) reading, "I shall not . . . quote from *H. Helmholtz* (1821-1894), though he is important for his emphasis on *unconscious inference.*" However, he did quote from Wundt, whom he described not as a psychologist but as a "German physiologist" who had held that "Our proper activity is unconscious" and who had once written (p. 160):

> Our mind is so fortunately equipped, that it brings us the most important bases for our thoughts without our having the least knowledge of this work of elaboration. Only the results of it become conscious. This unconscious mind is for us like an unknown being who creates and produces for us, and finally throws the ripe fruits in our lap.

Whyte failed to cite the precise source of the latter quotation. However, at the end of the book he did supply a single bibliographic reference to Wundt. This one concerned an early publication in which Wundt had discussed "contributions to the theory of sensory perception."[11] At the time—during the 1860s—Wundt was working at Heidelberg as a physiologist; since Whyte had called Wundt a physiologist, it seems likely that the quotation came from this early publication. Moreover, as noted by Boring (1950, pp. 318–319), the book "contains a brief discussion of unconscious inference (*unbewusster Schluss:* the phrase is used) as the mechanism of perception."

Whether the theory of unconscious inference was original with Wundt may be questioned. As also noted by Boring (1950, p. 309), Helmholtz had developed the essentials of the theory around 1855, a few years before Wundt wrote on the subject. In fact, in the words of Boring, "Wundt admitted that . . . the theory belongs more to Helmholtz." Furthermore, as applied to physiological optics, Helmholtz certainly did very much more with the theory.

In some respects this question of priority with regard to unconscious inference is not momentous in view of the fact that by 1880[12] both Helmholtz and Wundt had ceased to endorse the concept. Consequently, Whyte should not have listed Wundt and Helmholtz among those who endorsed a belief in "the unconscious before Freud." It will be recalled that James had called attention to their "recantation" in his *Principles* of 1890. Wundt himself was very definite in his rejection of the unconscious, as shown in this passage wherein he concluded that belief in the unconscious is metaphysically untenable (1897, p. 196):

> We can know nothing of the unconscious or, what amounts to the same thing for psychology, a material process which is not immediately perceived but merely assumed hypothetically on the basis of metaphysical presuppositions. Such metaphysical assumptions are merely devices to cover up an incomplete or entirely wanting psychological observation.

This serves as a reminder of the important psychological observation made by Helmholtz when he came to realize that what he had once attributed to unconscious reasoning was more definitely related to the automatism of habit. It was this changed interpretation of the concept of unconscious reasoning James had called a "recantation." Ellenberger failed to take this changed interpretation into account. Instead, in allusion to what Helmholtz had stated in the 1859 edition of the *Physiological Optics,* he declared (1970, p. 313):

> Helmholtz discovered the phenomenon of "unconscious inference": we perceive the objects not as they impress our sense organs, but "as they

---

[11] The book's title in German was virtually the same, namely, *Beiträge zur Theorie der Sinneswahrnehmung.* Although the book as a whole has not been translated, the introduction concerned with the "methods in Psychology" has been translated and is now available in Shipley's *Classics in Psychology* (1961).

[12] Helmholtz in his essay of 1879 explained why he had decided to cease employing the phrase "unconscious inference." Moreover, as noted by Titchener (1929, p. 6), Wundt had already rejected "the unconscious as a principle of psychological explanation" as early as 1874.

> should be." Perception is a kind of instantaneous and unconscious reconstruction of what our past experience taught us about the object.

From the context it appears that for Ellenberger this discovery of unconscious inference was congruent with influences leading to the emergence of belief in mind as unconscious, especially as such belief came to be reflected in post-Freudian psychiatry. At all events, the chapter in which Helmholtz's discovery is introduced covers the period from 1880 to 1900 and is entitled "On the Threshold of a New Dynamic Psychiatry." It is a long chapter of some seventy-five pages and close to two hundred and fifty bibliographic notes; but the name of James is missing from these notes. As in Whyte there was no mention of Helmholtz's "recantation" as James had reported in his *Principles.* In the case of Whyte this is understandable, since there is no mention of the *Principles* in his survey of *The Unconscious before Freud.* In the case of Ellenberger however, as shown in the following quotation, there was very explicit recognition of the *Principles* (pp. 762–763):

> In the field of psychology the important event was the publication of William James's *Principles of Psychology.* The well-known Harvard psychologist had been working for twelve years on the book, which was the first major work of its kind to appear in the United States, and had an immediate and lasting success on both sides of the Atlantic. This textbook treated not only various aspects of experimental psychology but problems of hypnosis, dual personality, and psychical research as well.

It is to be noted that Ellenberger had nothing to say about the way the "textbook" treated problems of the unconscious in general and unconscious inference in particular. Although there are numerous references to Hartmann and to Schopenhauer as nineteenth-century "discoverers" of the unconscious, there is no reference to James as a critic of their views. Nor is there any reference to James's systematic presentation of the ten arguments advanced in support of belief in mental states as unconscious along with his replies to these arguments. There is no mention of the fact that with specific reference to the question of perception as unconscious inference James had also rendered a negative verdict. In short, neither Ellenberger nor Whyte devotes any space to the negative stand taken by James on this or on any other question pertaining to mind as unconscious. No reader of their volumes would ever suspect that James had once indicated belief in mental states as unconscious as "the sovereign means for believing what one likes in psychology, and of turning what might become a science into a tumbling-ground for whimsies."

Actually, in neither of these books are any of James's teachings given more than incidental attention. Moreover, and this is important, even when mentioned they are so presented as to suggest that James is to be included among those listed as "discoverers" of the unconscious. Whyte (p. 168), for example, includes the name of James among those who, along with Charcot,

Janet, and Breuer, "made contributions before 1899 when Freud's *Interpretation of Dreams* was published." Furthermore, Ellenberger interpreted James's interest in automatic writing as implicit endorsement of belief in mind as unconscious. He made this quite definite by writing that "Frederic Myers and William James understood that automatic writing provided a means of access to the unconscious" (p. 121).

Both Myers and James were interested in automatic writing, particularly as it might have a bearing on so-called psychic phenomena. As will be brought out in a later section, Myers was closely identified with the investigation of such phenomena and was one of the founders of the Society for Psychical Research in England, just as James was instrumental in establishing a similar society in America. Furthermore, both James and Myers endeavored to have psychical research conform to the canons of *scientific* research. Whether interest in this research also implied tacit endorsement of the unconscious is to be questioned. Otherwise it would mean that for James the unconscious had ceased to be a "tumbling-ground for whimsies" and that he had become more accepting of views he had once rejected–views of Leibnitz, Hartmann, and Schopenhauer. Just what it did mean for James calls for separate consideration.

WILLIAM JAMES AND PSYCHICAL RESEARCH

There can be no question about James's active support of investigations of so-called psychical phenomena.[13] This is evident from his discussion of "mediumships" in the *Principles* (Vol. I, pp. 393-400), in the course of which he dealt with automatic writing, the trance states of the mediums, and reports of departed spirits or alien agencies being in "control" of the medium. In this general context he wrote (p. 396):

> I am myself persuaded by abundant acquaintance with the trances of one medium that the 'control' may be altogether different from any *possible* waking self of the person. . . . I record my bare opinion here unsupported by the evidence, not, of course, in order to convert anyone to my view, but because I am persuaded that a serious study of these trance-phenomena is one of the greatest needs of psychology, and think that my personal confession may possibly draw a reader or two into a field which the *soi-disant* 'scientist' usually refuses to explore.

It is important to note that James did not venture to describe the exact nature of the "control" operative during the trance. In this one instance he appeared to be convinced of the existence of a genuine if perplexing phenomenon. By implication he was ruling out the possibility of fraud, deception,

---

[13] An excellent introductory survey of the nature and scope of James's support of these investigations is to be found in the work by Perry (1935, Vol. II, pp. 154–172). For a later and more comprehensive account of James's affiliation with psychical research see the 1960 volume by Murphy and Ballou.

or trickery of any kind. As a phenomenon it was to be taken seriously as worthy of scientific investigation and called for critical examination by psychologists since it belonged to "trance-phenomena" whose study constituted "one of the greatest needs of psychology."

Now, in the opinion of James, his willingness to have "psychic" phenomena studied as bona fide psychological issues has been misunderstood or misinterpreted as indicative of a belief in spirits or ghosts. At all events, when he was called a "spiritist" he resented and denied it. According to Perry (Vol. II, pp. 348–349), James Leuba had published an article on "Professor William James' Interpretation of Religious Experience" in which, among other statements, he reported that in his book concerned with this kind of experience James had introduced the "imaginary shadows of spirit agents" and that the reader of the book finds that "ghosts pop out of the very places he had just shown you to be empty." In a letter written on April 17, 1904, James took issue with such statements in this blunt fashion:

> Dear Leuba,
>
> I have read your article with great interest, admiring its clearness of statement, and rejoicing in the way in which you go to the heart of my contentions, straight and without floundering. Only of your characterization of my thesis as that of "spirit-intervention" do I complain. No reader . . . could possibly guess that the only spirit that I contend for is "God." Unless he knows my book he will suppose that I am a "spiritist" out and out, which I am not. This is unfair.

Unfortunately, this disclaimer continues to be overlooked or ignored. For instance, even Ellenberger (1970, p. 837) refers to James as one of the "spiritists." It may be that some justification for calling James a spiritist has to do with his belief in God as a spirit; but this belief is subject to misinterpretation unless qualified by reference to the following explanation James included in the same letter to Leuba (Perry, Vol. II, pp. 350–351):

> My personal position is simple. I have no living sense of commerce with a God. I envy those who have, for I know that the addition of such a sense would help me greatly. The Divine, for my active life, is limited to impersonal and abstract concepts which, as ideals, interest and determine me, but do so faintly in comparison with what a feeling of God might effect, if I had one. This, to be sure, is largely a matter of intensity, but a shade of intensity may make one's whole centre of moral energy shift. Now, although I am so devoid of Gottesbewusstsein in the directer and stronger sense, yet there is *something in me* which *makes response* when I hear utterances from that quarter made by others. I recognize the deeper voice. Something tells me: *"thither lies truth"*—and I am sure it is not old theistic prejudices of infancy. Those in my case were Christian, but I have grown so out of Christianity that entanglement therewith on the part of mystical utterance has to be abstracted from and overcome, before I can listen. Call this, if you like, my mystical *germ*. It is a very common germ. It creates the rank and

> file of believers. As it withstands in my case, so it will withstand in most cases, all purely atheistic criticism, but *interpretative* criticism (not of the mere "hysteria" and "nerves" order) it can energetically combine with.

The foregoing explanation of James's analysis of the concept of God was intended to answer Leuba's attack directed against James's analysis of the psychology of religion as presented in the Gifford Lectures at Edinburgh in 1901-1902 and published under the title of *The Varieties of Religious Experience–A Study of Human Nature.* This was the book in which Leuba thought James had been taking "spirit agents" and "ghosts" seriously. As James insisted, it was contrary to fact and "unfair" for Leuba to make such a statement. Even his recognition of God as a spirit, James was saying, was not the same as making God a ghost or shadowy apparition. He even denied having "a feeling of God"; his notion of God or the Divine was both "impersonal and abstract." Being impersonal his God had to be nonanthropomorphic and being abstract his God had to be nonmaterial in the sense that any abstraction such as justice or circularity or infinity has to be nonmaterial. Possibly it was in this sense that James was thinking of God as a spirit.[14] If so, he failed to make this explicit in the *Varieties.*

Incidentally, Ellenberger was familiar with the *Varieties* and alludes to it as supplying "evidence of the Divine" in a restricted sense. This was introduced at the close of a discussion concerned with Janet's "deep preoccupation with religion" and his interest not only in the psychological analysis of religious belief but also in spiritism as an "attempt to converse . . . with disembodied spirits" (pp. 394-400). Since James was also professionally identified with religious experience and with psychical research, it is easy to understand why Ellenberger thought of James as a spiritist. Furthermore, even though James denied being one, some of his basic attitudes toward psychical research and religion are hard to reconcile with this denial. In reacting to the paranormal, the mystical, and the supernatural, he was more inclined to side with the claims of the spiritualists than with those of skeptics. At least there was no a priori conviction of the spiritualist's claims as utter nonsense.

FROM THE PARANORMAL TO THE SPIRITUAL

That James took psychical research seriously was evident in his comments in the *Principles.* In fact, he was identified with the movement while engaged in writing his psychology during the decade of the 1880s. This was the decade

---

[14]With reference to the way James thought of God, Perry introduced this clarifying comment (Vol. II, pp. 358-359):

> He insisted upon retaining not only the ideality but also the actuality of God–as a conscious power beyond, with which one may come into beneficent contact; he believed in the triumph, through this same power, of the cause of righteousness to which his moral will was pledged; and he entertained a hopeful half-belief in personal immortality.

when both the British and American movements were established, the British Society for Psychical Research founded in 1882 and the American one in 1884. James was a member of the American society from 1884 until his death in 1910, and, as noted by Perry, served as vice-president for eighteen years and as president for two years. Two different letters James wrote around 1884–1885 and from which Perry cited the following excerpts reflect James's purpose in supporting investigation of the paranormal (Vol. II, p. 160):

> We are founding here a "Society for Psychical Research," under which innocent sounding name ghosts, second sight, spiritualism and all sorts of hobgoblins are going to be "investigated" by the most high-toned and "cultured" members of the community.
>
> I take it the urgent thing . . . is to ascertain in a manner so thorough as to constitute *evidence* that will be accepted by outsiders, just what the *phenomenal conditions of certain* phenomenal occurrences are. Not till that is done, can spiritualistic or anti-spiritualistic theories be even mooted. I'm sure that the more we can steer clear of theories at first, the better. . . . *"Facts"* are what are wanted.

It is important to emphasize that James was on the alert for the possible discovery of such paranormal "facts" while he was writing the *Principles.* This is so because, as will be brought out shortly, James has sometimes been listed as having endorsed the hypothesis of *unconscious* mental processes on the basis of findings reported in the literature of psychical research. Since he had such findings in mind while engaged in writing Volume I of the *Principles,* it is hard to believe that he interpreted any or all of them as justifying endorsement of this hypothesis. Otherwise what he wrote about "mediumships" in Chapter 10 (pp. 393-400) should have induced him to revise or retract what he had written in Chapter 6 (pp. 162–176) about the existence of unconscious mental states.

In the course of time, however, James appeared to favor "spiritualistic" interpretations not only with respect to the "facts" reported by psychical researchers, but also with respect to religious experiences reported by the devout. In 1904, the very year in which he had assured Leuba that he was not an out and out spiritist, he had occasion to indicate in what sense one might believe in a "spiritual reality." This took place when he consented to reply to a questionnaire dealing with religious belief. The way he disposed of two of the questions will shed light on the issue under consideration. As excerpted from the questionnaire by Murphy and Ballou, the first one reads (1960, pp. 272-273):

> *Question:* Is God an attitude of the Universe toward you? *Answer:* Yes, but more conscious. "God," to me, is not the only spiritual reality to believe in. Religion means primarily a universe of spiritual relations surrounding the earthly practical ones, not merely relations of "value," but agencies and their activities. I suppose that the chief premise for my hospitality towards the religious testimony of others is my con-

> viction that "normal" or "sane" consciousness is so small a part of actual experience. Whate'er be true, it is not true exclusively, as philistine scientific opinion assumes. The other kinds of consciousness bear witness to a much wider universe of experiences, from which our belief selects and emphasizes such parts as best satisfy our needs.

And the second one reads (p. 274):

> *Question:* Do you believe in personal immortality? *Answer:* Never keenly, but more strongly as I grow older.

In his answer to the first question James introduced a distinction between two kinds of consciousness: (*a*) ordinary or "normal" consciousness concerned with a narrow segment of "actual experience," and (*b*) the kind concerned with a "wider" realm of experiences indicative of "a universe of spiritual relations." Just what is implied by this latter realm will be considered later. For the time being it is enough to note that the distinction in question was described in terms of an antithesis between "earthly" relations on the one hand and "spiritual" relations on the other. It is also well to note that the answer to the second question, with its acknowledgment of a growing belief in personal immortality, is also suggestive of belief in the existence of a separate spiritual realm.

Actually James was doing no more than defending *belief* in a spiritual world and in personal immortality. He was not ready to transform his belief about such matters into dogmatic convictions. This was clear from his review of F. W. H. Myers' *Human Personality and Its Survival of Bodily Death.* As one of the pioneer participants in psychical research Myers had been persuaded of the spiritistic implications of many paranormal phenomena. In the volume under review his object had been to demonstrate what they signified for the survival hypothesis. It was a long review and there is no need to consider it in detail. For present purposes it will suffice to introduce an early introductory paragraph and a later concluding one. The early one serves as a reminder of what James took to be the correct attitude with which to investigate and evaluate paranormal reports. As quoted by Murphy and Ballou, this paragraph reads as follows (1960, p. 227):

> Anyone with a healthy sense for evidence, a sense not methodically blunted by the sectarianism of "science," ought now, it seems to me, to feel that exalted sensibilities and memories, veridical phantasms, haunted houses, trances with super-normal faculty, and even experimental thought-transference, are natural kinds of phenomena which ought, just like other natural events, to be followed up with scientific curiosity.

The later, concluding paragraph (p. 236) serves to indicate that James had reservations regarding the truth of what Myers had to say about a spiritual world in general and about immortality in particular:

> As regards the truth of his theory, as contradistinguished from its formal merits as a constructive effort, it is certainly too early for anyone to pass dogmatic judgment. Most readers, even those who admire the scheme as a whole, will doubtless shrink from yielding credence to it unreservedly. It will seem like skating over ice too thin for any intellect less nimble than Myers' to place its feet on boldly.

ON *BELIEF* IN THE SUPERNATURAL AND IMMORTALITY

James was thus unable to give his unqualified endorsement to the Myers theory. In finding it "too early for anyone to pass dogmatic judgment" he was urging postponement of a final verdict until coercive evidence—either positive or negative—made it possible to render a verdict. By urging suspension of judgment he was evidently going on record as opposed to those who seem to dismiss any spiritistic theory in the name of "science," although he was not unmindful of the fact that belief in spiritualism might suggest a concomitant belief in the supernatural and thus be at variance with the concept of natural law as understood by the world of science. Nevertheless, in a "Postscript" to his book on *The Varieties of Religious Experience* he faced this issue and concluded with endorsement of a qualified supernaturalism in these words (1902, p. 523):

> In spite of its being so shocking to reigning intellectual tastes, I believe that a candid consideration of piecemeal supernaturalism and a complete discussion of all its metaphysical bearings will show it to be the hypothesis by which the largest number of legitimate requirements are met. That, of course, would be a program for other books than this; what I now say sufficiently indicates to the philosophic reader the place where I belong.

As a matter of fact, James had paved the way for possible endorsement of this hypothesis some years before writing his "Postscript" to the *Varieties,* in 1898 when he delivered the "Ingersoll Lecture on the Immortality of Man" at Harvard. The lecture was published under the title of *Human Immortality: Two Supposed Objections to the Doctrine.* As suggested by the title, the lecture was not so much concerned with the truth or validity of the doctrine as with theoretical justification for possible *belief* in the doctrine. In particular, he was concerned with the argument that belief in human immortality is hard or impossible to justify since mind or personality is obviously a function of the brain and consequently would cease to exist with the death of the brain.

This argument, James pointed out, assumes mental events to be functionally dependent upon brain tissue in the sense of being a product of brain metabolism, just as books can be said to be a product of the printing press. But James refused to accept this argument as an irrefutable objection. Functional dependence, he also pointed out, may be conceived of in such a way as to have the brain function as a *transmissive* mechanism rather than just as a *productive* mechanism. Instead of producing thoughts its brain tracts might be receiving them from the "outside" in a manner comparable to the way in which telegraphic wires receive and *transmit* messages coming from "outside" the wires. Apart from its bearing on the subject of immortality, Murphy once called attention to the broader implications of this Jamesian suggestion by interpreting it as follows (1949, p. 207):

> Another solution for the mind-body problem was offered by James in the form of a new variety of dualism. . . . The brain, he suggested, may be not the *basis* for mental life, but merely the agency which *transmits* psychic realities into the terms which organisms use in their relations to their environment. . . .He felt that something of immense value could be learned from phenomena which appeared to him to indicate that the organism comes into contact with superbiological forces. The relation of man to reality seemed to include much that was not to be found in the biological structure of personality.

According to Perry, James took this transmission theory of brain action seriously. It was not introduced as an ad hoc theory when preparing the Ingersoll lecture, but rather, as explained by Perry (Vol. II, pp. 132–133):

> This idea that the brain, instead of creating mind, merely strains and canalizes it was an idea that James had long entertained, and an idea which seemed to him entirely congruent with the alleged phenomena of psychical research. It was here formulated in dualistic terms, as though body and mind were different stuffs or substances. He was still holding in reserve that "phenomenism" in which this dualism was to be overcome. But the transmission theory was clearly an anticipation of the hypothesis developed in his later metaphysics and philosophy of religion, in which the mystical and similar experiences were interpreted as an overflow of superhuman mentality through a lowering of the normal threshold.

What Perry called "superhuman mentality" is the same as what Murphy called "superbiological forces." Both phrases suggest the extraordinary, the mystical, or the supernatural. Although James did not employ these phrases, he did entertain a bold hypothesis to which they are applicable as descriptively appropriate. This hypothesis assumed the existence of a kind of vast reservoir of consciousness or mind capable of acting on the brain from the "outside." In a chapter on mysticism in the *Varieties* James alluded to such a reservoir as the "cosmic consciousness." This term, James reported, was first introduced by Dr. R. M. Bucke, a Canadian psychiatrist, who had experienced this kind of consciousness in his own person and who then studied it in others. As a mystical experience it was difficult to describe, but Bucke tried to say something about it in the following passage quoted by James from Bucke's book on the subject (1902, p. 398):

> The prime characteristic of cosmic consciousness is a consciousness of the cosmos, that is, of the life and order of the universe. Along with the consciousness of the cosmos there occurs an intellectual enlighten-

> ment which alone would place the individual on a new plane of existence—would make him almost a member of a new species. To this is added a state of moral exaltation, an indescribable feeling of elevation, elation, and joyousness, and a quickening of the moral senses, which is fully as striking and more important than is the enhanced intellectual power. With these come what may be called a sense of immortality, a consciousness of eternal life, not a conviction that he shall have this, but the consciousness that he has it already.

In his Ingersoll lecture James had not employed the term *cosmic consciousness,*[15] but he had anticipated the concept when he wrote about a "mother-sea" of consciousness in the universe. This notion was intended to provide for a possible independent spiritual realm as called for by the transmission theory. Belief in the existence of such a realm was implicit in a belief in immortality. Under the circumstances James found Bucke's cosmic consciousness with its suggestion of a "sense of immortality" a welcome alternative to his mother-sea of consciousness. Both terms are obviously congruent with the "spiritistic" presuppositions of ardent devotees of psychical research. In this connection Perry called attention to the fact that James changed the meaning of the concept of a mother-sea in the second edition of *Human Immortality.* In the first edition it was presented as a vast, generalized sea of consciousness in which the identity of individual souls was not assured. However, in the second edition, James "revised his hypothesis, making the mother-sea consist of a collection of individual spirits, each existing there in complete and truer form than in what filters through to this phenomenal life" (Vol. II, p. 137).

It ought to be obvious that this revised hypothesis reflects the climate of belief sometimes engendered at a seance, in which the medium while in a trance purportedly is receiving information from a departed spirit. In accordance with the transmission theory the information, as Perry put it, would be filtering through to the medium from the communicating spirit. In formulating this hypothesis, James was not doing anything more than disposing of a supposed "scientific" argument advanced by those opposed to belief in immortality; he did not regard the hypothesis as confirmed. From this viewpoint, as previously noted, he did not regard himself as a "spiritist." Furthermore, his Ingersoll lecture had nothing to do with *proof* for the existence of immortal spirits, it merely ventured to safeguard the right to *believe* in an immortal soul for those who felt so disposed.

FROM PSYCHOLOGICAL RESEARCH TO PSYCHICAL RESEARCH

In safeguarding the right to *believe* in a soul James was echoing a sentiment he had already voiced in the *Principles.* In explaining why he was not

---

[15]The lecture was delivered in 1898 and Bucke's book *Cosmic Consciousness* was not published until 1901.

basing his psychology on the theory of a soul he first noted that "*the IMMEDIATELY KNOWN thing which on the mental side is in apposition with the entire brain-process is the state of consciousness and not the soul itself*" and that the "wisest course" for psychology to follow would be one "*which contents itself with verifiable laws, and seeks only to be clear, and to avoid unsafe hypotheses.*" And then he added (Vol. I, p. 182):

> By keeping to it, our psychology will remain positivistic and non-metaphysical; and although this is only a provisional halting-place, and things must some day be more thoroughly thought out, we shall abide there in this book, and . . . we shall take no account of the soul. *The spiritualist reader may nevertheless believe in the soul if he will*; whilst the positivistic one who wishes to give a tinge of mystery to the expression of his positivism can continue to say that nature in her unfathomable designs has mixed us of clay and flame, of brain and mind, that the two things hang indubitably together and determine each other's being, but how or why, no mortal may ever know. (Italics added.)

From the foregoing it is evident that James deemed it "wisest" for scientific psychology to play safe by dispensing with metaphysical commitments and also by restricting its research to problems capable of being settled by means of relevant evidence. This, of course, was the same as urging restriction to testable hypotheses. By implication James seemed to be contrasting "unsafe hypotheses" with those that are testable or verifiable. In deciding to write a psychology without a soul he, in effect, was treating the soul-theory as an unsafe hypothesis—there was no way of subjecting it to proof or disproof by known psychological techniques of investigation.

However, once he became familiar with the field of psychical research he acted as if this field might accomplish what psychology could not. At all events, as previously stressed, he was willing to support the quest for facts psychical research might bring to light. He had little to say about this quest in writing the *Principles*, but he definitely had it in mind in preparing his Ingersoll lecture and when it came to preparing his lectures on religious experience he continued to have psychical research in mind. For instance, in connection with the subject of immortality he mentioned three prominent leaders of psychical research in the final pages of the *Varieties* when, with specific reference to "spirit-return," he had this to say (1902, p. 524):

> It seems to me that it is eminently a case for facts to testify. Facts, I think, are yet lacking to prove 'spirit-return,' though I have the highest respect for the patient labors of Messrs. Myers, Hodgson, and Hyslop, and am somewhat impressed by their favorable conclusions.

The work of Myers impressed James particularly. In fact, at one point in the *Varieties* in his lecture on conversion he had occasion to refer to and approve of an important "discovery" made by Myers that in the opinion of some writers has been taken to mean discovery of the unconscious. For example, in his book *Unconsciousness* James G. Miller contrasted James's rejection of the concept in the *Principles* with his endorsement of it in the *Varieties* (1942, p. 16). Actually, there was some mention of the work of Myers in the *Principles* (Vol. I, p. 400) which, as will be made evident in the next section, was directly related to the "discovery" in question. Had James interpreted this as discovery of the unconscious, it seems that he not only would have called attention to the reasons for his endorsement of what he had rejected so vehemently in an earlier chapter but that he also would have introduced an appropriate explanatory note in the earlier chapter. Since such was not the case, James does not seem to have regarded Myers' "discovery" as identical with discovery of the unconscious—at least not the kind of unconscious he had rejected. Whether it was related to any other kind of concept of the unconscious is a possibility calling for more discussion.

F. W. H. MYERS AND HIS "DISCOVERY"

Frederic William Henry Myers (1843-1901) majored in the classics at Cambridge University, taught Latin early in his career, and then served as a school inspector for a short time. In other words, he had not started as a student of psychical research, but by middle age he had become actively identified with topics either directly or indirectly related to psychical research. In fact, as mentioned earlier, he helped found the Society for Psychical Research in 1882. Before long he was an active contributor to the society's publications as he reported on his investigations of mediumistic seances, on double personality, on automatic writing, on what he called experimental hypnotism, and on topics traditionally classified as occult phenomena. Had the term been known in his day, his field of interest would have been called parapsychology.

Nevertheless, even though Myers was not identified with the field of psychology, as distinguished from parapsychology, James paid tribute to him as one who had advanced the cause of psychology. His tribute, as incorporated in his lecture on religious conversion, took the following form (1902, p. 233):

> I cannot but think that the most important step forward that has occurred in psychology since I have been a student of that science is the discovery, first made in 1886, that, in certain subjects at least, there is not only the consciousness of the ordinary field, with its usual centre and margin, but an addition thereto in the shape of a set of memories, thoughts, and feelings which are extra-marginal and outside of the primary consciousness altogether, but yet must be classed as conscious facts of some sort, able to reveal their presence by unmistakable signs. I call this the most important step forward because, unlike the other advances which psychology has made, this discovery has revealed to us an entirely unsuspected peculiarity in the constitution of human nature. No other step forward which psychology has made can proffer any such claim as this.
>
> In particular this discovery of a consciousness existing beyond the

> field, or subliminally as Mr. Myers terms it, casts light on many phenomena of religious biography.

Unfortunately, James failed to elaborate upon the exact nature of this 1886 discovery, as if he expected his audience to be somewhat familiar with such "an important forward step." Still, in retrospect it is difficult to think of any development during 1886 that stands out as a unique contribution to psychology's progress. It may be that he was thinking of a discovery first made *around* 1886. At all events, as previously noted, in the *Principles* he referred to a "highly important series of articles" written by Myers and "especially" one published in May 1885. It thus seems almost certain that the key to the discovery is to be found in this series of articles. They all dealt with automatic writing and what Myers suggested as the far-reaching possible significance of the products of such writing. In what respect these suggestions can be construed as revealing a momentous original discovery, as James indicated, is not immediately obvious from James's account of it in the lecture on conversion. He evidently thought of it as different from any preceding psychological finding, since, in his words, "it was first made in 1886." Accordingly, to repeat, it could not have been discovery of the unconscious because men like Leibnitz, Schopenhauer, and Hartmann had written about the unconscious prior to 1886.

In this connection it is relevant to note another point in the lecture—that the discovery does not apply to *all,* but only to "certain subjects." No comparable reservation is ordinarily applied to the unconscious. At least Freudian and other "dynamic" practitioners do not act as if only certain of their patients possess an unconscious. It is not uncommon, however, to attribute alleged "psychic powers" not to all human beings, but only to "certain subjects." To discover the existence of such "powers" in some subjects would be the equivalent of revealing what James described as "an entirely unsuspected peculiarity in the constitution of human nature." James thus seems to have regarded the discovery as a product of psychical research.

In addition to its relevance for psychical research James also regarded the Myers discovery as shedding light on certain phases of religious experience. This accounts for the fact that James first called attention to it in his chapter on religious conversion. He was thinking of conversion not as a matter of ritualistic convenience but as a vitally important process of inner change having an effect on personal values and self-regard. In the words of James (1902, p. 189):

> To be converted, to be regenerated, to receive grace, to experience religion, to gain an assurance, are so many phrases which denote the process, gradual or sudden, by which a self hitherto divided, and consciously wrong, inferior and unhappy, becomes unified and consciously right, superior and happy, in consequence of its firmer hold upon religious realities. This at least is what conversion signifies in general terms,

whether or not we believe that a direct divine operation is needed to bring such a moral change about.

The conversion experience, as described by James, thus involves a transformation from being "*consciously* wrong" to being "*consciously* right." To this extent there is no appeal to an *unconscious* process. In fact, in this same chapter on conversion James had occasion to call one reference to such a process a "misnomer." This was in allusion to what had come to be called "unconscious cerebration." In the contexts to which the phrase had been applied, James wrote (p. 207) that the word "unconscious" is "almost certainly a misnomer" and ought to be "replaced by the vaguer term 'subconscious' or 'subliminal.'" Apparently James preferred such "vaguer" terms as synonyms for what he had also described as Myers' discovery of an "extra-marginal" consciousness.

James failed to indicate why he regarded words like *subliminal* and *extra-marginal* as vaguer than the word *unconscious,* the word they were intended to replace. Interestingly enough, as will soon be brought out, Myers himself did not hesitate to employ the word *unconscious* from time to time; but James eschewed the word. In fact, in his initial reference to Myers as a student of automatic writing, he attributed the automatism in question to *dissociation* and not to the unconscious (1890, Vol. I, p. 399). This constitutes another bit of evidence showing that for James the Myers discovery of an extra-marginal consciousness was not the discovery of the unconscious. Furthermore, it seems he was thinking of this extra-marginal or subliminal consciousness as vague not so much in the sense of something being hazy and obscure, but more in the sense of something so rich in its potential as to preclude prediction of its eventual progress or development. To appreciate the nature of this potential for growth requires understanding of the concept of subliminal consciousness as introduced by Myers, and interpreted by James.

THE CONCEPT OF SUBLIMINAL CONSCIOUSNESS

It should be obvious that in the present context the word *subliminal* is not to be equated with its laboratory use in psychophysical studies of subliminal stimuli. That such stimuli may influence behavior was commonplace knowledge in psychological circles years before Myers had become interested in psychical research. Stated differently, aside from the adjective *subliminal,* his "discovery" had nothing to do with measurement of threshold values and kindred psychophysical studies. Otherwise his "discovery" would not have been a discovery.

In the course of reviewing Myers' articles[16] on automatic writing and

---

[16]Myers wrote three articles on the subject of automatic writing, all of which were published in the *Proceedings of the Society for Psychical Research.* The first one was first

related topics it became evident that, unlike James, he had no misgivings about referring to mind as unconscious. When James, as may be recalled, had written about "this discovery of a consciousness existing beyond the field, or subliminally as Mr. Myers terms it," he neglected to show that Mr. Myers had also termed it as existing unconsciously. In fact, although Myers seemed to employ the words as synonymous, he made more frequent use of the word *unconscious.* By way of illustration consider the following excerpts from one of his papers on automatic writing, in which he was reporting on results of various suggestions made to hypnotized subjects (1887, p. 238, p. 239, p.244, p. 245, and pp. 256–257):

> For the line was merely this,—that any suggestion uttered by M. Janet in a brusque tone of command reached the *unconscious self* alone: any other remark reached the subject—awake or somnambulic—in the ordinary way.
>
> The command thus given had a persistent effect, and while the awakened Louise continued to chatter as usual with other persons, her *unconscious self* wrote brief and scrawling responses to M. Janet's questions.
>
> . . . of what actions can we ever venture to assert that they are absolutely *unconscious,* absolutely unrememberable?
>
> . . . but Adrienne, who had risen out of the *Unconscious,* had sunk into the *Unconscious* again,—must I say?—for evermore.
>
> We can no longer draw a broad line between the conscious and the *unconscious,* and say that what a man is conscious of is part of his true self, and that phenomena, however complex, which never enter into his consciousness, must be considered as lying outside his true identity. (All italics added.)

Whether the word *subliminal* can be substituted for the word *unconscious* in each of the preceding excerpts is to be questioned, especially if subliminal is taken to mean extra-marginal. The latter connotation is the one James preferred and may be one reason he did not follow Myers in the use of the term *unconscious.* Nevertheless, he was justified in assuming that for Myers the unconscious was extra-marginal in the sense of being sensitive to external influences. Such sensitivity is necessarily a prerequisite for James's supposition of brain mechanisms being transmissive. Myers provided for such transmissive functions by attributing some products of automatic writing to telepathic influences. As he put it, "we have seen cause not unfrequently to associate telepathic impulses—both in their inception and in their reception—with the

---

published under the title of "On a Telepathic Explanation of Some So-Called Spiritualistic Phenomena" in 1884, II: 217–237. In referring to it later he changed the title to read "Automatic Writing—I" because, as he realized, the first title was too "cumbrous." The second article, "Automatic Writing—II," appeared in 1885, III: 1–63, and "Automatic Writing—III" appeared in 1887, III: 209–261.

unconscious rather than conscious operations of the brain" (1887, p. 210). He called attention to such external influences most explicitly by noting that "in nine cases out of ten the automatist attributes his writing to some influence external to himself." He then had this to say about the problem involved as treated in an earlier one of his papers (1887, p. 213):

> With this, then, as the problem before us, I propose now to develop in a fresh direction a suggestion made, and partly acted upon, in my last paper. I there dwelt on my conviction that if we are to understand *supernormal* phenomena–phenomena transcending, apparently, the stage of evolution at which we have admittedly arrived, –we must first compare them, as fully as possible, both with *normal* and with *abnormal* phenomena; –meaning by abnormal phenomena those which, while diverging from the ordinary standard, fall below or, at least, do not transcend it. I insisted also that we must expect that supernormal phenomena, if they occur at all, will show many points of resemblance to abnormal–nay, to positively morbid–phenomena, without therefore themselves necessarily deserving to be classed as morbid in any degree. When unfamiliar impulses arise in the organism–whether these impulses be evolutive or dissolutive in character–their readiest *paths of externalisation* are likely to be somewhat similar; –just as . . . the same kind of ache in the gums may indicate to our sensation either the formation of an abscess or the growth of a tooth.

Myers, as shown in the next paragraph, regarded the latter distinction as never having been made before and was thus possibly revealing one respect in which James was later to credit him with having been first:

> I cannot find that this principle is set forth in an accredited textbook. Yet I must believe that it will come to be recognized as a guiding principle in psycho-physiological inquiry; nay, that this view will be seen to have been inevitable so soon as external signs of psychological facts were grasped with a certain degree of precision. Thus far the cerebral-psychical changes which go on after the frame has once been built up have been watched by the psychologist mainly in their evolutive, by the physiologist mainly in their dissolutive aspect.

One of the evolutive aspects that constituted an undercurrent of Myers' investigations had to do with possible proof for the immortality of the unconscious or subliminal self, or what Myers also designated as a transcendental self. In an article entitled "Human Personality in the Light of Hypnotic Suggestion" he dealt with this issue quite bluntly and unambiguously. After outlining the scope of conditions to be investigated by the method of "experimental psychology in its strictest sense"–a scope embracing supernormal, spontaneous, and induced mental states[17]–he had this to say about one of his own convictions (1885, p. 2):

---

[17]As explained by Myers, these three terms all designate abnormal conditions. He failed to cite specific examples of the *supernormal* states, apparently assuming the meaning to

> My own conviction is that we possess—and can nearly prove it—some kind of soul, or spirit, or transcendental self, which even in this life occasionally manifests powers beyond the powers of our physical organism, and which very probably survives the grave. Thus much I am bound in candour to say, lest in what follows I should seem to be mystifying the reader, or sailing under colours not my own.

Many years later, around 1900, Myers wrote a book for the purpose of completely proving what, as just indicated, he could only "nearly prove" in 1885. During the intervening years his experiences with automatic writing and with mediumistic seances had brought about this change from strong belief to utter certainty regarding the supernormal powers of the transcendental self and its probable status as an immortal spirit. For him it appeared certain that on occasion information supplied by a medium while in a trance could not possibly be a product of her own mind. Moreover, as mentioned earlier in this chapter, James himself in the *Principles* had once stated that he was persuaded by his "abundant acquaintance with the trances of one medium" that in her trance condition she had *facts* to report of which she had been 100 percent ignorant in her normal waking self. He again gave expression to belief in such possible "spiritual" influences coming from without in this statement in the *Varieties* (pp. 242–243):

> The lower manifestations of the Subliminal,[18] indeed, fall within the resources of the personal subject: his ordinary sense-material, inattentively taken in and subconsciously remembered and combined, will account for all his usual automatisms. But just as our primary wide-awake consciousness throws open our senses to the touch of things material, so it is logically conceivable that *if there be* higher spiritual agencies that can directly touch us, the psychological condition of their doing so *might be* our possession of a subconscious region which alone should yield access to them. The hubbub of the waking life might close a door which in the dreamy Subliminal might remain ajar or open. . . . If there be higher powers able to impress us, they may get access to us only through the subliminal door.

From the foregoing it seems that James was not quite ready to share Myers' spiritistic convictions. At all events he appeared to have reservations about some of Myers' certainties, as shown by the italicized subjunctive phrase in which James in effect wondered "if there be" spiritual powers. This raises a question concerning the extent to which James was prepared to

---

be self-evident as applicable to "mental and physical conditions of all kinds." Under *spontaneous* states he included "sleep and dreams, somnambulism, trance, hysteria, automatism, alternating consciousness, epilepsy, insanity, death and dissolution." In contrast to such spontaneous states he listed this series of *induced* states: "narcotism, hypnotic catalepsy, hypnotic somnambulism, and the like, which afford . . . an unequalled insight into the mysteries of man."

[18] Just why James wrote thus with a capital *S* was not explained. The use of the definite pronoun in the phrase "*the* Subliminal" connotes a specific entity possibly in the form of a "higher spiritual agency," mentioned in this same paragraph as "logically conceivable."

endorse the views expressed by Myers. In fact, this question was once put to James very directly and he dealt with it with comparable directness.

ANSWER TO A CHALLENGING QUESTION

The question was put to James by James Ward (1843–1925) a distinguished Cambridge University psychologist. He and James, as noted by Perry, "had been acquainted since 1880, and had corresponded on psychological questions." When the *Varieties* was published James saw to it that Ward received a copy. This resulted in an interchange of letters during July of 1902 in the first one of which, among other comments, Ward had this to say about James's evident approval of the views of Myers (Perry, Vol. II, pp. 648–649):

> I do not, of course, object to your taking the subconscious for granted, but I feel you go too far in accepting Myers' views as so much "gospel truth." So far as I can see the entire presentative content of subconsciousness is derivative: it consists, as you seem to admit, of memories or suggestions. It would, I think, be substantially true to say: "There is nothing in subconsciousness—in the way of idea, at least—that was not first in consciousness." Religious ideas, then, cannot have originated there: the most that can be said is that they may be transfigured and quickened by emotions that have emerged thence. Subconsciousness may be the source of an illumination inexplicable enough to the subject experiencing it, but it cannot, I think, be a source of revelation. . . .
>
> On the one hand, all seems to turn on the extent to which the subconscious door is open or shut, and here the individual is helpless; but, on the other, you still talk of the *will* to believe: "we and God," you say, "have business with each other; and *in opening ourselves to his influence* our deepest destiny is fulfilled." . . . No doubt the relation of the human and the divine wills is a hard, perhaps a hopeless problem, but without some genuine "synergism" an admitted fact, I don't see how anything worth the name of religion is possible. Yet you seem to make it a matter of enthusiasm in the bad sense, of "obsession" and the like: in fact you seem to bring religion so much into line with what is fundamentally pathological, that if I did not know you better, I should be tempted to regard your whole discourse as a practical joke!

In his reply to the letter James, after an introductory solicitous inquiry about Ward's health in the opening paragraph, continued with the next paragraph as follows (Vol. II, 649–650):

> As for what you say of my results, I am moved to make a brief comment. I don't accept all Myers' opinions as "gospel truth," quite the reverse. But I think Myers' *problem*, the "exploration of the subliminal," to be the most important definite investigation opened of late in psychology, and I think of Myers' way of going at it on the whole admirable. Who has brought together and simplified as much as he? Have you seen an obituary article on his relation to psychology by me in the S.P.R. *Proceedings* of last year?

> As for the derivative nature of the subliminal, it *certainly* in my view is not entire. The existence of supernormal memory . . . and supernormal cognitions . . . proves that there *is* a region for exploration, and that Myers' problem is genuinely important. The relation of it all to religion is through mysticism. I *can't* ignore the vital prominence of that sort of experience in the religious life. I have fully admitted the necessary cooperation of intellect in elaborating the results, and think you misapprehend me as saying "all feeling and no reason."
>
> But I feel sure that contemplative reason would produce no religion . . . unless there were in addition some of these other non-rational intuitive processes to clinch persuasion.

Evidently James conceived of the subliminal as, at least to some degree, a product of influences unique to the field of psychical research in contradistinction to the field of psychological research. This is indicated by his answer to Ward's contention regarding *all* subliminal content having been derived from what had been the normal content of consciousness. In effect James argued *some* content is of "supernormal" origin and, as related to religion, has to do with "mysticism" and "intuitive processes." Implicitly he credited Myers with having shown the bearing of such supernormal findings on the progress of psychology. That is why he called Ward's attention to the obituary article concerned with Myers' relation to psychology. This article is important because it supplies a convenient digest of James's reasons for once having written the Myers discovery to be "the most important step forward that has occurred in psychology since I have been a student of that science."

The high points of the James article were presented at a meeting in London of the Society for Psychical Research on Friday, March 8, 1901. As reported in the Society's *Journal,*[19] the meeting was "devoted to a memorial to F. W. H. Myers," with special prominence given to these minutes of the meeting (pp. 54-56):

> Mr. J. G. Piddington then read extracts from a paper by Professor William James on Frederic Myers' services to Psychology. Mr. James began by pointing out that the quest which Myers had put before himself was that of immortality, and that his contributions to Psychology were incidental to that quest. But the service which he rendered to Psychology was nevertheless of a very original and striking kind. It was Myers who first definitely opened up the whole region of the subconscious mind, and devised methods for investigating its resources, by crystal gazing, automatic writing, trance speaking, and the like. His great achievement was to bring unity into an assemblage of heterogeneous phenomena; to show the analogies and resemblances between things seemingly so wide apart as hallucination, demonical possession, hysteria, and the visions of genius; to weave them into a system.
>
> Myers showed that the great region of mental activity, which he termed the subliminal, contained matter of various kinds, various in its origins and in its utility; some mere rubbish, lapsed fragments of memory;

[19] *Journal of the Society for Psychical Research,* 1901-1902, X.

some the stuff of which day-dreams are made; but here and there we come across indications of faculties and modes of perception superior to those of common waking life.

The corner-stone of Myers' system was the conception that the "consciousness" of the classic psychology is but a portion of a larger whole—an organism in perpetual process of evolution. His evolutionary conception of consciousness was, in the writer's view, an hypothesis of first-rate philosophic importance and might be destined to play a leading part in the psychology of the future. Whether Myers' hypotheses were, in fact, justified or not, they were at any rate far more plausible than those of the classic psychology. Nature was everywhere gothic not classic; and Myers, in contrast to the clearly defined and nicely articulated consciousness of the old psychology, presented us with a vast aggregate of half-shaped, half-systematized, and partly incoherent phenomena—a veritable jungle such as nature herself is wont to show the explorer.

The writer then contrasted the official view of the consciousness which survives death, an abstract mentality living on spiritual truth, and communicating ideal wisdom—the academic platonizing Sunday-school conception—with the view of human survival presented by Myers.

Whatever verdict might ultimately be passed upon his work, he would, it was likely, be long remembered as the pioneer who staked out and claimed for science a vast tract of mental wilderness.

Just as James's letter to Ward reflected endorsement of the "supernormal," so do the preceding extracts from his memorial tribute to Myers. It is clearly evident, for example, in his references to "indications of faculties and modes of perception superior to those of common waking life" and "the consciousness which survives death." However, as James indicated, Myers' "contributions to psychology" were not directly dependent upon this quest for proof of immortality; they were incidental by-products of this quest. Moreover, since they were described as being "of a very original and striking kind," they must embody the essence of Myers' discovery. James also characterized Myers as a "pioneer" whose "hypotheses" impressed him as being more "plausible" than those of traditional psychology even if they should turn out not to have been justified. This is a perplexing statement. Hypotheses are to be judged by means of evidence confirming their validity and not by their inherent plausibility. Does this mean that James was thinking of Myers' discovery as a function of one or more of these plausible hypotheses? If so, it may have been more of a conjecture than a genuine discovery.

THE MYERS DISCOVERY: FACT OR CONJECTURE?

Whether the Myers "discovery" was as "original and striking" as James believed is to be questioned. Had it really been dramatically revelatory of something crucially important and hitherto unknown, Myers' name would be familiar to all serious students of psychology and most textbooks of general psychology would be keeping his memory alive. In other words, his discovery does not appear to have been as momentous as the discoveries made by men like Newton, Darwin, Roentgen, Helmholtz, Mendel, and Pasteur. Furthermore, equating the discovery with subliminal processes may not have been as original as James indicated. The very term *subliminal* was an outgrowth of Fechner's efforts to measure barely perceptible or subconscious sensory impressions, and some decades before Myers the existence of impressions below the level of awareness had also been postulated by Herbart. Unlike Myers', their views of the subliminal were not derivatives of psychical research. As James realized, this made Myers' views of the extra-marginal or subliminal consciousness uniquely different from any view advanced prior to 1886. It was *sui generis* and thus, as James thought, could be hailed as a discovery and an important forward step for psychology.

Even though Myers' discovery was a derivative of psychical research, James could welcome it as a contribution to the future of psychology; for he, unlike the majority of his psychological contemporaries, took such research seriously. He had personally participated in the critical examination of trance phenomena at mediumistic seances. Also, after due examination of the relevant evidence he became persuaded of the reality of mental telepathy–he had become convinced that it is possible for one mind to communicate with another mind directly and independently of any known process of sense perception.[20]

James had also become convinced of the existence of subliminal processes that might render such telepathic communication possible. This is evident from what he included in his review of Myers' book *Human Personality and Its Survival of Bodily Death,* quoted here from the review by Murphy and Ballou (1960, p. 228):

> There *is* a subliminal region of life which opens fitfully into a supraliminal region. The only doubt is as to whether it be general in human beings, or whether it be not limited to a few hypnotic and hysteric subjects. . . .
>
> The subliminal regions being thus established as an actuality, the next question is as to its farther limits, where it exists. My subliminal, for instance, has my ordinary consciousness for one of its environments, but has it additional environments on the remoter side? Has it direct relations of intercourse, for example, with the consciousness, subliminal or supraliminal of other men?

By way of additional explanation James supplied the following account of the subliminal self's relation to the spiritual world as conceived by Myers (1960, p. 230):

---

[20]Telepathy is not quite the same as extrasensory perception or ESP. The latter term refers to direct awareness of some condition or event without activation of any known sensory process as is reported to occur when designs on ESP cards are "perceived" even though the cards are hidden or placed face down. On the other hand, telepathy has to do with "reading" another's mind and not with non-sensory awareness of an impersonal event.

> From its intercourse with this spiritual world the subliminal self of each of us may draw strength and communicate it to the supraliminal life. The "energizing of life" seems, in fact, to be one of its functions. The reparativeness of sleep, the curative effects of self-suggestion, the "up-rushing" inspirations of genius, the regenerative influences of prayer and of religious self-surrender, the strength of belief which mystical experiences give, are all ascribed by Myers to the "dynamogeny" of the spiritual world, upon which we are enabled to make drafts of power by virtue of our connection with our subliminal.

In these two quotations James appears to have summarized his reasons for regarding Myers' account of the subliminal as a genuine *discovery.* As a description it is more detailed and clarifying than the account given in the *Varieties.* It is now quite clear that the "discovery" is contingent upon belief in the reality of a spiritual world and its impact on the life of man. Evidence for the existence of such a world was almost entirely a product of psychical research. Like modern reports coming from centers of parapsychology the reports coming from centers of psychical research failed to dissipate the latent skepticism of the psychological world as a whole. For the majority of psychologists in James's day neither mental telepathy nor the "dynamogeny of the spiritual world" were judged to be discoveries of psychological reality. At best they were deemed to be unconfirmed hypotheses or interesting conjectures. Similarly, the claims of contemporary students of parapsychology for the factual status of extrasensory perception continue to meet with objections by many psychologists for whom the evidence upon which such claims is based is not at all coercive. As they see it, ESP is not a fact in the sense in which color blindness, dyslexia, and the blind spot are facts. Stated a little differently, ESP has not yet been discovered as the latter three facts were once discovered. In terms of this perspective, James to the contrary notwithstanding, the Myers account of the subliminal region was more conjecture than discovery.

CONCERNING THE SUBLIMINAL AND THE UNCONSCIOUS

Even as conjecture, Myers' views of the subliminal are not to be construed as foreshadowings of the Freudian unconscious nor as endorsement of any of the views of the unconscious James had examined and rejected in the *Principles.* In fact, as may be recalled, even though Myers had repeatedly used the word *unconscious* as a synonym for the word *subliminal,* James never did so. At no time in writing about Myers' discovery did he refer to it as discovery of the unconscious. It was always discovery of the subliminal or extra-marginal. This means that he was still giving a negative answer to the question raised at the beginning of this chapter, "Do unconscious mental states exist?" Stated differently, in connection with Myers' discovery he was recognizing the existence of subliminal or subconscious mental states and denying the existence of unconscious mental states.

Nevertheless, as already mentioned, it is precisely in connection with Myers' discovery as presented in the *Varieties* that some authors have listed James as finally having come to endorse the concept of the unconscious despite his earlier rejection of it in the *Principles.* In fairness to them it should be realized that there is one passage in the chapter on conversion which taken by itself reads as if James may have had the Freudian unconscious in mind. This is the passage (1902, pp. 234-235):

> In the wonderful explorations by Binet, Janet, Breuer, Freud, Mason, Prince, and others of the subliminal consciousness of patients with hysteria, we have revealed to us whole systems of underground life, in the shape of memories of a painful sort which lead a parasitic existence, buried outside of the primary fields of consciousness, and making irruptions thereto with hallucinations, pains, convulsions, paralyses of feeling and of motion, and the whole procession of symptoms of hysteric disease of body and of mind. Alter or abolish by suggestion these subconscious memories, and the patient immediately gets well. His symptoms were automatisms, in Mr. Myers' sense of the word.

Careful attention to the details of this passage will show that it does not constitute recognition and approval of Freud's dynamic unconscious. As if mindful of his former misgivings concerning mental states as unconscious, James seems to have been deliberate in his avoidance of the word *unconscious.* Instead the passage mentions "the subliminal consciousness" and "subconscious memories." Subliminal and subconscious are, of course, synonymous terms, but they are not terms of which Freud would have approved. In his *Interpretation of Dreams* he explains that "subconscious" is to be avoided because it tends to "stress the equivalence of what is psychical to what is conscious" (p. 615). Accordingly, the subconscious for both James and Freud is unrelated to the concept of mind as unconscious.

Furthermore, the entire passage is concerned with the subconscious of victims of hysteria and their automatisms. By implication "the whole procession of symptoms" ascribed to their subconscious is unique to them as patients and is not to be ascribed to mankind as a whole. For Freud, on the other hand, the unconscious was not unique to a given class of patients but was viewed as characteristic of everyone's psychological endowment. In this connection it may be recalled that when it came to treating his patients Freud used free association rather than the technique of suggestion mentioned by James. According to James, once the memories buried in the subliminal are dislodged by suggestion "the patient immediately gets well." This kind of brief psychotherapy is very different from the months or years of psychoanalytic probing required to dislodge memories buried in the unconscious.

Some of the other men listed by James as having contributed to the study of hysteria were more directly concerned with the subconscious than was Freud. Consider the names of Binet and Janet, since James had discussed their contributions in one section of the *Principles,* a fairly long section entitled "'Unconsciousness' in Hysterics" (Vol. I, pp. 202-214). The table of contents gives this more explicit caption: "The 'unconsciousness' of hysterics not genuine" (p. x). In general, James accounted for the symptomatology of hysteria—the anomalies of sensation and motion—in terms of the concept of dissociation, the kind of division of consciousness Binet had called "double consciousness."

Both Binet and Janet, as noted by James, attributed these anomalies to dissociation. With specific reference to induced or suggested loss of cutaneous sensibility James reported that they "have shown that during the times of anesthesia, and co-existing with it, *sensibility to the anaesthetic parts is also there, in the form of a secondary consciousness* entirely cut off from the primary or normal one, but susceptible of being *tapped* and made to testify to its existence in various odd ways" (p. 203). Automatic writing is one of these odd ways, but many others were employed.

As James interpreted such findings, hysterical abnormalities are not indicative of mind as dissòciated or split into one set of conscious processes and another set of unconscious ones. For James, both of the dissociated or split sets are conscious. Whether such splitting or dissociation may occur in the mentally healthy or just in the hysterically predisposed was a problematic issue, concerning which James wrote as follows (Vol. I, p. 210):

> How far this splitting up of the mind into separate consciousnesses may exist in each one of us is a problem. M. Janet holds that it is only possible where there is abnormal weakness, and consequently a defect of unifying co-ordinating power. An hysterical woman abandons part of her consciousness because she is too weak nervously to hold it together. The abandoned part meanwhile may solidify into a secondary or subconscious self. In a perfectly sound subject, on the other hand, what is dropped out of mind at one moment keeps coming back at the next.

Notice that Janet is said to have referred to his patient's "secondary or sub-conscious self" and not to her unconscious self. This appears to be a distinction of which Janet would have approved. In his writings there are repeated allusions to "subconscious fixed ideas" and no mention of unconscious fixed ideas. In fact, the concept of subconscious fixed ideas was original with Janet. There have been some who interpreted Janet's analysis of the nature and origin of these subconscious ideas as not too different from the psychoanalytic teachings of Freud, giving rise to a rumor that Freud was indebted to Janet for the essential conceptual foundation of psychoanalysis. Needless to say, this sort of rumor was bitterly resented by Freud. As reported by Ernest Jones (Vol. III, pp. 213-214), he even gave expression to this resentment late in life after he had been asked whether he would care to receive a visit from Janet. In a letter written in April, 1937, to one of his close associates he explained why he "will not see Janet," in particular objecting to "the libel" which French writers had spread concerning his having "stolen"

Janet's ideas.[21] Janet could have cleared Freud's name by denouncing the libelous falsehood, but this never happened.

Janet was *persona non grata* to Freud for another reason, especially pertinent in the present context since it has to do with what Freud took to be Janet's disparagement of the unconscious by his dismissing the concept of mind as unconscious as "just a manner of speaking." This provoked Freud to disparage Janet's scientific thinking: "You can get an idea of his scientific level from his utterance that the unconscious is *une façon de parler.*" From this it seems evident that Freud did not regard Janet as having contributed to the discovery of the unconscious, as some writers have suggested. Whyte, for example, definitely implies this by listing Janet's name among those concerned with "the successive discovery . . . of the unconscious mind" (1960, p. 196). And Ellenberger makes this very explicit in his long chapter devoted to the life and influence of Janet (1970, pp. 331–417). On the very first page of this chapter, contrary to Freud's repudiation of his alleged indebtedness to Janet, Ellenberger declares Janet's "work" to have been "one of the main sources for Freud."

All things considered, it should now be evident that Freud would not have welcomed the statement by James to the effect that he along with Janet had engaged in the study of "the subliminal consciousness of patients with hysteria." As already indicated, Freud had misgivings about subliminal or subconscious processes, as well as about any influence of Janet's investigation of such processes on his own exploration of the unconscious. Under the circumstances it should also be evident that the passage in which the foregoing statement was made is just another allusion to James's recognition of the

---

[21] The use of the term "stolen" suggests that the French writers accused Freud of having availed himself of Janet's ideas without acknowledging the source. If so, then Freud's indignant protest is entirely justified, for there are several places in the different volumes of Freud's *Collected Papers* in which his indebtedness to or agreement with Janet is acknowledged. In Volume I, for example, in connection with a discussion of the difference between organic and hysterical paralyses Freud wrote (p. 55), "On this point I must agree completely with the views expressed by Janet in the latest numbers of the *Archives de Neurologie.*" In "The Unconscious in Psycho-Analysis," Janet is given credit for having been the "first" to have advanced a certain theory concerned with posthypnotic suggestibility. As expressed by Freud the credit took this form (1912, p. 261):

> A post-hypnotic suggestion is a laboratory product, an artificial product. But if we adopt the theory of hysterical phenomena first put forward by Pierre Janet and elaborated by Breuer and myself, we shall not be at a loss for plenty of natural facts showing the psychological character of the post-hypnotic suggestion even more clearly and distinctly.

Finally, to cite one more example, in his paper "On the History of the Psycho-Analytic Movement" Freud, as shown in the following quotation, after voicing dissatisfaction with Janet ended with a word of commendation (1914, pp. 32-33):

> In Paris itself, a conviction still seems to reign (to which Janet himself gave eloquent expression at the Congress in London in 1913) that everything good in psychoanalysis is a repetition of Janet's views with insignificant modifications, and that everything else in it is bad. . . . Even though we deny his claims, however, we cannot forget the value of his work on the psychology of the neuroses.

hopes for Myers' discovery of the subliminal and is not in any way related to Freud's concept of the unconscious.

This should not be interpreted as meaning rejection of all Freudian insights on the part of James. After all, the passage in question was written at the turn of the century when Freud's ideas were not yet widely known. Even his most important book, *The Interpretation of Dreams,* which had been published in 1899, was obscure at the time James was writing the *Varieties.* As pointed out by Strachey in his introduction to the English translation of Freud's book (p. xx), by 1905 only 351 copies of the book had been sold. It is not likely that James had come across one of these copies when writing his lectures on religious experience; at least there is no mention of the book in the *Varieties.* Some years later, James did have occasion to consider Freud's dream theory, especially as it might be related to the kind of functional psychology James came to sponsor, but this was not tantamount to belated endorsement of the Freudian or any other kind of unconscious.

There is no way of knowing how Freud would have dealt with James's critique of the unconscious. He may not have been familiar with it—in his extensive bibliography in the different editions of the volume on dreams there is no mention of the *Principles.* In fact, Jones indicates very definitely (Vol. I, p. 373) that Freud had not read James's classic at the time he was developing his theory of mind as unconscious. Nor does Jones indicate that he ever read it. If he had come across the sections concerned with the arguments critical of the unconscious, it is conceivable that he would have been as unenthusiastic about James as he had been about Janet. Nevertheless, as will be brought out in the next chapter, the time came when he welcomed what he took to be James's approval of and hopes for his psychoanalytic psychology.

SUMMARY REVIEW

In retrospect it can now be seen that virtually all the issues introduced in this chapter are either direct or indirect outgrowths of James's consistently negative answer to this basic question: "Do unconscious mental states exist?" Dealing with this question involved consideration of the following topics:

1. The petites perceptions of Leibnitz and his argument to the effect that inaudible sounds of a single wave must be heard unconsciously if the roar of an ocean is to be apperceived. This argument, James noted, involves the fallacy of division.
2. The behavior of neither sleepwalkers nor hypnotized subjects requires an assumption of control exercised by unconscious mental processes.
3. Like difficulty in recalling dreams, so posthypnotic amnesia suggests dissociation rather than repression by the unconscious.
4. The posthypnotic execution of an experimenter's requests is a form of delayed reaction explicable as the outcome of a determining tendency rather than as the product of an unconscious motive.

5. James regarded the concept of unconscious motivation as questionable because its advocates so often seem to assume that once we become conscious of a hitherto unknown aspect of a given motive for a past action, that aspect must have been resident in the unconscious all along. This involves the fallacy of sensationalism or atomism.
6. The foregoing fallacy was also discussed in connection with intellectual confusion stemming from failure to recognize the difference between entertaining an idea and subsequently coming to know many more things about the given idea.
7. As James saw it, when ideas are not being thought and when acts of skill are not being performed their potential reinstatement is a function of the neurology of memory as contrasted with their supposititious preservation in a hypothetical unconscious.
8. Another aspect of the preceding issue was discussed in terms of Herbart's concept of an apperceptive mass.
9. Attention was called to the fact that, as James noted, both Wundt and Helmholtz changed from their early acceptance of the concept of unconscious inference to their later "recantation."
10. It follows from the above that, contrary to the opinion of some recent writers, neither Wundt nor Helmholtz are to be listed as having endorsed the concept of mind as unconscious.
11. The "basic process" stressed by Helmholtz referred to the transition from preoccupation with details in the early stages of learning to the automatism of habit in the final stages. No need, then, to posit a transfer of the preoccupation to an unconscious mind.
12. Discussion of James's interest in automatic writing, trance states, and religious experience as related to questions of spiritism and the unconscious.
13. Consideration of James's identification with psychical research and his defense of *belief* in the supernatural and immortality involved discussion of (*a*) the concept of natural law; (*b*) the distinction between transmissive and productive brain mechanisms; and (*c*) the concept of cosmic consciousness.
14. James regarded the goals of psychical research as different from the goals of psychological research.
15. The discovery of the subliminal by Myers and its implications for psychical research and some phases of religion as perceived by James.
16. Conclusions regarding the existence of a spiritistic realm when inferred from the concept of subliminal consciousness are conjectures rather than discoveries.
17. The subliminal or subconscious of Binet and Janet is not to be confused with the unconscious of Freud.
18. For Freud the subconscious was an untenable concept.
19. Janet was *persona non grata* to Freud.
20. Freud was ignorant of the *Principles.*

A CONCLUDING COMMENT

In listing his objections to the concept of mind as unconscious in the *Principles* of 1890 and in the *Varieties* of 1902 James did not have the Freudian unconscious in mind. Consequently, taken strictly, his rejection of the concept as outlined in the present chapter is not to be construed as a rejection of the Freudian unconscious. Neither is it to be interpreted as an endorsement of Freud's views, as some writers were led to believe. What he thought about these views in later years will be dealt with in the course of the next chapter.

What merits explicit recognition at this point is the fact that by 1890 James, Wundt, and Helmholtz as founding fathers of psychology as science—like Ebbinghaus some two decades earlier—were taking a dim view of the concept of unconscious mental states. In other words, by the turn of the century, with the advent of Freud, academic psychology had already given due consideration to the unconscious and found it irreconcilable with hopes for the development of a genuine science of psychology.

REFERENCES

Abrams, S. 1971. "The Psychoanalytic Unconscious." In *The Unconscious Today,* edited by M. Kanzer. New York: International Universities Press.

Beldoch, M. 1972. "Science as Fiction." *Psychotherapy and Social Science Review* 6: 12–18.

Boring, E. G. 1950. *A History of Experimental Psychology.* New York: Appleton-Century-Crofts.

Brett, G. S. 1912. *A History of Psychology,* Vol. I. London: George Allen & Unwin, Ltd.

Ellenberger, E. 1970. *The Discovery of the Unconscious.* New York: Basic Books, Inc.

English, H. B., and English, A. C. 1958. *A Comprehensive Dictionary of Psychological and Psychoanalytical Terms.* New York: Longmans, Green and Co.

Freud, S. *The Interpretation of Dreams.* Translated by James Strachey. New York: Basic Books, Inc. (Original edition first published in 1899.)

——. 1938. "Some Elementary Lessons in Psycho-Analysis." In *The Standard Edition of the Complete Psychological Works of Sigmund Freud,* translated by James Strachey, Vol. XXIII, pp. 279-286. London: The Hogarth Press.

Hartshorne, C 1968. *The Philosophy and Psychology of Sensation.* Port Washington, N.Y.: Kennikot Press, Inc. (First published in 1934.)

Helmholtz, H. 1965. "On Perception and the Unconscious Conclusion." In *A Source Book in the History of Psychology,* edited by R. J. Herrnstein and E. G. Boring. Cambridge: Harvard University Press.

Hilgard, E. R. 1971. "Hypnotic Phenomena: The Struggle for Scientific Acceptance." *American Scientist* 59: 567–577.

Hunter, W. S. 1913. "Delayed Reaction in Animals and Children." *Behavior Monographs* 2, No. 6, p. 86.

James, W. 1890. *Principles of Psychology,* Vols. I and II. New York: Henry Holt and Co.

——. 1898. *Human Immortality: Two Supposed Objections to the Doctrine.* Boston: Houghton Mifflin Co.

——. 1902. *The Varieties of Religious Experience–A Study in Human Nature.* New York: Longmans, Green and Co.

Jones, E. 1953, 1957. *The Life and Work of Sigmund Freud,* Vol. I and Vol. III (respectively). New York: Basic Books, Inc.

Lashley, K. S. 1963. *Brain Mechanisms and Intelligence.* New York: Dover Publications, Inc. (First published in 1929.)

Miller, J. G. 1942. *Unconsciousness.* New York: John Wiley & Sons, Inc.

Mühl, A. 1930. *Automatic Writing.* Dresden: Theodor Steinkopff.

Murphy, G. 1947. *Personality.* New York: Harper & Bros.

——. 1949. *Historical Introduction to Modern Psychology.* New York: Harcourt, Brace and Co.

Murphy, G., and Ballou, R. O. 1960. *William James on Psychical Research.* New York: The Viking Press.

Myers, F. W. H. 1885. "Human Personality in the Light of Hypnotic Suggestion." In *Proceedings of the Society for Psychical Research* III: 1–24.

——. 1887. "Automatic Writing–III." In *Proceedings of the Society for Psychical Research* III: 290–261.

Perry, R. B. 1935. *The Thought and Character of William James,* Vols. I and II. Boston: Little, Brown and Co.

Pietsch, P. 1972. "Shuffle Brain." *Harper's Magazine* 244: 41–46.

Prince, M. 1906. *The Dissociation of a Personality.* New York: Longmans, Green and Co.

Shipley, T., ed. 1961. *Classics in Psychology.* New York: Philosophical Library.

Sperry, R. W. 1969. "A Modified Concept of Consciousness." *Psychological Review* 76: 532–536.

——. 1970. "An Objective Approach to Subjective Experience: Further Explanation of a Hypothesis." *Psychological Review* 77: 585–590.

Titchener, E B. 1929. *Systematic Psychology: Prolegomena.* New York: The Macmillan Co.

Warren, R. M., and Warren, R. P. 1968. *Helmholtz on Perception: Its Physiology and Development.* New York: John Wiley & Sons, Inc.

Weisskopf, V. F. 1972. "The Significance of Science." *Science* 176: 138–146.

Whyte, L. L. 1960. *The Unconscious before Freud.* New York: Basic Books, Inc.

Wundt, W. 1897. *Outlines of Psychology.* Translated with the cooperation of the author by C. H. Judd. Leipzig: Wilhelm Engelmann.

——. 1961. "Introduction: On the Methods in Psychology." In *Classics in Psychology,* edited by T. Shipley, pp. 51–78. New York: Philosophical Library.

4

Freud's Psychical Unconscious

As noted from time to time on previous pages, James equated belief in mind as unconscious with belief in a myth, or, at best, belief in a dubious paradox. That is why he never equated the concept of subliminal processes with the concept of unconscious *mental* processes. In his view, belief in mind as unconscious was a hindrance to the promotion of a scientific psychology. On the other hand, for Freud the unconscious was a scientific finding of the first magnitude; in fact, he regarded it as a science in its own right. He once wrote: "The future will probably attribute far greater importance to psychoanalysis as the science of the unconscious than as a therapeutic procedure" (1929, p. 673).

When Freud was writing his *Traumdeutung,* or *The Interpretation of Dreams,* he was mindful of academic opposition to his views. This is not to say that he was mindful of what James had written in his criticisms of the unconscious, for James is not mentioned in the long bibliography at the end of the work. Furthermore, according to Jones (Vol. I, p. 373), Freud "was not very given to reading books on psychology." Thus one can be reasonably confident that he had not read the *Principles* of James. Nevertheless, he must have been familiar with some psychological texts because he contrasted his views with those to be found in such works.

CONCERNING FREUD'S CLASH WITH ACADEMIC PSYCHOLOGY

Actually, Freud did not mention any texts by name, but referred to them in general. This is made evident in the following passage from the *Tramdeu-*

tung, in which Freud contrasts his "psychologizing" as a "physician" with that of the "philosophers" or academic psychologists (pp. 611-612):

> So far we have been psychologizing on our own account. It is time now to consider the theoretical views which govern present-day psychology and to examine their relation to our hypotheses. The problem of the unconscious in psychology is . . . less *a* psychological problem than *the* problem of psychology. So long as psychology dealt with this problem by a verbal explanation to the effect that 'psychical' *meant* 'conscious' and that to speak of 'unconscious psychical processes' was palpable nonsense, any psychological evaluation of the observations made by physicians upon abnormal mental states was out of the question. The physician and the philosopher can only come together if they both recognize that the term 'unconscious psychical processes' is 'the appropriate and justified expression of a solidly established fact.' The physician can only shrug his shoulders when he is assured that 'consciousness is an indispensable characteristic of what is psychical,' and perhaps, if he still feels enough respect for the utterances of philosophers, he may presume that they have not been dealing with the same thing or working at the same science. For even a single understanding observation of a neurotic's mental life or a single analysis of a dream must leave him with an unshakable conviction that the most complicated and most rational thought-processes, which can surely not be denied the name of psychical processes, can occur without exciting the subject's consciousness. It is true that the physician cannot learn of these unconscious processes until they have produced some effect upon consciousness which can be communicated or observed. But this conscious effect may exhibit a psychical character quite different from that of the unconscious process, so that internal perception cannot possibly regard the one as a substitute for the other. The physician must feel at liberty to proceed by *inference* from the conscious effect to the unconscious psychical process. He thus learns that the conscious effect is only a remote psychical result of the unconscious process and that the latter has not become conscious as such; and moreover that the latter was present and operative even without betraying its existence in any way to consciousness.

This was Freud's answer to those who had opposed belief in the unconscious, as James had. From their viewpoint it is "palpable nonsense" to believe in unconscious consciousness. As philosopher-psychologists they lacked the clinical experience of physicians with "abnormal mental states" and hence relied exclusively on "a verbal explanation." Had they been familiar with these states they would not have been baffled by the paradox of unconscious consciousness. Their confrontation with clinical cases of hysteria and other kinds of mental abnormality would have exposed the inadequacy of their verbal explanations. It would have made them realize, so Freud argued, that a psychical process was not always the same as a conscious process and, presumably, they would have been convinced of the real existence of an unconscious psychical process. Instead of being a myth, as James seemed to hold, it was regarded as "a solidly established fact." However, this "fact," Freud indicated, is concealed from the neurotic's "internal perception" and, of course, from the physician's direct observation. As a result, the only way the existence of such a "fact" can be established is by inference.

A NEGLECTED PROBLEM

Having made a distinction between the meaning of a conscious process as contrasted with the meaning of a psychical process, Freud unfortunately neglected to elaborate upon the distinction. He failed to specify just what characteristics are to be attributed to the inferred psychical process. The one characteristic mentioned refers to thinking: by observing the "neurotic's mental life" the physician "must" be convinced of the occurrence of "thought-processes" even though his patient is ignorant of their occurrence. Furthermore, since such processes are obviously "psychical" or mental, for the neurotic to be oblivious of them established their unconscious existence. So Freud seemed to argue, but in doing so he glossed over the problem of a dependable criterion by means of which the psychical or mental status of an event or process is to be determined.

This constituted a problem because he had objected to having the word "psychical" mean the same as the word "conscious." In other words, he would have objected to this generalization: the unconscious is a derivative of the conscious in the sense that, for example, actions attributed to an unconscious wish presuppose knowledge of wishing as a conscious process. By extension, the implication is that other comparable phrases such as unconscious thought or unconscious protest involve acquaintance with thinking and protesting as personal happenings for the phrases to be meaningful. Broadly speaking, this is the equivalent of regarding consciousness as "an indispensable characteristic of what is psychical." But this is precisely what Freud denied, though he neglected to indicate what other characteristic is to be substituted if given events are to be classified as *psychical* events. The word *psychical* in this context is a literal translation of the German adjective *psychische* which Freud employed. In the given context it would be better to translate it as meaning *mental* events, so as to avoid the connotation of the word *psychical* suggested by reference to psychical research with its halo of the occult and as distinguished from ordinary psychological research.

Accordingly, for Freud the unconscious was deemed to be a psychical realm only in the sense of being a *mental,* but not a *conscious* realm. He was at pains to emphasize this distinction. In a footnote (p. 612) he reports his satisfaction at having come across an author who, in support of this distinction, had quoted this sentence from Henry Maudsley's 1867 volume entitled *The Physiology and Pathology of the Mind:*[1] "It is a truth which cannot be

[1]It may be that Freud was misled by having been supplied with a mistaken title for Maudsley's book, since in the *Traumdeutung* bibliography it is listed as *Psychology and Pathology of the Mind* (p. 644). Unless he also had come across the quotation in the

too distinctly borne in mind that consciousness is not co-extensive with mind." Incidentally, as will be explained later, this is only a portion of Maudsley's sentence, since the original ends with a qualifying clause. However, for the time being, this may be disregarded and the formulation given in the footnote be accepted as it stands.

MAUDSLEY ON MIND AS DIFFERENT FROM CONSCIOUSNESS

Contrary to what Freud seemed to believe, this sentence may have nothing to do with the concept of an unconscious mind as he conceived it. Maudsley's whole approach to mental life reflected the outlook of a physiological psychologist rather than that of a psychoanalyst. This is evident from the way historians have dealt with his work. Brett, for example, has classified him with writers who attempt "to reduce psychology to a form of physiology" (1921, p. 191). And Zilboorg, to cite another example, reflects a similar physiological bias by declaring Maudsley to have been "purely materialistic" since "to him mental diseases were brain diseases" (1941, p. 421).

As a matter of fact, from one viewpoint Maudsley's statement about consciousness not being co-extensive with mind comes close to being a truism. After all, at any instant of time one is conscious of but a minute segment of the totality of knowledge, skills, feelings, interests, memories, and kindred constituents implicit in the concept of mind. A man's knowledge of language is not co-extensive with the words of which he is momentarily conscious. Should he possess an educated mind and have knowledge of Latin, French, mathematics, history, literature, current events, architecture, and law, the scope of his mind would obviously never be co-extensive with the scope of his consciousness. Furthermore, his educated mind is a product of learning and as such implies consciousness to the extent that all learning entails sensory stimulation, a modicum of attention, perception, memory, understanding, and similar components of man's cognitive apparatus. From this empiristic viewpoint mind would appear to be a derivative of consciousness and not a derivative of a mysterious unconscious. This seems to be what Maudsley may have meant by his sentence.[2]

---

book itself, he might have been justified in taking it for granted that Maudsley had been primarily interested in the psychology rather than the physiology of mind. Incidentally, the same error occurred in Boring's history, for he too lists the title as *Psychology* and not *Physiology and Pathology of Mind* (1950, p. 660).

[2]There is no assurance that Maudsley would have employed this precise way of clarifying his distinction between mind and consciousness. In explaining why "mind and consciousness are not synonymous" he attributed mind to a state of "statical equilibrium" of the brain and consciousness to its "manifested energy," with the former involving much vaster "mental organization" than the latter. This is the way he alluded to this distinction (1893, p. 29):

> Mental power exists in statical equilibrium as well as in manifested energy; . . . no man can call to mind at any moment the thousandth part of his knowledge. How

The latter interpretation of Maudsley's sentence is in line with James's approving references to Maudsley's psychology. In his chapter on habit, for example, by way of showing the transition from conscious acts to automatic or habitual acts James quotes this passage from Maudsley's book (Vol. I, pp. 113-114):

> If an act became no easier after being done several times, if the careful direction of consciousness were necessary to its accomplishment on each occasion, it is evident that the whole activity of a lifetime might be confined to one or two deeds—that no progress could take place in development. A man might be occupied all day in dressing and undressing himself; the attitude of his body would absorb all his attention and energy; the washing of his hands or the fastening of a button would be as difficult to him on each occasion as to the child on its first trial; and he would, furthermore, be completely exhausted by his exertions. Think of the pains necessary to teach a child to stand, of the many efforts which it must make, and of the ease with which it at last stands, unconscious of any effort. For while secondarily automatic acts are accomplished with comparatively little weariness—in this regard approaching the organic movements, or the original reflex movements—the conscious effort of the will soon produces exhaustion. A spinal cord without . . . memory would simply be an idiotic spinal cord. . . . It is impossible for an individual to realize how much he owes to its automatic agency until disease has impaired its functions.

The stand taken by Maudsley was entirely in accord with the fundamentals of a functionalist psychology and as such could be welcomed by James. From the context it is evident that Maudsley was not thinking of a "psychical" unconscious as conceived by Freud. Furthermore, his account of the nature of "secondarily automatic acts" is reminiscent of Helmholtz's basic process as described in the previous chapter. Recall that Helmholtz accounted for the automatism of habit without invoking the doctrine of unconscious inference. This means that neither he nor Maudsley attributed retention or preservation of such automatism to an unconscious mind—rather, as a product of repetition and drill, and like any readily reactivated past event, it was to be attributed to the neurology of memory. James expressed this very simply and directly when, after letting *n* stand for a past event, he wrote (Vol. I, p. 655):

> The *retention* of *n* . . . is no mysterious storing up of an 'idea' in an unconscious state. It is not a fact of the mental order at all. It is a purely physical phenomenon, a morphological feature, the presence of 'paths' . . . in the finest recesses of the brain's tissue.

---

utterly helpless is consciousness to give any account of the statical condition of mind! But as statical mind is in reality the statical condition of the nervous substrata which minister to its manifestations, it is plain that, if we ever are to know anything of mental organization, it is to the progress of physiology that we must look for information.

It thus appears that both Helmholtz and Maudsley would have agreed with this Jamesian interpretation of the nature of retention. Reduced to its essentials it might have struck them as a commonsense interpretation. In an everyday example, James was arguing that even though we have forgotten our high school geometry it is not entirely obliterated, since it can be relearned in significantly less time than was required for its initial mastery some thirty years ago. What was retained, James held, was some kind of neural change in the tissues of the brain and not some ghosts of mathematical ideas stored up in an unconscious state.

It is entirely conceivable that at one time Freud might have agreed with this explanation. At all events, there is a passage in his *Interpretation of Dreams* suggestive of this possibility. The English version reads: "Even when investigation shows that the primary exciting cause of a phenomenon is psychical, deeper research will one day trace the path further and discover an organic basis for the mental event. But, if at the moment we cannot see beyond the mental, that is no reason for denying its existence"[3] (pp. 41-42).

As applied to Maudsley's differentiation between mind and consciousness this would mean that with respect to the instance of ordinary associative memory, such as a request for specific information, hearing the request would exemplify the "psychical" or "exciting cause" of the elicited response. To be more specific: were a teacher to ask a pupil, "What is the capital of Alaska?" the pupil would be *conscious* of the question and would have to search his *mind* for the answer. In view of the vast number of geographic and other items of retained information he has accumulated in previous years his *mind* is manifestly more extensive than his momentary awareness of the question. As retained items they are *organic* rather than psychical and also *unconscious* until brought to *mind* in the quest for an answer to the question. The quest will continue until there is recall of "Juneau" as the correct answer; but this does not mean that prior to its recall the idea of Juneau *qua* idea had been existing in some nonorganic state of unconscious consciousness.

Maudsley's distinction between mind and consciousness, contrary to Freud's interpretation, thus has nothing to do with the concept of an unconscious mind. Instead, it has to do with the psychical as currently experienced, in contradistinction to the cumulative results of what has already been experienced—the kind of distinction once made by Titchener when he defined consciousness as "the sum-total of mental processes occurring *now*" as distinguished from the definition of mind as "the sum-total of mental processes occurring in the lifetime of an individual" (1917, p. 19). In this formulation

---

[3]This is my somewhat free and not literal translation. The original in the *Traumdeutung* reads as follows (1922, p. 30):

> Selbst wo das Psychische sich bei der Erforschung als der primäre Anlass eines Phänomens erkennen lässt, wird ein tieferes Eindringen die Fortsetzung des Weges bis zur organischen Begründung des Seelischen einmal zu finden wissen. Wo aber das Psychische für unsere derzeitige Erkenntnis die Endstation bedeuten müsste, da braucht es darum nicht geleugnet zu werden.

Titchener was not regarding mind as a free-floating realm of unconscious consciousness freed from the influence of brain processes. He made this clear in an alternative definition of mind as "the sum-total of human experience considered as dependent upon a nervous system" (p. 16). Of course, he also regarded consciousness as dependent upon a nervous system. In this respect he described mind and consciousness as "almost identical." In other respects he found the chief difference to be the one to which Maudsley had called attention: namely, that mind is more extensive in scope than consciousness. Generally, he treated mind and consciousness as synonymous concepts.

Titchener was in substantial agreement with the opinion of John Hughlings Jackson, one of Maudsley's contemporaries[4] and one of the founding fathers of modern clinical neurology, for in an article concerned with the evolution of the nervous system Jackson had this to say about a possible distinction between mind and consciousness (Vol. II, p. 85):

> I take consciousness and mind to be synonymous terms; if all consciousness is lost all mind is lost. Unconscious states of mind are sometimes spoken of, which seems to me to involve a contradiction. That there may be activities of lower nervous arrangements of the highest centres, which have no attendant psychical states, and which yet lead to next activities of the very highest nervous arrangements of those centres whose activities have attendant psychical states, I can easily understand. But these prior activities are states of the nervous system, not any sort of states of mind.

As Jackson suggests here and as he brought out even more clearly in other sections of the same article, not all nervous states are concomitants of mental or conscious states, even though all mental or conscious states are concomitants of nervous states. From this viewpoint he rejected the contention of those who talked about "unconscious states of mind" as if undisturbed by the contradiction implicit in talk about unconscious consciousness; he was cognizant of the contradiction and reacted accordingly. This deserves explicit mention. Recall that Freud had indicated that only "philosophers" as contrasted with "physicians" would be troubled by the concept of "unconscious psychical processes," yet Jackson was a physician and an active one. Moreover, although not engaged in medical practice, both James and Wundt had been trained as physicians and they too shared Jackson's negative view of the concept.

It is true, of course, that Freud was referring to physicians whose work entailed experience with abnormalities of mental life. Still, both Jackson and James had such experience, and even Wundt as a philosopher-psychologist was familiar with such abnormalities through his wide reading. The same can be said about Titchener, Wundt's erudite disciple, who was also a wide reader.

---

[4] As indicated by the year of their birth, there can be no question about their status as contemporaries: both men were born in 1835. Jackson died in 1911 and Maudsley in 1918.

As just pointed out, Titchener's views of mind and consciousness were essentially in agreement with the distinction proposed by Maudsley. Indeed, with reference to the bearing of this distinction on the mind-body problem in general and on the problem of the unconscious in particular, Titchener came close to expressing the views of Jackson, of Wundt, and of James. Each of these men, it seems safe to say, would have been in substantial agreement with the following Titchenerian views (1917, pp. 39–40):

> The nervous system does not cause, but it does explain mind. It explains mind as the map of a country explains the fragmentary glimpses of hills and rivers and towns that we catch on our journey through it. In a word, reference to the nervous system introduces into psychology just that unity and coherence which a strictly descriptive psychology cannot achieve.
>
> Mind lapses every night, and reforms every morning; but the bodily processes go on, in sleep and in waking. An idea drops out of memory, to recur, perhaps quite unexpectedly, many years later; but the bodily processes have been going on without interruption. Reference to the body does not add one iota to the data of psychology, to the sum of introspections. It does furnish us with an explanatory principle for psychology; it does enable us to systematise our introspective data. Indeed, if we refuse to explain mind by body, we must accept the one or the other of two, equally unsatisfactory alternatives: we must either rest content with a simple description of mental experience, or must invent an *unconscious mind* to give coherence and continuity to the conscious. Both courses have been tried. But, if we take the first, we never arrive at a science of psychology and if we take the second, we voluntarily leave the sphere of fact for the *sphere of fiction.* (Italics added.)

Before leaving this issue it is well to note that Maudsley, along with Jackson and James, might be said to have anticipated Titchener's misgivings concerning the unconscious. This is evident from a section of his *Physiology of Mind* in which the question of unconscious ideas was under consideration. Toward the end of this section Maudsley gave his answer to the question in this forthright conclusion (1893, p. 71):

> Another objection to the doctrine of unconscious ideas, is that we only know ideas through consciousness, and consciousness through ideas; the expression unconscious idea, is as absurd, therefore, as that of unconscious consciousness. . . . It is this which is the absurdity; for the idea, like the definite movement of muscle, is the function not the structure, not the statical element, but the element in action; we might as well speak of the movement of blowing the nose as being laid up inactive in the muscles or their nerve-centres (which, after all, in a certain sense it is, for the young child can't blow its nose), as talk of unconscious ideas stored up in the mind.

Had Freud read the preceding paragraph and others like it in Maudsley's book, he obviously would not have thought of Maudsley as a champion of the doctrine of unconscious ideas. In fact, to revert to Freud's contrast between the psychologizing of physicians and philosophers, he might have been troubled to find Maudsley, the physician, agreeing with philosophers that "to speak of unconscious psychical processes" is "palpable nonsense," or what Maudsley had called an absurdity. It thus seems likely that Freud, in the absence of immediate access to Maudsley's writings, had been restricted to the single sentence dealing with Maudsley's contention regarding mind as more extensive than consciousness. Furthermore, he had to depend on the meaning of this sentence in the context of the thesis being expounded by the writer who had quoted the sentence. Under the circumstances he was more apt to be influenced by the writer's objective than by Maudsley's original objective; hence his misinterpretation of Maudsley's distinction between mind and consciousness.

CONCERNING A MISINTERPRETATION OF MAUDSLEY

Upon consulting the *Traumdeutung* it was found that the sentence attributed to Maudsley was printed in German; consequently, Freud had not been dealing with the English original. Nor did he mention Maudsley's name in connection with the sentence as is the case in the English translation. Evidently, James Strachey, the translator, by consulting the text from which Freud had been quoting, had succeeded in tracking down the name of the writer of the sentence in question. Then, instead of translating the German version,[5] he copied the words as they appeared in the English original. This means that Strachey was quoting Maudsley and not translating the German sentence. However, he did adhere to the latter to the extent of disregarding a portion of Maudsley's sentence that had not been included in the German. The full sentence in the *Physiology of Mind* with the disregarded section indicated by italics reads as follows (1893, p. 25): "It is a truth which cannot be too distinctly borne in mind, that consciousness is not co-extensive with mind, *that it is not mind but an incidental accompaniment of mind.*"

By way of explanation for such disparagement of the importance of consciousness, Maudsley wrote it seemed "conceivable" that "a man might be as good a reasoning machine without as he is with consciousness" provided his nervous system were being influenced by afferent impulses now associated with consciousness and also provided one had technical devices by means of which to observe "the results of the cerebral operations from without." Had Maudsley been writing in the modern era he could have given voice to the same general explanation by comparing man as "a reasoning machine" with the "reasoning" of computers. In terms of this comparison it is "conceivable"

---

[5]This is the German version (1922, p. 451): "Es ist eine Wahrheit, die man nicht ausdrücklich genug hervorheben kann, dass Bewusstsein und Seele nicht Begriffe von gleicher Ausdehnung sind."

that he might have argued that just as computers are unconscious so mind as "a reasoning machine" might also be unconscious. But this would not be the equivalent of the dynamic unconscious Freud perceived in the dreams, memory lapses, and phobias of his patients.

Under the circumstances, in the absence of the qualifying clause and without Maudsley's explanation, Freud had to read his own meaning into the statement about mind and consciousness not being co-extensive. Taken out of context it is, manifestly, subject to a variety of interpretations. Apparently Freud took it to mean that mind encompasses consciousness. In doing so he seemed to equate mind with the unconscious in the sense of making it the repository of unconscious ideas despite their connotation of unconscious consciousness. Such an interpretation is obviously at variance with the drift of Maudsley's thinking. Moreover, by a perplexing *tour de force,* and again contrary to Maudsley's thinking, he made consciousness a derivative of the unconscious. This is made clear in the following quotation taken from the section containing Maudsley's statement (pp. 612-613):

> It is essential to abandon the overvaluation of the property of being conscious before it becomes possible to form any correct view of the origin of what is mental. . . . The unconscious is the larger sphere, which includes within it the smaller sphere of the conscious. Everything conscious has an unconscious preliminary stage; whereas what is unconscious may remain at that stage and nevertheless claim to be regarded as having the full value of a psychical process. The unconscious is the true psychical reality; *in its innermost nature it is as much unknown to us as the reality of the external world, and it is as incompletely presented by the data of consciousness as is the external world by the communications of our sense organs.*

It is well to realize that Freud deemed the last statement concerned with the unconscious as "the true psychical reality" so significant as to call for italicized emphasis. He had reached the conclusion at the threshold of his career, for the statement is taken from the last section of the *Traumdeutung* and this had been published in 1899. It is also well to realize that Freud continued to uphold the same conclusion at the close of his career. In an unfinished paper written in 1938, about a year before his death, he reverted to the same theme. The paper—probably his very last manuscript—was called "Some Elementary Lessons in Psycho-Analysis" and the conclusion he had arrived at some forty years earlier had survived all the intervening years as shown in this one of the "elementary lessons" (1938, p. 283):

> Everyone—or almost everyone—was agreed that what is mental really *has* a common quality in which its essence is expressed: namely, the quality of *being conscious*—unique, indescribable, but needing no description. All that is conscious, they said, is mental, and conversely, all that is mental is conscious: that is self-evident and to contradict it is nonsense. It cannot be said that this decision threw much light upon the nature of the mental; for consciousness is one of the fundamental

> facts of our life and our researches come up against it like a blank wall and can find no path beyond it. . . . If ever human thought found itself in an *impasse* it was here.
>
> Psycho-analysis escaped such difficulties . . . by energetically denying the equation between what is mental and what is conscious. No; being conscious cannot be the essence of what is mental. It is only a *quality* of what is mental, and an unstable quality at that—one that is far oftener absent than present. The mental, whatever its nature may be, is in itself unconscious and probably similar in kind to all the other natural processes of which we have obtained knowledge.

As may be recalled, this 1938 paper was mentioned in the previous chapter in connection with the phenomenon of posthypnotic suggestibility; there will be occasion to mention it again in the next chapter. Even though it failed to be completed, it is obviously an important paper—highlighting some of the issues which, in retrospect toward the final months of his life, Freud had singled out for special comment because of their distinctive psychoanalytic implications. Presumably they were intended to serve as means of facilitating understanding and acceptance of these implications. In some ways, for Freud, they were all bound up with this central issue, namely, his contention that being conscious is not the essence of mind because, as he had already maintained so many years earlier, "the unconscious is the true psychical reality." He had even maintained that consciousness is a derivative of this unconscious psychical reality. As previously noted, this is a perplexing conclusion the meaning and validity of which cannot be determined without prior clarification of Freud's concept of the "true psychical reality."

CONCERNING FREUD'S PSYCHICAL REALITY

According to Freud, as we have seen, psychoanalysis might be defined as the science of the unconscious. He even predicted the future will probably reveal it to have been more important as this kind of a science than as a technique for treating personality disorders. The concept of mind as unconscious was thus made the foundation of psychoanalytic psychology. For obvious reasons, Freud stood ready to safeguard the concept from adverse criticism. In his view, to question its scientific status as James and others had done was the equivalent of an attack on psychoanalysis itself. Adverse criticism was a threat to it both as science and as therapeutic art.

A chief criticism of the unconscious had stressed the contradiction involved in the notion of a consciousness which is also unconscious. Freud had this criticism in mind when he took those "philosophers" to task who had rejected the idea of "unconscious psychical processes" as "palpable nonsense." As philosopher-psychologists they had equated the psychical with the conscious. Their stand had been given definite expression as far back as 1886 by John Dewey when he wrote: "Consciousness is necessary for the definition of what is in itself unconscious" (p. 2).

In short, for them the phenomenon of consciousness was made a *sine qua non* for psychical reality. This meant that any process designated as a psychical or mental process was presumed to involve consciousness either directly or indirectly. For example, with reference to the automatism of habit, as in signing one's name or drinking from a cup, conscious control may be said to have been so reduced as to have transformed what had once been fully conscious effortful maneuvers into quasi-reflex automatisms. As a functionalist Dewey would have accounted for such "unconscious," well entrenched habitual acts in terms of their history as what had started out as fully conscious acts.

This kind of explanation is in accord with a fundamental doctrine of functional psychology concerning the guiding role of consciousness in the acquisition of knowledge and skill. Progress in learning, according to the doctrine, is characterized by a shift from the strain of conscious attention to new problems to the free and easy or virtually "unconscious" disposition of these problems once mastery has been achieved. The shift, in other words, is from the conscious to the unconscious or, at least, from the more conscious to the less conscious. This kind of shift was implicit in the psychical reality of functional psychology.

Although Freud, as far as known, had never familiarized himself with the writings of Dewey and other functional psychologists, his disparagement of the role of consciousness suffices to stamp him as opposed to their view of psychical reality as marked by the shift from the conscious to the unconscious. Instead, he reversed this by making it a shift from the unconscious to the conscious; hence, as he maintained, "the unconscious is the true psychical reality." This amounts to deriving consciousness from an unconscious consciousness. By means of this reversal Freud appears to have tried to circumvent the objection of those who, in his words, had criticized the concept of "unconscious psychical processes" as "palpable nonsense."

On the surface, it is more of a dogmatic denial than a clarifying disposition of the objection. Moreover, since Freud viewed the "nature" of the unconscious as unknown, it is hard to understand how it could serve as the basis for an explanation of the "nature" of consciousness. After all, enlightenment calls for the transition from the known to the unknown and not the other way around. Freud appears to have disregarded this truism by seeming to explain the light of consciousness by an appeal to the darkness of the unconscious. As a procedure it is reminiscent of this maxim as quoted by James in the name of a contemporary philosopher (Vol. I, p. 347): "Whatever you are *totally* ignorant of, assert to be the explanation of everything else."

In all fairness, the foregoing maxim is actually not applicable to Freud's view of the unconscious as being "the true psychical reality." As he saw it, the nature of the unconscious is not *totally* unknown to us. Reference to the italicized sentence of the quotation dealing with the "overvaluation" of consciousness indicates that Freud was careful to restrict our ignorance of the unconscious to "its innermost nature" and thus, by implication, not to *all* of it. It will also be noticed that he regarded this kind of ignorance as comparable to our ignorance of "the reality of the external world." There was no additional explanation of this allusion to the external world as unknown, as if he expected it to be readily comprehensible without further comment. Another way to put this would be to say that he seemed to expect his readers to be sufficiently familiar with the metaphysics of Kant to understand the allusion to be a reflection of Kant's distinction between noumenal and phenomenal worlds. This distinction, as noted in Chapter 2, had already been recognized by von Hartmann in his philosophy of the unconscious; in fact, it may be recalled that von Hartmann wrote as if Kant should be listed among discoverers of the unconscious. This raises a question about the possible bearing of Kant's philosophy on Freud's psychology.

WAS FREUD INFLUENCED BY KANT?

Since, as just indicated, Freud appears to have made use of Kant's concept of a noumenal world, it is really unnecessary to ask whether he was influenced by Kant—the question has already been answered in the affirmative. Nevertheless, it is not an altogether superfluous question, because not all students of Freud would agree with this answer. Wolman, for example, in his book dealing with "the meaning of Freudian psychology," declares that "Freud was opposed to the idealistic German philosophy of Kant" (1968, p. 95). Wolman failed to say more about this and also failed to supply a pertinent bibliographic reference, so it is hard to know how this is to be interpreted. Does it mean that Freud had expressed opposition to specific Kantian teachings, and if so which ones? Or does it refer to total rejection of all things Kantian? It certainly cannot refer to such extreme anti-Kantianism. As a matter of fact, Freud once voiced his indebtedness to Kant with particular reference to the notion of mental processes being unconscious. This was in his 1915 paper "The Unconscious" and took this form (p. 171):

> The psycho-analytic assumption of unconscious mental activity appears to us, on the one hand, as a further expansion of the primitive animism which caused us to see copies of our own consciousness all around us, and, on the other hand, as an extension of the corrections undertaken by Kant of our views on external perception. Just as Kant warned us not to overlook the fact that our perceptions are subjectively conditioned and must not be regarded as identical with what is perceived though unknowable, so psycho-analysis warns us not to equate perceptions by means of consciousness with the unconscious mental processes which are their object.

Freud seems to have been familiar with many other Kantian concepts and evidently expected his readers to share this familiarity. Thus, in *The Interpretation of Dreams* there is mention of Kant's categorical imperative (p. 68) in a matter-of-fact way without a word of explanation. On a later page (p. 503) there is the same kind of casual reference to Kant's view of the concept of time. He again dealt with the latter concept in a letter written in 1938 some months before his death. In it, after suggesting that "it might be that the idea of time is connected with the work of" our perceptual consciousness, he wrote, "Kant would then be in the right if we replace his old-fashioned 'a priori' by our modern introspection of the psychical apparatus. It should be the same with space, causality, etc." (Jones, Vol. III, p. 466.)

In this reference to "space, causality, etc." there is an obvious indication of familiarity with the famous Kantian categories of understanding. They have to do with ways in which, according to Kant, man's intellect deals with sensory phenomena as judgments are made with respect to causal relationships, differences in quantity and quality, contingent as contrasted with inevitable changes, and other fundamental modes of organizing experience. Kant regarded them as characteristic of the inherent structure of man's reason. As such, although acting on the data of sensory experience they were deemed to be independent of and not derivatives of sensory experience. Freud seems to have had reference to these Kantian categories in writing about what he called man's "psychical apparatus."

In connection with this reference to "psychical apparatus" recall that Freud did not use *psychical* as a synonym for the word *conscious.* Instead, he used it to present the "unconscious psychical process" as what he called "a solidly established fact." In doing so, however, he had failed to specify precisely how a *psychical* process was to be recognized since, by hypothesis, it was to be differentiated from any conscious process. He did indicate it to be characteristic of "thought-processes" and hence by implication made the act of thinking the differentiating criterion, so that any thoughtful act would be a *psychical* act in contradistinction to any act of thoughtless awareness. This makes for a distinction between thinking on the one hand and meaningless sensory awareness on the other, or between insightful understanding as contrasted with mere sentience in the abstract. It is the kind of distinction Kant had once epitomized in this way: "The understanding cannot see. The senses cannot think. Only by their union can knowledge be produced."

In some ways this Kantian distinction amounts to a detailed elaboration of the logic implicit in Aristotle's distinction between the intellectual soul and the sentient soul—the former being unique to man as the rational animal. The distinction is also implicit in Locke's recognition of the origin and development of our ideas as influenced by the conjoint operation of sensation and reflection. His famous *Essay Concerning Human Understanding,* in which the nature and scope of this operation is subjected to careful analysis, might thus be regarded as having foreshadowed the Kantian distinction. In general, these and similar historical precedents converge on a central theme—the distinctive role of active reason as the hallmark of mind. This theme is reflected in Aristotle's intellectual soul, in the Cartesian *res cogitans,* in the rationalism of Spinoza, in Locke's reflection, and in Kant's pure reason. And it is also reflected in what Freud had called *the primacy of the intellect.*

FREUD ON THE PRIMACY OF INTELLECT

In popularizations of Freudian psychology the imperiousness of the sex drive and other instincts is likely to be stressed. Cravings, urges, and wishes dominate talk about sublimation, the symbolism of dreams, and so-called Freudian slips, as if in this popular view Freud had transformed Aristotle's concept of man as a rational animal into man as an instinctual animal driven by aroused id impulses or the dynamism of repressed ideas. From this viewpoint Freud's psychology appears to be an anti-intellectualistic psychology and it is easy to find evidence seeming to support this interpretation. However, there is also opposing evidence which ought not to be overlooked before arriving at a final conclusion. For example, in his monograph *The Future of an Illusion* Freud noted the bearing of rational considerations on factors involved in coping with the phenomenon of repression in this statement (1934, p. 77): "The time has probably come to replace the consequences of repression by the results of *rational* mental effort" (italics added). Note that there is no reference to a rationalizing mental effort. This merits special mention because the psychoanalytic recognition of rationalization as a fact has sometimes been interpreted as a Freudian description of man as being a rationalizing rather than a rational animal. That this constitutes a misinterpretation of Freud's position is further indicated by his use of a phrase like "primacy of the intellect" and not primacy of instinct. What he meant by the intellect's primacy is made clear in this famous passage (1934, p. 93):

> We may insist as much as we like that the human intellect is weak in comparison with human instincts and be right in doing so. But, nevertheless, there is something peculiar about this weakness. The voice of the intellect is a soft one, but it does not rest until it has gained a hearing. Ultimately, after endlessly repeated rebuffs, it succeeds.

This tribute to the eventual triumph of the voice of the intellect may make it easier to understand what Freud seems to have meant by his somewhat enigmatic identification of the unconscious with the mental or the psychical as distinguished from the conscious. Such identification was evident in statements to the effect that "the mental is itself unconscious," that "being conscious cannot be the essence of what is mental," that the unconscious is "the true psychical reality," and that "what is mental" is not the same as "what is conscious." Statements of this kind all reflect what seems to have been one of Freud's firm convictions as expressed in his *Interpretation of Dreams* of 1899 in these italicized words (p. 593): "*the most complicated achievements of thought are possible without the assistance of consciousness.*" It was again reflected close to thirty years later with his recognition of "the primacy of the intellect" in the *Future of an Illusion.*

This recognition of a difference between thought or intellect on the one hand and consciousness on the other made it possible for Freud to come to terms with the paradox of unconscious consciousness. It was as if the preceding statements could be rendered less enigmatic by being rephrased in the light of the difference in question. Thus, he might have made thinking "the true psychical reality." Analogously, he might have written "being conscious cannot be the essence of what is intellectual." As already mentioned, in terms of this differentiation between the intellectual and the sensory Freud can be said to have been in accord with a venerable philosophic tradition–especially Kant's contribution to this tradition. The broader implications of this tradition on Freud's concept of the unconscious will be considered in a later chapter.

Actually, Freud may have been even more influenced by the views of Herbart, Kant's successor at the University of Königsberg, than by Kant's views. Johann Friedrich Herbart was both philosopher and psychologist; in fact, he was more directly concerned with laying the groundwork for a scientific psychology than was Kant. In some respects he might also be said to have laid the groundwork for that which emerged as psychoanalytic psychology, since some of his teachings regarding the dynamics of thinking are striking anticipations of some of Freud's teachings.

HERBART ON THE DYNAMICS OF THINKING

A section of the previous chapter was devoted to an account of Herbart's concept of an *apperceptive mass,* with particular reference to its importance for educational planning at the classroom level. It was pointed out that the concept of apperceptive mass is closely related to Freud's concept of the *preconscious.* The latter concept refers to the totality of readily available items of information at an individual's disposal; hence the preconscious may be thought of as a background or reservoir of such information. But this is not the only respect in which a Herbartian concept appears to foreshadow a later Freudian concept.

Other respects in which such resemblances between the two kinds of psychology have been detected inlcude Herbartian references to repressed ideas, to ideational conflict, and to related aspects of the dynamics of thinking. In his biography of Freud, Ernest Jones has devoted several pages to these resemblances between Herbartian and Freudian teachings (Vol. I, pp. 371–376). Although he was unable to demonstrate that Freud had ever come across Herbart's writings, he did find that in his last year of attendance at the *Gymnasium* Freud was introduced to an exposition of Herbart's psychology in a textbook written by Gustaf Lindner. In this book, as noted by Jones, the youthful Freud was confronted with this sentence: "A result of the fusion of ideas proves that ideas which were once in consciousness and for any reason have been repressed (*verdrängt*) out of it are not lost, but in certain circumstances may return" (p. 374).

In his long chapter "Sigmund Freud and Psychoanalysis" Ellenberger also called attention to Herbartian anticipation of some cardinal Freudian teachings. By way of showing that Herbart's psychology was "one of the main sources of psychoanalysis" he wrote as follows (1970, p. 536):

> Herbart taught the dynamic concept of a fluctuating threshold between the conscious and the unconscious, of conflicts between representations that struggle with each other to gain access to the conscious and are repressed by stronger ones but strive to return, or else produce an indirect effect in consciousness, and the notion of chains of associations that cross each other at nodal points, but also of "free emerging associations," the idea that mental processes as a whole are ruled by a striving for equilibrium. All this is to be found in psychoanalysis, though sometimes in modified form. Whether Freud read Herbart is not known, but it is sure that he had been introduced to Herbart's psychology . . . through Lindner's textbook.

It thus seems to be evident that Freud was indebted to Herbart for the foundation of what developed into psychoanalytic psychology. In the course of this development, however, Freud had occasion to introduce many concepts and interpretations of non-Herbartian lineage. To a large extent they were original with Freud. After all, unlike Herbart, he was concentrating on psychopathology and not on education. This may explain why, unlike Freud, Herbart never entertained such notions as Oedipus complex, the id as a caldron of seething impulsiveness, latent dream content, a tyrannical superego, penis envy, anxiety neurosis, or the psychopathology of everyday life. In the language of Herbart, such notions were original with and unique to Freud's apperceptive mass.

FROM HERBART TO JAMES AND FROM JAMES TO FREUD

To the extent that psychoanalysis reflected Herbartian psychology it might be expected that James would have entertained serious misgivings about psychoanalytic psychology. At all events, there is no question about his distrust of the soundness of Herbart's views. He had reason to object to the Herbartian dynamics of ideational association, since, as indicated in this famous passage, he denied that *ideas* are ever associated (Vol. I, p. 554):

> *Association,* so far as the word stands for an *effect, is between THINGS THOUGHT OF–it is THINGS, not ideas, which are associated in the mind.* We ought to talk of the association of *objects,* not of the association of *ideas.* And so far as association stands for a cause, it is between *processes in the brain*–it is these which, by being associated in certain ways, determine what successive objects shall be thought.

On a later page in the same chapter (p. 603) James referred to Herbart's "mythological supposition" to the effect that "each idea is a permanently existing entity" able to gain entrance into "the theatre of consciousness" only by usurping the place of "another idea previously there." The displaced idea was relegated to the unconscious by sinking below the threshold where it continues to reside until it can once again rise above the threshold into the realm of consciousness. In fact, James characterized talk about such sinking and rising of ideas and their fusions and inhibitions as "glib Herbartian jargon" which seemed to him to be "almost hideous." Furthermore, James also questioned Herbart's use of the term *apperception* (Vol. II, pp. 107-111). In general, he objected to the term because it had been subjected to varying interpretations by different philosophers.[6] More specifically, as applied to Herbart's notion of apperceptive mass James rendered this opinion (p. 107): "We gain no insight into what really occurs either in the mind or in the brain by calling all these things the 'apperceiving mass,' though, of course, this may upon occasion be convenient."[7]

All the foregoing objections to Herbart's psychology, it is well to remember, appeared in 1890. In view of their vehemence and definiteness one might have anticipated that James would have objected to any future psychology emerging out of such Herbartian presuppositions. As already indicated, psychoanalysis proved to be such a future psychology. As a movement it was still struggling for recognition in the early years of the present century. However, in 1909 Freud appeared as an invited lecturer at Clark University[8] in Worcester, Massachusetts, in connection with the vicennial celebration of the founding of the university. This was Freud's first and only visit to the United States. A small group of first generation psychoanalysts were also in attendance–including Ferenczi, Brill, Jung, and Jones. Distinguished first generation American psychologists were there too–men such as James,[9] Titchener, and

---

[6]Kant had used the word in the phrase "transcendental unity of apperception" by way of accounting for mind as integrated rather than disintegrated. Before Kant the word had been used in a different sense by Leibnitz. Furthermore, after both Kant and Herbart, Wundt employed the word with a still different meaning.

[7]Many decades after James this possible convenience of the term continued to be recognized. For example, in their psychological dictionary English and English had this to say about the apperceptive mass (pp. 37-38):

> Though the term is now little used, the doctrine that understanding and learning depend upon discovering relationships between the facts presented and the learner's already existing experience is the basis of practically all educational theory, and of much educational practice. Apperception is defined in terms of the outmoded psychology of *mental content*, but the facts referred to are important and deserve restatement in terms of behavior and performance.

[8]Freud's lectures and those of the other participants at the Clark University Celebration were translated and published in *The American Journal of Psychology*, 1910, XXI: 181-328. In 1973 the Arno Press reprinted these lectures in their series of *Classics in Psychology* in a volume entitled *Lectures Delivered at The 20th Anniversary Celebration of Clark University*.

[9]Although this was the first and only time James met with Freud, he had heard of Freud many years before this meeting. In fact he had alluded to Freud as early as 1894. This was in connection with a review of the article by Breuer and Freud "On the Psychic Mechanisms of Hysterical Phenomena." After referring to it as an "important paper" he had the following to say about it (1894, p. 199):

G. Stanley Hall. For Freud it was a momentous occasion. In fact, as reported by Jones (Vol. II, p. 57), when Freud had an honorary doctorate conferred upon him by the university "he was visibly moved" as he announced: "This is the first official recognition of our endeavors."

On the same page Jones indicates that Freud in writing about his Clark University lectures recalled James as having "followed the lectures with great interest" and then Freud added:

> He was very friendly to us and I shall never forget his parting words, said with his arm around my shoulder: "The future of psychology belongs to your work"–a remarkable saying when one reflects on his puritanical background.

In terms of his recall of the remark made by James concerning "the future of psychology" Freud was justified in believing his account of psychoanalysis had made a favorable impression on James. At all events the remark itself supplies no evidence of any unfavorable impression. Nevertheless, in a letter James had written shortly after his meeting with Freud one can note both favorable and unfavorable impressions. The letter, as cited by Ralph Barton Perry, mentions functional psychology and then continues with this passage (Vol. II, p. 122):

> Speaking of 'functional' psychology, Clark University . . . had a little international congress the other day in honor of the twentieth year of its existence. I went there for one day in order to see what Freud was like, and met also Jung of Zürich, who . . . made a very pleasant impression. I hope that Freud and his pupils will push their ideas to their utmost limits, so that we may learn what they are. They can't fail to throw light on human nature; but I confess that he made on me personally the impression of a man obsessed with fixed ideas. I can make nothing in my own case with his dream theories, and obviously 'symbolism' is a most dangerous method.

Despite his misgivings about symbolism as related to Freud's dream-theory, James did not despair of the theory's possible value for psychology–especially functional psychology. This is evident from a letter he wrote to Professor Mary W. Calkins on September 19, 1909. Since Freud's five lectures had been delivered during the week starting with Monday, September 6th and ending on Friday the 10th, James had not permitted many days to elapse before writing to Miss Calkins as follows (Perry, p. 123):

The distinguished neurologists who sign it stumbled accidentally on cures which enable them not only to give a general formula for the disease, but a general method for its treatment. Hysteria for them starts always from a shock, and is a 'disease of the memory.' Certain reminiscences of the shock fall into the subliminal consciousness, where they can only be discovered in 'hypnoid' states. . . . The cure is to draw them out in hypnotism, let them produce all their emotional effects, however violent, and *work themselves off.*

> My day at Clark University was very enjoyable. . . . I strongly suspect Freud, with his dream-theory, of being a regular *hallucinė*. But I hope that he and his disciples will push it to its limits, as undoubtedly it covers some facts, and will add to our understanding of "functional" psychology, which is the real psychology.

Since James was present at Clark University for but a single day, he could not have heard all five lectures. His judgment of "Freud and his pupils" must have been based upon what he saw and heard on this single day. In view of the fact that in both of the letters just cited the chief emphasis was on Freud's dream-theory, it seems likely that the lecture devoted to this theory was the one James attended. This may have been the third lecture, for, according to Jones (Vol. II, p. 212), the interpretation of dreams was discussed by Freud in his third lecture as supplying "the most secure basis of psychoanalysis."

This lecture was largely concerned with the technique of psychoanalysis and its reliance on free association in dealing with dream material as well as with Freudian interpretations of slips of the tongue and other parapraxes. Evidently, James interpreted the content of this lecture as related to investigations that might come to be of value for the future of functional psychology. Of course, this was not an unqualified endorsement. He was troubled by Freud's "fixed ideas" and by his inability to "make" something of the dream-theory with its reliance on the "dangerous method" of symbolism. However, in both letters he hoped that the Freudian investigations would continue and be pushed to their limits. In the first letter he granted that the investigations "can't fail to throw light on human nature" and in the letter to Miss Calkins he granted that the dream-theory "undoubtedly . . . covers some facts."

It thus seems clear from both letters that James was giving qualified endorsement to psychoanalytic investigations, especially as they might be presumed to enhance understanding of functional psychology. This is particularly interesting because functional psychology as a school or system was primarily concerned with the function of consciousness. Moreover, by 1909 functional psychology had become an established and well recognized movement. Consequently, it seems safe to regard James as having been referring to this movement rather than to his anticipations of the movement in the *Principles* of 1890.

Now the school of functional psychology stressed the function of consciousness as being instrumental in coping with difficulties and novel situations. Success in disposing of such problems, especially in the case of recurrent problems, made for a shift from conscious control to the autonomous control of well entrenched habit. This, so the functionalists taught, left mind or consciousness free to cope with new problems. Autonomous control whether in the form of habit or instinct or reflex mechanism was not attributed to vestigial consciousness as transformed into some mysterious unconscious consciousness. Functional psychology was thus clearly at variance with the Freudian unconscious. Under the circumstances, since James had equated functional psychology with the "real psychology," it is likely that when he said to Freud, "The future of psychology belongs to your work" he was not giving tacit endorsement to the hypothesis of an unconscious mind. Nevertheless, to revert to an earlier point, in other ways he expected Freud's work to "throw light on human nature"; but just what phases of the work impressed him must remain conjectural. Still, it is tempting to consider a few more or less plausible conjectures.

JAMES ON FREUD'S WORK: SOME CONJECTURES

One respect in which Freud's "work" might conceivably have impressed James as worthy of encouragement has to do with free association as the point of departure for the psychoanalytic study of mind. As introduced and applied by Freud this appears to have been the first systematic effort to obtain reports from the common man of the way ideas of all kinds occur to him when he is urged to give free rein to their spontaneous occurrence. James might well have recognized this as a pioneering attempt to subject what he had described as the *stream of consciousness* to systematic investigation. If so, then it is readily understandable that he hoped Freud and his pupils would "push" free association "to its limits."

Another respect in which the technique of free association might have been welcomed by James has to do with its bearing on what James had once called the "causal efficacy" of consciousness or ideation. He mentioned this in voicing his opposition to the theory of epiphenomenalism. The latter theory regarded consciousness as a mere by-product of brain activity in the way in which smoke from a factory's chimney is a by-product of machinery at work. According to this theory, consciousness does not do or cause anything any more than smoke produces a manufactured product. It was in opposition to this stand that James stressed the causal efficacy of ideas as they are experienced. By implication, in his reliance upon free association Freud can also be regarded as opposed to epiphenomenalism. Moreover, this is worth noting because Freud had started his professional career as a student of brain activity, as a neurologist. His interest in psychology in general and psychopathology in particular was a later development. Broadly speaking, in fostering this interest he was helping to promote the two medical specialties of neurology and psychiatry, with the latter specialty giving explicit recognition to the causal efficacy of mind. James might have glimpsed this. Still, this is somewhat more speculative than the preceding conjectures.

Precisely why James could "make nothing" out of Freud's dream theory must also be limited to speculative considerations. It may be that James had trouble reconciling presuppositions of the dream theory with belief in the causal efficacy of consciousness. According to the dream theory, the dream as experienced is a product of unconscious forces. The latter forces account for the dream's meaning and, by hypothesis, this meaning is concealed in the unconscious. Analysis of the manifest content [illegible] of the dream as experienced is required in order to get at the latent content or the dream's real meaning. Stated differently, the unconscious latent content instigates or causes the conscious manifest content. If this be so, then causal efficacy is being attributed to the unconscious rather than to consciousness. It is as if consciousness of the dream is made a by-product of unconscious psychical processes and this would constitute a variant of the theory of epiphenomenalism to which James, as just pointed out, had been opposed. Assuming that James had been aware of this implication as he was listening to Freud's lecture, it is not hard to understand why he was troubled by the dream theory.

This brings up the important question of motivation in general and the concept of unconscious motivation in particular. Of course, long before Freud academic psychology had dealt with the subject of motivation as indicated by chapters on instinct and emotion as spurs to behavior. However, these chapters dealt with motivation from the perspective of normal psychology. But now in the present context it is being considered from the perspective of one of the founding fathers of medical psychology. Both Freud and those influenced by his teachings came to regard this entire issue as the central factor in what came to be called a dynamic psychiatry. Furthermore, those whose professional thinking is governed by belief in and devotion to this central factor are said to be analytically oriented.

As dynamic and analytically oriented practitioners they may be affiliated with any one of a variety of schools of psychotherapy. Thus, there are classical Freudian as well as neo-Freudian and non-Freudian schools. Despite marked differences in doctrine among these rival schools, they do not differ in their recognition of the reality and importance of unconscious motivation. But this does not mean agreement with regard to what each school attributes to the unconscious.

There are some provocative issues arising out of this clash between rival analytic schools on the one hand and their differing views of the concept of motivation on the other—especially the concept of unconscious motivation. Furthermore, as will be brought out in the next chapter, some of these issues may be construed as elaborations of or, in some instances, as deviations from Freud's psychical unconscious as discussed in the present chapter.

REFERENCES

Boring, E. G. 1950. *A History of Experimental Psychology.* New York: Appleton-Century-Crofts.

Brett, G. S. 1921. *A History of Psychology,* Vol. III. London: George Allen & Unwin, Ltd.

Dewey, J. 1893. *Psychology,* 3rd Edition. New York: Harper & Brothers. (First published in 1886.)

Ellenberger, H. F. 1970. *The Discovery of the Unconscious—The History and Evolution of Dynamic Psychiatry.* New York: Basic Books, Inc.

English, H. B., and English, A. C. 1958. *A Comprehensive Dictionary of Psychological and Psychoanalytical Terms.* New York: Longmans, Green and Co.

Freud, S. 1915. "The Unconscious." In *The Standard Edition of the Complete Psychological Works of Sigmund Freud,* translated by James Strachey, Vol. XIV, pp. 159–215.

——. *The Interpretation of Dreams.* Translated by James Strachey, New York: Basic Books, Inc.

——. 1922. *Die Traumdeutung.* Leipzig and Wien: Franz Deuticke.

——. 1929. "Psychoanalysis." In *Encyclopaedia Britannica,* Vol. 18, pp. 672-674.

——. 1934. *The Future of an Illusion.* London: The Hogarth Press.

——. 1938. "Some Elementary Lessons in Psycho-Analysis." In *The Standard Edition of Sigmund Freud,* Vol. XXIII, pp. 279-286.

Jackson, J. H. 1958. "Remarks on Evolution and Dissolution of the Nervous System." In *Selected Writings of John Hughlings Jackson,* Vol. II, edited by J. Taylor. New York: Basic Books, Inc.

James, W. 1890. *The Principles of Psychology,* Vols. I and II. New York: Henry Holt and Company.

——. 1894. Review of "Ueber den psychischen Mechanismus hysterischer Phänomene," by J. Breuer and S. Freud. *Psychological Review* 1: 199.

Jones, E. 1953, 1955, 1957. *The Life and Work of Sigmund Freud,* Vol. I, Vol. II, and Vol. III (respectively). New York: Basic Books, Inc.

Maudsley, H. 1893. *The Physiology of Mind* ("Being the First Part of a Third Edition" of *The Physiology and Pathology of Mind* of 1867). New York: D. Appleton and Company.

Perry, R. B. 1935. *The Thought and Character of William James,* Vol. II. Boston: Little, Brown and Company.

Titchener, E. B. 1917. *A Text-Book of Psychology.* New York: The Macmillan Company.

Wolman, B. B. 1968. *The Unconscious Mind–The Meaning of Freudian Psychology.* Englewood Cliffs, New Jersey: Prentice-Hall, Inc.

Zilboorg, G. 1941. *A History of Medical Psychology.* New York: W. W. Norton & Company, Inc.

5

The Unconscious and Theories of Motivation

During the early decades of the present century both psychology and psychiatry became increasingly dynamic. This is another way of noting that both fields began to devote more attention to the subject of motivation. However, in general, there was a difference in underlying attitude toward the subject: psychiatrists were chiefly interested in the motivational dynamics of their patients and psychologists were mainly concerned with the influence of motivation on human and animal behavior, especially as subject to experimental control. As a result dynamic psychiatry was centered in clinical studies as contrasted with the laboratory studies characteristic of dynamic psychology. One consequence of this difference was that the concept of unconscious motivation tended to dominate the clinical or psychiatric orientation while no such emphasis governed the orientation of the experimental psychologists. The difference in orientation was already recognized by Freud when he contrasted the "physician's" belief in and acceptance of unconscious mental processes with the skepticism regarding the existence of such processes on the part of "university professors"—a clash between medical psychology on the one hand and academic psychology on the other. The implications of this clash constitute the central themes of the present chapter and, in some respects, the emergence of these themes might be said to have been foreshadowed or symbolized by the differing psychological orientation of James and Freud as touched upon in the last two chapters. What they stood for in the history of psychology epitomized the nature of the clash in question and their one personal meeting may be regarded as symbolic of that clash. This made it a historic meeting.

A HISTORIC MEETING

As noted in the last chapter, the only time William James and Sigmund Freud ever met was on September 8, 1909. This was on the occasion of the third of Freud's five lectures at Clark University's vicennial celebration. The lecture James heard referred to the strict determinism of all mental processes as reflected in blunders, jokes, hysterical symptoms, Jung's association experiments, and especially in the formation of dreams. Freely translated, Freud had this to say about the importance of dream interpretation for understanding of the unconscious (1910, p. 32):

> In reality the interpretation of dreams is the royal road to knowledge of the unconscious. It is the most certain foundation of psychoanalysis and the realm in which every worker has to seek his own proof and his own instruction. When I am asked, how can one become a psychoanalyst, then I answer, by the study of one's own dreams.

In the lecture James thus heard about the dynamics and distortion of wish-fulfillment as dream-work transforms latent into manifest content. He also heard about the way the unconscious has to make use of special symbolism for the expression of "sexueller Komplexe." And toward the end of the lecture (p. 39) there was renewed emphasis on the motivational implications of the psychoanalyst's "strict belief in the determination of mental life." For him there is nothing accidental or arbitrary in all that man thinks, feels, and does; he is on the alert for detecting the manifold of motives operative in mental life. In this respect he differs from those of us who seem to rest content with reliance upon a single psychic *cause* ("einer einzigen psychischen Ursache") in place of the manifold of *motives* ("mehrfache Motivierung"). In short, even in this single lecture James was exposed to the salient characteristics Freud attributed to the concept of a dynamic unconscious.

In retrospect, this meeting of James and Freud stands out as memorable because it marked the coming together of a leading academic psychologist and a leading medical psychologist–a leading critic of the unconscious was face to face with a leading champion of the unconscious.

This is not to be interpreted as meaning that they were mindful of being sponsors of divergent stands at the time of their brief meeting. Indeed, as reported on an earlier page, Freud was especially moved by the fact that James was not only "very friendly" but also by the fact that with his arm around Freud's shoulder he said, "The future of psychology belongs to your work." This word of encouragement along with the words he heard upon being awarded an honorary doctorate made a deep impression upon Freud. As he saw it, after a decade of neglect by the world of learning, psychoanalysis was at last being accorded the accolade of academic recognition. In his own words it was, "The first official recognition of our endeavors."

In all likelihood the meeting was far more momentous for Freud than for James. It took place when James's career was drawing to a close, for he died less than a year later on August 26, 1910. In the case of Freud the meeting might be said to have come at the start of three decades of creative writing and increasing influence. Under the circumstances it is conceivable that Freud might have taken James's remark about "the future of psychology" to have been an implicit request to carry on the unfinished tasks of a colleague whose days were numbered. It is tempting to read fulfillment of such a request in the fact that, as previously noted, Freud had this to say about his hopes for the probable outcome of his own unfinished labors: "The future will probably attribute far greater importance to psycho-analysis as the science of the unconscious than as a therapeutic procedure." As a "science" this was envisaged as more of a contribution to psychology than to psychiatry.

Obviously, there is no way of determining just how Freud interpreted the remark made by James. It is virtually certain though that, since he had not read James's *Principles,* he was not likely to have thought of James as one who might have entertained misgivings about the prospects of a "science of the unconscious." For this reason it may be that for him it was as if when fully expressed James had predicted, "The future of psychology belongs to your work as an investigator of the unconscious."

Actually, as brought out in the letters James had written about his meeting with Freud and as discussed in Chapter 4, there would have been no justification for the latter interpretation of what James may have meant to say. This is so primarily because James among other reactions to Freud's lecture mentioned his hope that in the future Freud and his disciples would contribute to the progress of functional psychology. As may be recalled, he even declared this to be "the real psychology." It was "real" in the sense that functional psychology was concerned with the phylogenetic and ontogenetic importance of consciousness as manifested by problem-solving maneuvers when faced with difficulties. In brief, for the functionalist consciousness was endowed with causal efficacy and was not dismissed as an inert epiphenomenon in the biological scheme of things. However, in terms of Freud's perspective, mind or conscious acts were subordinated to the unconscious[1] and thus his "real" psychology was different from James's functionalism.

Even though Freud was not familiar with what James had written about belief in states of mind as unconscious becoming "the sovereign means for believing what one likes in psychology," he was familiar with what others had written against endorsement of the latter belief. Thus in his monograph "The Unconscious" (1915, p. 170) he stated: "Those who have resisted the assumption of an unconscious *psychical* are not likely to be ready to exchange it for an unconscious *consciousness.*" Of course, as just noted, had he realized that James belonged to "those" unable "to accept" the paradox of an unconscious

---

[1] Such subordination was mentioned by Freud in different contexts at various times. For the present, by way of reminder, it is enough to note that in his paper entitled "A Note on the Unconscious in Psycho-Analysis" (1912, p. 264) he had maintained that "every psychical act begins as an unconscious one, and it may either remain so or go on developing into consciousness, according as it meets with resistance or not."

consciousness, he might have been perplexed about the meaning of James's encouraging observation concerning the future of psychoanalysis. However, had he had access to the letters in which James had commented on his impressions of his day at the Clark University meeting, his perplexity might have vanished. He would have realized that James, although critical of the dream theory and uneasy about Freud's "fixed ideas," nevertheless saw factual data emerging from the study of dreams and light being shed on the nature of human nature as psychoanalysts proceed "to push their ideas to their utmost limits."

James was thus obviously ambivalent with reference to his judgment of Freud's teachings. He approved of some and disapproved of others. Such ambivalence or discriminating selectivity involves an issue sometimes referred to as the contrast or conflict between scientific as opposed to "orthodox" viewpoints. Although this issue is not directly related to the question of unconscious motivation, it does have some indirect bearing. Moreover, its broader implications are too important to be ignored. Consequently, even though it entails a digression from the main theme of the present chapter, some of these implications will be outlined in the next section. It may even come to be viewed as a meaningful and clarifying digression.

SCIENCE VERSUS ORTHODOXY

As applied to psychology in general James's ambivalence with respect to psychoanalysis can be reduced to this blunt question: Does identification with a given school of psychology imply agreement with every single one of its distinctive teachings or theories? James, as just pointed out, was unable to agree with Freud's theory of the unconscious or with his treatment of dream symbolism. At best one might say James was sympathetic with the promise of what psychoanalytic research might bring to light, but was not thereby identifying with psychoanalysis in the spirit of one of Freud's disciples. Hence one might ask, were Freud's acknowledged disciples constrained to agree with *all* of his teachings? Stated a little differently, were they to reject a few of his teachings, might they still call themselves psychoanalysts? Or to put this in a somewhat broader perspective: Does active affiliation with a school of psychology entail consistent endorsement of whatever the leaders of the school chance to espouse? If so, then the follower of the school might be accused of inconsistency were he to be selective by discriminating between personally acceptable and unacceptable teachings.

However, as should be obvious, such selectivity, from the viewpoint of science, does not entail inconsistency. In this respect science differs from the kind of party loyalty some regard as a political virtue. To question specific teachings or doctrines in terms of relevant supporting evidence is deemed to be a scientific virtue. In the absence of such questioning science tends to be replaced by dogma, and this means orthodoxies to defend and heresies to oppose.

Furthermore, with specific reference to psychoanalysis and its offshoots, it has become rather common to hear talk about orthodox Freudians or orthodox Jungians or Adlerians, Rankians, and others. As a consequence, it is necessary to be mindful of denominational differences associated with names like psychoanalysis, analytic psychology, individual psychology, and Rank's dynamic relationship psychology. As might be expected, followers of these differing psychologies developed their own accounts of man's unconscious with the result, for example, that the Freudian unconscious is not to be confused with the Jungian unconscious.

This state of affairs has given rise to debates concerning minimum essentials of belief in order to qualify as an adherent of any one of these psychologies. As a matter of expository convenience, consideration of this issue will be restricted to psychoanalytic psychology by asking whether those who call themselves psychoanalysts must be prepared to endorse every teaching Freud came to sponsor. To put this a little differently: What teachings may be rejected without thereby losing one's identity as a psychoanalyst? Put still differently: Are there any distinctively Jungian or Adlerian teachings a psychoanalyst may endorse without thereby depriving himself of the right to call himself a psychoanalyst? Can he reject Freud's death instinct, endorse Jung's racial unconscious and Adler's masculine protest, and continue as a member in good standing in one of the psychoanalytic institutes? Would he jeopardize his standing if, like James, he had serious doubts about the concept of mind as unconscious?

Actually, this last question is not altogether rhetorical. Within the last few years an analytically trained psychiatrist, Richard Rabkin, took it seriously by writing an article entitled "Is the Unconscious Necessary?" The details of his article will be considered in the next chapter, but in the present context it will suffice to note that among other conclusions reached was this one which, by implication, justified James and others in their doubts (1969, p. 577): "The behavioral scientist or practitioner . . . who cannot ask the question in the title of this paper, is limited in his capacity for inquiry." Needless to add, there is little likelihood of obtaining the same answer to Rabkin's question from different psychoanalysts, especially if they were asked to elaborate upon their answers.

What one psychoanalyst stresses as an essential teaching may be dismissed as nonessential by another. As once pointed out by Judd Marmor (1949), the differences among psychoanalysts are such that "there is no close unity among psychoanalysts . . . either in theory or practice." There are some who can no longer endorse Freud's libido theory, others who regard it as both valid and indispensable, and still others who have subjected it to drastic reinterpretation. Indeed, as Ruth Munroe (1955, p. 16) has made very clear, there are "non-libido schools" of psychoanalytic thought each of which has replaced the libido theory with its own interpretation of motivational dynamics. Similarly, not all who identify themselves as psychoanalysts necessarily agree with Freud's teachings regarding a death instinct, the origin of religious beliefs, mental telepathy, the possible significance of numerology, and the unconscious wish as responsible for most of our blunders, memory lapses, and errors of omission and commission.

In her book entitled *Schools of Psychoanalytic Thought* Munroe includes accounts of the schools associated with the names of different leaders such as Adler, Jung, Rank, Horney, Fromm, and Sullivan. Although, as individuals, not all of these heads of schools would have described themselves as psychoanalysts, all would have regarded themselves as being analytically oriented. In that sense, despite their disavowal of affiliation with the orthodox Freudian school, they continued to reflect endorsement of and active interest in Freud's emphasis on the importance of the analysis of unconscious motives. This explains why Munroe identified these differing schools with psychoanalytic thought.

Even though members of psychoanalytic schools differ among themselves in their evaluation of specific Freudian teachings, might there not be some teachings upon which they would be in agreement? Another way to formulate this question is to ask, are there any respects in which those who pride themselves on being analytically oriented have anything in common aside from giving themselves a common professional label? It is hard to find an answer to this question by turning to Freud's writings. In fact, Freud does not seem to have regarded psychoanalysis as a finished system whose tenets will never have to be modified or possibly rejected or replaced by other teachings.

He was well aware of the difficulty of presenting psychoanalytic teachings so as to overcome the resistance of critical thinkers who insist upon proof for given conclusions. This is evident from a point he raised in his last paper—the 1938 paper concerned with elementary lessons in psychoanalysis and already considered in the previous chapter. He had this to say about anticipated difficulties in getting the "lay public" to agree with his conclusions (1938, pp. 281, 283):

> And there is then a danger that a critical hearer may shake his head and say: 'All this sounds most peculiar: where does the fellow get it from?'
>
> . . . Psychoanalysis has little prospect of becoming popular. It is not merely that much of what it has to say offends people's feelings. Almost as much difficulty is created by the fact that our science involves a number of *hypotheses—it is hard to say whether they should be regarded as postulates or as products of our researches*—which are bound to seem very strange to ordinary modes of thought and which fundamentally contradict current views. (Italics added.)

The references to hypotheses and postulates suggest that in his retrospective survey of the status of psychoanalysis Freud was no longer certain about what he had established on the basis of clinical research and what he may have taken for granted in terms of tacit assumption. Since he neglected to supply specific instances of these areas of uncertainty, it is impossible to know how he would have disposed of the question regarding the essentials or central core of psychoanalytic teachings.

It is certain though that he wanted these teachings to be classified as contributions to psychology rather than medicine, for he was explicit in describing psychoanalysis as "a part of the mental science of psychology" (p. 377). By his use of the word *part* he was thus recognizing the restricted scope of psychoanalysis as contrasted with the broader range of psychology as a whole. Unfortunately, he failed to elaborate upon this either by showing what the "part" includes or what it excludes. Had he done so, he might have supplied his answer to the question of psychoanalytic essentials.

JONES ON ESSENTIALS OF PSYCHOANALYSIS

One psychoanalyst who did venture to supply an answer to the question was Ernest Jones. As a member of Freud's inner circle and a lifetime student of Freud's writings his answer, conceivably, might approximate something Freud might have said had the question been put to him. But this is entirely speculative. What is not speculative is that Jones actually came to grips with this problem of unity among practitioners who label themselves psychoanalysts. In a paper published in 1946 Jones concluded that "the impossibility of this ideal is being recognized and it is being replaced by the more practicable . . . endeavor to distinguish between what constitute the essential characteristics of psychoanalysis and what are superimposed and more varying features." As he saw it, these "essential characteristics" call for (1) "the study of mental processes of which we are unaware" to get at the instigators of behavior in accordance with the doctrine of psychic determinism; (2) the employment of "the free association technique" for the purpose of exposing such instigators or determinants; and (3) attention to the relevance and importance of "the phenomena of transference and resistance."

These three interrelated essential characteristics of psychoanalysis thus made the psychoanalyst a student of motivation in general and of hidden motives in particular. Jones was careful to point out that such hidden motives even though the patient is ignorant or "unaware" of them are nevertheless to be classified as *mental* processes. This, of course, reflects one meaning of the word *unconscious.* Furthermore, the fact that such unconscious motives could be brought to light by free association suggests that they were accessible to waking ideation, especially if resistances could be overcome or circumvented. This made the motive even when conceived of as inaccessible or hidden as much a mental process as an explicitly conscious motive. In terms of this perspective the Freudian unconscious becomes the repository of hidden motives and psychoanalysis becomes a method for enticing or luring them from their place of concealment despite resistance and transference. The three essential psychoanalytic characteristics proposed by Jones can thus be compressed into a single sentence, with the proviso that the detailed teachings of Freud and his followers are to be viewed either as elaborations of these characteristics or as nonessential accretions.

CONCERNING HIDDEN MOTIVES

It must be recognized that in stressing hidden motivation as an essential factor in the conceptual outlook of the psychoanalyst Jones was not making Freud the discoverer of hidden motivation. As noted in Chapter 2, even before Freud, in the words of James, there were those who had maintained that our "feelings towards people are perfect wells of motivation, unconscious of itself, which introspection brings to light." Nor was James the first to have called attention to the phenomenon, for Spinoza (1632-1677) appears to have anticipated both James and Freud. This was brought out in connection with a famous passage in which Spinoza had been discussing man's impotence when in "bondage" to emotion and impulse. The passage, broadly considered, had to do with the causation of desire and reads as follows (J. Ratner, ed., 1927, p. 253):

> A final cause, as it is called, is nothing . . . but human desire, in so far as this is considered as the principle or primary cause of anything. For example, when we say that the having a house to live in was the final cause of this or that house, we merely mean that a man, because he imagined the advantages of a domestic life, desired to build a house. Therefore, having a house to live in, in so far as it is considered as a final cause, is merely this particular desire, which is really an efficient cause, and is considered as primary, because *men are usually ignorant of the causes of their desires;* for, as I have often said, *we are conscious of our actions and desires, but ignorant of the causes by which we are determined to desire anything.* (Italics added.)

Neither James nor Freud introduced any reference to the foregoing passage; hence there is no way of knowing whether they would have agreed with Spinoza's distinction between the consciousness of desire and ignorance of the cause of desire. This distinction is, of course, not directly related to what James had stigmatized as a "tissue of confusion" in connection with the quest for allegedly hidden or unconscious motives. Nor does the distinction necessarily invalidate the importance Jones attributed to the unconscious as an *essential* characteristic of Freudian psychology.

Furthermore, it has no direct bearing on the employment of free association as a means of exploring the unconscious. As a technique this was original with Freud and, as previously noted, might also have impressed James as a promising means of learning more about the stream of consciousness. In view of what he had written in denial of mental states as unconscious he would not have expected the "more" to be revelatory of hidden motives. Whether this denial of unconscious motivation is to be construed as a denial of Spinoza's conclusions regarding the causation of desire is open to question.

The answer depends on the possibility of making a distinction between motivation and causation.

Neither James nor Freud considered this distinction and yet it is related to their views of psychology as science, especially if science be viewed as contingent upon the determinism implicit in the causal relationship. Accordingly, before dealing with the distinction directly it appears advisable to discuss the determinism contingency in its bearing on the concept of unconscious motivation.

DETERMINISM AND SCIENCE

Even though, as just indicated, neither James nor Freud had occasion to quote Spinoza in connection with their respective views of unconscious motivation, it might nevertheless be argued that Freud's views were more Spinozistic than those of James. Psychic determinism, as Jones made clear, is an essential characteristic of psychoanalytic psychology, just as scientific determinism was an outstanding and fundamental tenet of Spinoza's philosophy. This, of course, means that the doctrine of free will was alien to the latter philosophy as well as to the former psychology. James, on the other hand, although granting the force of arguments advanced by sponsors of determinism, refused to consider these arguments as altogether "coercive." This is evident from a passage in the *Principles* in which he had this to say about the possibility of eventually being able to establish the "truth" of free will or indeterminism (Vol. II, pp. 573–574):

> Doubt of this particular truth will probably be open to the end of time, and the utmost that a believer in free-will can *ever* do will be to show that the deterministic arguments are not coercive. That they are seductive, I am the last to deny; nor do I deny that effort may be needed to keep the faith in freedom, when they press upon it, upright in the mind.

Incidentally, James granted that his defense of free will was prompted by "ethical rather than psychological" considerations.[2] He seems to have equated determinism with fatalism. Fatalistic determinism as a doctrine is the equivalent of Calvinistic predestination without any saving clause to allow for the

---

[2] James appears to have equated the ethical considerations with "moral freedom." He was concerned with the free will problem long before publication of the *Principles*. In fact, as cited by Murphy and Ballou (1960, p. 6), James made an entry in his diary on April 30, 1870, in which, among other comments, he had this to say about the possibility of belief in free will being illusory:

> At any rate, I will assume for the present—until next year—that it is no illusion. My first act of free will shall be to believe in free will. For the remainder of the year, I will abstain from the mere speculation and comtemplative *Grübelei* in which my nature takes most delight, and voluntarily cultivate the feeling of moral freedom, by reading books favorable to it, as well as by acting.

miracle of divine grace. However, Spinoza's determinism was not a fatalistic one in the sense of holding the destiny of the remote future to have been settled by the distant past. He did not believe some omniscient agency could now foretell the scores of all future games, the number of dogs to be born in the year 5000, and the geometry grades of all the Canadian students studying geometry next semester. This sort of belief involves a teleological determinism by believing all the happenings in the world to be moving toward some fixed goal or predetermined end. In the words of Ratner (p. xxxvi) this is to "confuse a perverted determinism of ends with a scientific determinism of means." James had evidently overlooked this distinction, since his espousal of free will is indicative of opposition to a determinism of ends along with failure to consider the alternative of a determinism of means.

Had James given due consideration to the concept of a determinism of means then, as Spinoza had, he would have rejected the free will doctrine. In agreement with Spinoza he would have understood that determinism rather than free will is in accord with the realization of man's quest for moral excellence. In fact, Spinoza's excursion into the field of psychology was occasioned by his basic concern with this quest. That is why his psychology is to be found in his *Ethics.* James, on the other hand, as already implied, found it difficult to reconcile the free will doctrine with the science of psychology. He made this explicit toward the end of the *Principles* (Vol. II, p. 573) when he wrote that because the "grounds of his opinion" for favoring the alternative of indeterminism are "ethical rather than psychological, he prefers to exclude them from the present book." This comes close to reserving indeterminism for ethics and determinism for psychology. In effect James was arguing that the doctrine of free will was difficult to reconcile with his efforts to establish the foundations for a science of psychology; hence the decision "to exclude" the doctrine from the *Principles.*

In other words, it was as if James recognized the world of science to be a deterministic world as reflected in the underlying dependability of causal relations implicit in laws of physics and laws of chemistry. Without eventual establishment of analogous laws of psychology there could be no science of psychology. In this connection it is of interest to note that the deterministic outlook of Spinoza, as a thoroughgoing naturalistic outlook, included recognition of what Spinoza designated as "sure mental laws" (Ratner, p. 47). Moreover, Freud's psychic determinism made psychoanalysis dependent upon such "sure mental laws," just as James had made psychology dependent on such laws by excluding indeterminism from the realm of psychology as science. Broadly considered, all three–Spinoza, James, and Freud–were thus regarding human behavior as a product of causal laws falling within the scope of a scientific determinism as expressed in causal laws whose discovery might, at least in theory, render prediction and control of behavior possible. Whether such causal laws are also laws of motivation is a separate issue to be disposed of by a return to the previously mentioned distinction between motivation and causation.

ON THE DISTINCTION BETWEEN MOTIVATION AND CAUSATION

By way of introduction it may prove clarifying to say someting more about Freud's neglect of this distinction. He and many of his followers have interpreted psychic determinism so broadly as to render all human behavior *motivated* behavior; so, by hypothesis, there is no unmotivated behavior. As is common knowledge, Freud attributed slips of the tongue, the "forgetting" of appointments, blunders and accidents, and other "chance" events to the influence of motives concealed in the unconscious. Often, in recognition of their origin, such motives were designated as Freudian wishes or Freudian slips. Even seemingly innocent or casual remarks like "pleased to meet you" or "regards to the family" came to be subjected to psychoanalytic probing for their unconscious determinants. Some years ago this gave rise to an apocryphal report about a man who chanced to meet his psychoanalyst on the street and called, "Good morning!" only to be halted and confronted with a challenging question, "What did you mean by that remark?" A variant of the anecdote, as reflected in the language of gesture, is suggested by the words of an old popular song to the effect that "every little movement has a meaning all its own." These two anecdotes point up the essence of psychic determinism, namely, that the real meaning of speech and action will turn out to be a product of ungratified desire or some unfulfilled aspiration. Thus it will be the outcome of motivational dynamics as influenced by conscious and unconscious determinants, but especially by the unconscious ones.

As previously noted, if *all* such determinants be classified as motives, there can be no unmotivated behavior. Freud does not seem to have been particularly concerned with this issue. At least he never gave direct expression to a generalization like, "There can be no unmotivated behavior." Moreover, in his investigation of what he called the psychopathology of everyday life he was not seeking instances of unmotivated behavior. Instead he appears to have been primarily interested in calling attention to hitherto overlooked motives operative in behavior commonly regarded as due to chance, accident, carelessness, fatigue, weakness, distraction, clumsiness, or some other nonmotivational conventional explanation for man's blunders, mishaps, failures, or ineptitudes. His book dealing with the psychopathology in question is replete with instances of the covert motives analysis had shown to be involved in the foregoing array. The book fails to include a section supplying examples of nonmotivated behavior, however. Lack of such a section may have induced many readers to interpret Freud's central thesis as meaning denial of the occurrence of nonmotivated behavior. For them it was as if Freud had written, "All behavior is instigated by one or more motives or one or more desires."

In terms of this hypothetical sentence motives are made the equivalent of desires; hence imperious motives are experienced as strong desires. When starving we hunger for food, when choking we crave air, and when lonely we yearn for companionship. All such hungers, cravings, and yearnings as experienced desires are conscious experiences and ordinarily induce action of some sort.

In this connection it is pertinent to revert to Spinoza's distinction between knowledge of desire and ignorance of the cause of desire. In the previously cited passage Spinoza had declared "men are usually ignorant of the causes of their desires" and that "we are conscious of our actions and desires, but ignorant of the causes by which we are determined to desire anything."

SPINOZA'S DISTINCTION BETWEEN DESIRES AND THEIR CAUSES

To the modern reader it may seem obvious that Spinoza's distinction between desires and their causes constitutes an anticipation of the Freudian concept of unconscious motivation. Support for this interpretation may be suggested by equating Spinoza's reference to ignorance with one meaning of the word *unconscious*. If so, then he might just as well have written, "men are usually unconscious of the causes of their desires." However, to regard this reformulation as the equivalent of what Freud meant by unconscious motivation may not be justified.

It may well be that Spinoza would have found the notion of unconscious motivation incomprehensible. He employed the word *desire* in a manner reminiscent of the Greek *orexis* or, as Wolfson has explained (1934, Vol. II, pp. 165-167), its Latin equivalent *cupiditas* as shown in a passage in the *Ethics* in which the orectic or conative nature of "desire (*cupiditas*)" is suggested by defining it as the faculty "by which the mind seeks a thing or turns away from it." For Spinoza this made *cupiditas* a conscious process as expressed in his statement about our being "conscious of our . . . desires." It would be in keeping with Spinoza's thought to regard *cupiditas* as approximating one of the modern meanings of *motive*. For example, in their dictionary English and English (1958, p. 331) define motive as "that which one consciously assigns as the basis of his behavior" and then explained that when first introduced "*motive* strongly carried the meaning of a *conscious* factor, something of which one was aware."

Accordingly, this original connotation of words like *desire* or *motive* is altogether at variance with the notion of unconscious desire or unconscious motive. In other words, it is as if Spinoza had written, "We are conscious of our motives, but ignorant or unconscious of their causes or determinants." Unfortunately, he did not supply any clarifying examples of the sense in which he was differentiating motives from their causes. It may be that he was thinking of rather familiar instances having to do with the arousal of interest as illustrated by a question like, "What causes some children to be fascinated by the study of algebra while others find the subject dull and forbidding?" Analogously, some children appear to be spontaneously motivated to study history or music or botany or Italian or carpentry, while others—the so-called academic dropouts—may not be motivated to study anything. Thus, the ordinary student's intrinsic interest in some one subject supplies a possible interpretation of Spinoza's meaning: the student may know what he desires to study, but not know what causes him to desire it.[3] This comes closer to being unconscious causation as contrasted with unconscious motivation.

There is another possible interpretation of what Spinoza had in mind in making his distinction between motivation and causation. This calls for reconsideration of the concept of *desire.* His analysis of desire revealed it to be more complex than indicated by the previously mentioned attractive and aversive implications of the word *cupiditas.* As he saw it, the concept includes the entire gamut of human longings or strivings. For him, as shown in the following quotation, desire involves both emotional and conative features and may give rise to what we moderns think of as mental conflict (Ratner, p. 218):

> By the word "desire," therefore, I understand all the efforts, impulses, appetites, and volitions of a man, which vary according to his changing disposition, and not unfrequently and so opposed to one another that he is drawn hither and thither, and knows not whither he ought to turn.

It is advisable to avoid thinking of the use of the phrase "volitions of man" as meaning what popular psychology refers to as will power. Instead the phrase is a derivative of the Latin *volo* meaning "I wish"; hence in his concept of desire Spinoza might be said to have anticipated the dynamics of the wish some two centuries before Freud. Furthermore, in this connection and at the risk of a slight digression, it might also be said his concept of desire anticipated the James-Lange theory of emotion by a similar time span. This calls for a word of explanation.

SPINOZA'S THEORY OF EMOTION

Spinoza recognized three basic or primary emotions–joy, sorrow, and desire. Moreover, in reflecting upon the nature of emotion per se he recognized its connection with widespread physiological changes. He made this quite explicit when he defined emotion as "the modifications of the body, by which the power of acting of the body itself is increased, diminished, helped, or hindered, together with the ideas of these modifications" (Ratner, p. 213).

---

[3]Incidental support for this interpretation of the educational scene came to light in a news item some years ago. On July 18, 1972, the *Wall Street Journal* published an article by Gary North of the Foundation for Economic Education concerned with a review of recent books critical of American public schools. Mr. North was espcially impressed with a book edited by Frederick Mosteller and Daniel Moynihan entitled *On Equality of Educational Opportunity* (New York: Random House, 1972). In the present context the following comment cited by Mr. North is particularly pertinent: "As of 1972, 'we are still ignorant of what makes education tick for children and of why what works for some doesn't seem to for others' (Gilbert & Mosteller)."

Had James come across this definition and had he cited it in his chapter on emotion, it is conceivable that what came to be called the James-Lange theory of emotion might have been called the *Spinoza-James* theory. This is so because there is a marked resemblance between what James wrote about emotion in the 1880s and what Spinoza had written some decades before the 1680s. In both versions bodily commotion is stressed as a sine qua non for any experience to be designated as emotional. In the following oft-quoted passage James made this the "vital point" of his theory (1890, Vol. II, p. 451):

> I now proceed to urge the vital point of my whole theory, which is this: *If we fancy some strong emotion, and then try to abstract from our consciousness of it all the feelings of its bodily symptoms, we find we have nothing left behind,* no "mind-stuff" out of which the emotion can be constituted, and that a cold and neutral state of intellectual perception is all that remains.

It is also worth noting that Freud appears to have arrived at a similar conclusion regarding feelings of visceral change as involved in affective experience. This was not based upon direct reference to the writings of Spinoza or James. In other words, independently of their views, Freud had this to say about the subject in his 1915 paper "The Unconscious" (p. 179): "Affectivity manifests itself essentially in motor (i.e., secretory and vasomotor) discharge resulting in an (internal) alteration of the subject's own body without reference to the external world; motility, in actions designed to affect changes in the external world." Moreover, Freud introduced this observation in a section concerned with "unconscious emotions" and in this connection it is of more than passing interest to call attention to the fact that Freud had reason to deny that emotions per se could be unconscious. He made this explicit in these two sentences (1915, p. 177):

> *It is surely of the essence of an emotion that we should be aware of it, i.e., that it should become known to consciousness. Thus the possibility of the attribute of unconsciousness would be completely excluded as far as emotions, feelings and affects are concerned.* (Italics added.)

It is thus obvious that Freud recognized a relationship between a person's awareness of emotion and "alteration" of his "own body." But he did not identify this with the James-Lange theory. In fact, in a later book he wrote that "the James-Lange theory . . . is utterly incomprehensible to us psychoanalysts" (1938, p. 344). Nevertheless, there was this recognition of bodily "alteration" as associated with emotion. Similarly, Spinoza associated emotion with "modifications" of the body and James with "bodily symptoms." Consequently, with respect to recognition of this kind of association, all three might be said to have been in agreement.

This agreement among the three with respect to emotion as related to bodily change is really not so strange. It is suggestive of rather commonplace knowledge. Most people know about circulatory, respiratory, muscular, and visceral changes associated with man's griefs, terrors, angers, loves, anxieties, lusts, excitements, depressions, and whatever else comes to be subsumed under the category of emotion. James included many rather detailed accounts of specific bodily symptoms associated with emotional expression. On the other hand Spinoza gave no series of specific examples illustrative of modifications of the body characteristic of emotional arousal. It may be that he deemed such a series unnecessary in view of the common man's familiarity with them. However, it may also be that in thinking about how these changes come about he realized the difficulty of accounting for them, of explaining how the pounding heart, labored breathing, and tense muscles of the enraged man "cause" him to "desire" to attack the object of his rage. Similarly, it might be asked how other patterns of bodily changes "cause" man to "desire" to flee from enemies, to help friends, to protect infants, to solve puzzles, to win games, to overcome rivals, and to plan for the future?

The foregoing question is based on the assumption that Spinoza, in regarding modifications of the body as essential concomitants of the life of emotion, was endowing these modifications with causal efficacy.[4] Furthermore, since he classified desire with its appetitive and aversive strivings as a primary emotion, he may have regarded bodily expressions of these strivings as "causes" of our "actions and desires." In terms of this interpretation it is as if he had written: "We are conscious of our actions and desires, but unconscious of the causes by which we are determined to strive for anything." Another way to put this is to say we may be aware of *what* we are doing, but not *why* we are doing it. Spinoza, as just mentioned, did not furnish many specific examples of this kind of broad generalization. However James, again independently of Spinoza, not only arrived at the same generalization but also clarified it by reference to commonplace observations.

In fact, he gave it rather detailed treatment in his famous chapter on instinct (Vol. II, Ch. 24). In some respects his treatment can be construed as descriptive of unconscious motivation not as Freud came to think of it but as Spinoza seems to have thought of it. This serves as a reminder of the fact that even in restricted contexts the unconscious is subject to more than one interpretation. However, in the present instance, to avoid misunderstanding it is well to limit James's treatment to the question of what instigates instinctive or unlearned behavior.

JAMES ON THE 'WHY?' OF INSTINCTIVE BEHAVIOR

In his treatment of instinct James disowned those older writings in which instinct was identified with "clairvoyant and prophetic power" enabling

[4]The "modifications" are those that came to be studied in terms of their adaptive significance for biological survival. Recall that Darwin had brought the issue to a sharp focus in his book of 1872, *The Expression of the Emotions in Men and Animals.* Still more detailed study occurred with discovery of endocrine modifications. An important and

animals to safeguard their welfare as if under divine guidance. Instead James stressed the relevance of neural mechanisms and anatomic structure. After defining instincts as manifestations of "the faculty of acting in such a way as to produce certain ends, without foresight of the ends, and without previous education in the performance," he added that "they are the functional correlatives of structure." This comes close to saying that birds fly not because they have a flight instinct, but because they have wings, and man breathes not because of a respiratory instinct, but because he has lungs. Paying attention to the function of the nervous system in the regulation of behavior, James noted, makes instinct "appear neither more nor less wonderful than all the other facts of life." He thus endeavored to limit his study of instinct to the factual and nonmystical.

In the light of this factual approach he raised a series of questions about man's everyday behavior. Among others he asked about instinctive reactions to cold, to sex, to food, and to other situations. To illustrate such reactions he asked: Why do men get close to a warm stove on cold days? Why do young men find young girls to be objects of fascinating interest? Why do men prefer meat and milk to straw and ditchwater? A biologist in viewing such instances of behavior might deem them to be useful in terms of survival value; but considerations of utility do not account for the 'why?' of each individual choice. Are the choices of the Lotharios and Don Juans of this world prompted by an interest in species survival?[5] In eating his dinner does the average person pause to ask himself why he is doing so? As James observed (Vol. II, pp. 386-387), such a person is not likely to be mindful of the need for nourishment in terms of ontogenetic survival. Instead he eats because:

> The food tastes good and makes him want more. If you ask him *why* he should want to eat more of what tastes like that, instead of revering you as a philosopher he will probably laugh at you for a fool. . . . It takes, in short, what Berkeley calls a mind debauched by learning to carry the process of making the natural seem strange, so far as to ask for the *why* of any instinctive human act. To the metaphysician alone can such questions occur as: Why do we smile, when pleased, and not scowl? Why are we unable to talk to a crowd as we talk to a single friend? Why does a particular maiden turn our wits so upside-down?

---

familiar example of such study culminated with the 1929 publication of W. B. Cannon's book dealing with emotional changes as influenced by the hormone adrenaline. Cannon's work stimulated further studies of this and other hormones, such as D. H. Funkenstein's 1955 article on the role of adrenaline and noradrenaline in fear and anger.

[5]This may seem so obvious as to strike many as self-evident. It is akin to pointing out that biological utility does not account for sex indulgence, especially by those who introduce contraceptive measures or those who masturbate or classify themselves as homosexual. Nevertheless, obvious as this may seem, it appears to have been questioned by B. F. Skinner. In a magazine article he had this to say about the "phylogenic" utility of sexual behavior (1972, p. 19):

> Until recently, the species could survive famine, pestilence, and other catastrophies only if its members procreated at every opportunity, and under such contingencies sexual contact became highly reinforcing. Sex is not reinforcing because it feels good; it is reinforcing *and* feels good for a common phylogenic reason.

> The common man can only say, "*Of course* we smile, *of course* our heart palpitates at the sight of the crowd, *of course* we love the maiden, that beautiful soul clad in that perfect form, so palpably and flagrantly made from all eternity to be loved!"

James was explicit in noting that instincts are subject to modification in the course of experience. With repetition of instinctive behavior it ceases to be blind impulsiveness with no foresight of ends to be expected. According to James, such modification is to be expected when "memories, associations, inferences, and expectations" cluster around instinctive impulses as a consequence of experience. It is well to recognize this because years later when the concept of instinct came to be attacked as scientifically questionable one reason for the attack had to do with the degree to which patterns of instinctive behavior are subject to change by learning. Some of those who introduced this argument seem to have failed to realize that James, as a defender of the concept, had already taken this argument into account in his analysis. As will be brought out in the next section, this argument was one of several directed against the concept in what came to be called the instinct controversy.

As just indicated, James made a distinction between instinct as exhibited initially by virtue of inherent neural organization and instinct as transformed or modified by the effects of experience. This marked recognition of the difference between unlearned and learned behavior and explained James's noting that it is fatuous to ask about the 'Why?' of unlearned behavior. In general, being impulsive, unlearned behavior is involuntary, spontaneous, unplanned, and unintentional. Furthermore, if motivated behavior be deemed voluntary, deliberate, planned, and intentional, then instinctive or unlearned behavior when unmodified by experience is not motivated behavior. Thus, in effect, James held that the young infant is impelled rather than motivated to fall asleep when tired, to cry when in pain, to stare at bright moving objects, to fill its lungs with air and its stomach with milk, to empty bladder and bowel, and to perspire when hot and shiver when cold.

All such instinctive reactions have their causes, but the causes are not motives. Only later when brought under voluntary control can they become products of motivation. Within limits an older child can succeed in holding his breath, in remaining awake though fatigued, in refusing to cry when hurt, and in inhibiting eliminative urges until reaching the toilet. As controlled behavior such behavior is motivated or intentional behavior; hence it would not be fatuous to ask about the 'Why?' of such behavior. This is implicit in what James had to say about instinctive behavior and its subsequent modification.

Actually, he did not elaborate explicitly upon the concept of motivation. Instead, man's instinctive impulses were viewed as the matrix giving rise to the springs of human action. James was thus attributing the driving forces of human nature to the dynamics of instinct. This doubtless accounts for the fact that his *Principles* contains no chapter on motivation and no section on what a later generation of psychologists listed as *drives* to animal and human behavior. At this juncture it seems appropriate to consider this shift from nineteenth-century interest in instinct to twentieth-century interest in drives.

THE SHIFT FROM INSTINCTS TO DRIVES

Until the time of World War I introductory textbooks of psychology contained no chapter on motivation, but they did devote space to the subject of instinct. By the time of World War II this was reversed: the books had a chapter on motivation, but no chapter on instinct. The reversal had been prompted by attacks on the concept of instinct starting around the 1920s. In large measure the attacks were directed at interpretations of human behavior regarded as expressions of fixed or stereotyped instincts given rise to innately determined patterns of reaction comparable to those characteristic of the nest-building of birds and the web-spinning of spiders. Even the relevance of the concept of heredity for psychology began to be questioned. The influence of experience and social tradition was played up and that of instinctive urges was played down. This so-called instinct controversy gave rise to a long list of articles and books.[6] For many engaged in the controversy the very word *instinct* became suspect as an acceptable scientific term, and before long the word *drive* began to be employed as an acceptable substitute[7] not only with reference to human behavior but also with reference to animal behavior. In fact, in the words of the ethologist W. H. Thorpe (pp. 17-18):

> . . . soon we had a whole host of 'drives' sufficient in variety and number to satisfy any nineteenth-century naturalist. And although there were many attempts to keep the term 'drive' for the undifferentiated activity and use the word 'motivation' for the directed activity, these were swept aside and we soon got hunger drives, thirst drives, homoeostatic drives, fear drives, self-preservatory drives, mating drives, excretory drives, sex drives, locomotory drives, nest-building drives, manipulation drives, migratory drives, anxiety drives, exploratory drives, fighting drives, fleeing drives, escape drives, social drives, pain-avoiding drives, respiratory drives, comfort drives, first-order drives and second-order drives, all in glorious confusion.

---

[6] An informative introduction to the controversy is to be found in the book of readings on the subject of instinct as selected and edited by R. C. Birney and R. C. Teevan. For a critical review of the subject from the perspective of animal ethology consult the volume *Learning and Instinct in Animals* by W. H. Thorpe. His Chapter 2, "The Nature of Drive and Its Place in the Theory of Instinct," is particularly relevant in the present context.

[7] Whether the word *drive* has a different meaning or connotation from the word *instinct* is subject to debate. The German word for drive is *Trieb,* so that *Triebkraft* stands for motive power and *Triebfeder* stands for motive. Freud has repeatedly employed the term *Sexualtrieb* and this has usually been translated as sexual instinct; however, it would be just as correct to translate it as sexual drive. This would accord with Eidelberg's definition of *Trieb* as "a powerful, striving, imperative force within a living organism, deeply rooted in its psychical nature and closely connected with the somatic sources from which it springs" (1968, p. 197).

This resulting confusion would have been deplored by Woodworth, the man who first gave currency to the word *drive* in psychological discussions. He was particularly interested in the dynamics of mental life and in 1918 gave formal expression to this interest with the publication of his *Dynamic Psychology.* He introduced the concept of drive in this direct fashion (p. 36):

> Once the point of view of a dynamic psychology is gained, two general problems come into sight, which may be named the problem of 'mechanism' and the problem of 'drive.' One is the problem, how we do a thing, and the other is the problem of what induces us to do it.

He was thus employing the concept of drive as a generic term to include factors or influences regarded as spurs or incitements to behavioral change. Woodworth did not introduce it as a replacement for the word *instinct*; at the time the instinct controversy had not yet made its appearance. Furthermore, as will be made evident in the next section, Woodworth's concern with drives and mechanisms was a result of his basic interest in the subject of motivation. In fact, he was not at all adverse to endorsing the concept of instinct, as he made clear in a chapter entitled "Native Equipment of Man." For example, he had this to say about a gregarious instinct (pp. 50–51):

> Herding together and playing together are typical instances of reactions to be classed under the gregarious instinct. When children, or adults, are together, we see also a tendency to become the leader, if possible, or to follow the leader when dominance has been established. These tendencies are probably instinctive rather than derived wholly from individual experience.

In the same chapter Woodworth also introduced the following distinction between instincts and native capacities (p. 60):

> Native capacities differ from instincts in that they do not provide ready-made reactions to stimuli. We do not expect the musically gifted child to break out in song at some special stimulus, and thus reveal his musical gift. We expect him to show an interest in music, to learn it readily, remember it well, and perhaps show some originality in the way of making up pieces for himself. His native gift amounts to a specific interest and an ability to learn specific things. The gifted individual is not one who can do certain things without learning, but who can learn those things very readily.

Some years after introducing his distinction between drives and mechanisms along with his recognition of the difference between native capacities and instincts, Woodworth registered his opposition to those who had questioned the scientific status of the concept of instinct. This was in the middle 1920s at the height of the instinct controversy. He voiced his opposition in a paper entitled "A Justification of the Concept of Instinct" and in doing so was possibly the first to call a halt to the concerted attack on the concept by leading psychologists and sociologists of the period. At the time, urging the elimination of the word *instinct* from the psychologist's scientific vocabulary was tantamount to being up-to-date and progressive. Consequently, Woodworth was not taking a popular stand. It was almost as if he had reason to protest that those who were now using his notion of drive in place of the traditional concept of instinct might be doing him an injustice, since he had never urged such replacement.

In his defense, Woodworth ventured to refute the major arguments that had been advanced against the concept. Thus there were some critics who had urged that behavior ascribed to an instinct can be analyzed into simpler component structures such as reflexes. As they saw it, it would be more in accord with scientific procedure to deal with such components and not with the more complex total performance. To this argument Woodworth replied that in all consistency the critics ought also object to having chemists talk about salts and acids and other compounds rather than talk about their constituent elements.

In addition, to those who had objected to instinct as a product of inheritance since in the final analysis what is inherited is some kind of structure, he had this to say (1927, pp. 136-137):

> It is urged that the notion of instinct, or inherited behavior, is superfluous because all that is inherited reduces to structure. The boomerang . . . is not thought of as having an instinct to return to the thrower, but simply as having a structure that makes the return inevitable. This objection ought to rule out reflex along with instinct—and habit as well, since what is retained in habit reduces to structure. Certainly, behavior can be inherited or retained only by way of structure (living structure, to be sure); but if we are to speak of behavior at all, we need behavior concepts. The fact that behavior depends on structure need not deter us from using concepts based on the facts of behavior, rather than on the often unknown facts of structure.

Years later, with advances in genetics, Woodworth's conclusion regarding such facts of structure received more detailed support of a kind that was not yet available in the 1920s. As brought out by Thorpe (pp. 16–17), there is good reason to assume the encoding of innate patterns of behavior in the DNA of the gene. Of course, both Woodworth and Thorpe were mindful of the need to discriminate between what might be attributed to such patterns as contrasted with changes in behavior due to learning, social tradition, and kindred nongenetic influences. Furthermore, especially in the case of animal behavior, it has been possible to control the effect of these influences by rearing individual animals in isolation. For example, it has long been known that songbirds even though brought up in solitude from the time of hatching will nevertheless, when more mature, give voice to the song characteristic of the species. Or to cite another example supplied by Thorpe

(p. 22), the young of the flying squirrel when reared by hand from the time of birth, if "given nuts, would go through all the motions of burying them in the bottom of the wire cage and then go away contented, even though the nuts were exposed to full view."

It is thus a matter of indifference whether this be called an instinct or a drive to bury nuts. In other words, reverting to an earlier point, in adding the word *drive* to the psychologist's professional vocabulary Woodworth was not thereby denying the relevance and scientific respectability of the concept of instinct. After all, as already suggested, his interest in the concepts of drives, native capacities, mechanisms, and instincts reflected his underlying interest in the development of a dynamic psychology. This called for inquiry into the origin, nature, and variety of human motives or the springs of human action. In broad perspective, just as Freud is often said to have given twentieth-century psychiatry its dynamic orientation, so Woodworth may be said to have given twentieth-century psychology its motivational or dynamic orientation.

WOODWORTH'S THEORY OF MOTIVATION: INTRODUCTION

As a student of James it is to be expected that Woodworth would have been in sympathy with the psychology of functionalism and its interest in finding a place for mind in the evolutionary process. This implies an interest in struggle, adaptive effort, goal-directed behavior, and similar aspects of motivation. That such an interest had gripped Woodworth early in his career is indicated by the fact that, as he recalls in his "Autobiography," back in his days as a graduate student in the 1890s he had told a fellow-student of a plan "to try and develop" what he called "motivology" (1932, p. 366). Later on in the autobiography he had this to say regarding the importance he came to attach to the subject of motivation, despite its more elusive nature when compared with the objectivity of studies of performance:

> Motivation always seemed to me a field worthy to be placed alongside of performance. That is, we need to know not only what the individual can do and how he does it, but also what induces him to do one thing rather than another and to put so much energy into what he does. We need a study of motivation in order to understand the selectivity of behavior and its varying energy. In my books I have sought repeatedly for a formula that should bring motives right down into the midst of performance instead of leaving them to float in a transcendental sphere.

This quest for the right formula made Woodworth's functionalism a dynamic functionalism. As Hilgard once put it (1956, p. 337), in the work of Woodworth one finds "the first functionalist to give a treatment of motivation in modern form." The point of departure for this treatment was focused on his distinction between drives and mechanisms. By means of this distinction he ventured to account for the "selectivity of behavior" as well as for "its varying energy."

For Woodworth the phrase "selectivity of behavior" referred to the problem of determining the facts responsible for specific choices in the way of foods, vocations, mates, recreations, friends, neighborhoods, religions, schools, clubs, clothes, careers, and any other manifestation of a significant preference or aversion. In effect he was asking, "How does it come about that people develop such a wide variety of interests?" Some people become devotees of the stock market and others of the church or of mathematics. There are people who are fascinated by baseball and others who are bored by it. Even among the players themselves preferences are revealed in terms of the specific positions selected. Not every player wants to be a pitcher or an outfielder. Similarly, among musicians some prefer to be harpists while others choose to play a wind instrument. In the field of medicine some physicians prefer research to private practice while still others decide to become hospital administrators, or medical missionaries or professors of medicine. There is no need to extend this list of the almost endless instances of ways in which human beings come to terms with opportunities for making particular choices. The ones mentioned suffice to indicate the vast scope of Woodworth's problem. He was among the first investigators to consider this issue of the origin of new interests, new motives, and new skills, along with the not infrequent concomitant decline of old interests, old motives, and old skills.

Woodworth's special attention to this issue had been sharpened by the stand taken by William McDougall (1871–1938) with specific reference to the energies of men or the springs of human behavior. In his influential *Introduction to Social Psychology* of 1908 McDougall had argued that it is especially important for progress in the social sciences for psychology to deal with the basic question of the nature and source of man's urges to action. As an answer to this question McDougall called attention to instincts as furnishing the conceptual basis for understanding the life of impulse and motivation. This is evident from the following two paragraphs from the *Social Psychology* as quoted by Woodworth (1918, pp. 63–64):

> We may say, then, that directly or indirectly the instincts are the prime movers of all human activity; by the conative or impulsive force of some instinct (or some habit derived from instinct), every train of thought, however cold and passionless it may seem, is borne along towards its end, and every bodily activity is initiated and sustained. The instinctive impulses determine the end of all activities and supply the driving power by which all mental activities are sustained; and all the complex intellectual apparatus of the most highly developed mind is but a means towards these ends, is but the instrument by which these impulses seek their satisfactions, while pleasure and pain do but serve to guide them in their choice of means.
>
> Take away these instinctive dispositions with their powerful impulses, and the organism would become incapable of activity of any kind;

it would lie inert and motionless like a wonderful clockwork whose mainspring had been removed or a steam-engine whose fires had been drawn.

In his account of the nature of these instincts or, as he later called them, these propensities, McDougall noted their intrinsic association with emotional dispositions. In fact, even before McDougall this had been noted by James who stressed its importance by writing in italics (1890, Vol. II, p. 442): "*Every object that excites an instinct excites an emotion as well.*" This sentence appears in the chapter on emotion and, as previously mentioned, for James the concept of emotion connoted bodily commotion. This amounts to saying that feelings and emotions involve the organism as a whole and lack the specificity of localization characteristic of sensations and reflexes. We can point to the spot that hurts and the examining physician can observe the pupillary reflex but neither he nor we can point to or observe the location of our hurt feelings, wounded pride, tender love, joyous triumph, burning anger, or any other such affective experience. In ordinary language this diffuse nature of affective experience is reflected in childlike statements like, "When angry, I'm angry all over," and, "When happy, I'm happy all over." There can thus be no question about the total organism being involved in emotional arousal. There can also be no question about the impulsive or conative nature of emotional arousal. In fear of fire there is an impulse to escape, just as in love for a baby there is an impulse to protect and safeguard.

The combination of feeling and impulse constitutive of emotion was stressed in McDougall's discussion of instinct. He recognized twelve such combinations of what he designated as "primary or simple instinctive tendencies." As he came to describe them they were illustrated in some detail, but for present purposes it will be enough to list the affective and impulse characteristics of each instinctive tendency as follows:

1. Anger with the concomitant desire or impulse to attack, destroy, punish, or discomfit the object of anger.
2. Fear with its impulse to get away from the fearsome situation or person.
3. Curiosity along with the feeling of wonder and the impulse to explore or investigate.
4. Disgust with the impulse to reject along with feelings of abhorrence.
5. The parental or mothering instinct characterized by tender emotion and protective impulses.
6. The mating instinct with its feelings of lust.
7. The nutritive instinct or the impulse to eat as experienced by feelings of hunger.
8. The gregarious instinct or the impulse for human association with feelings of loneliness when the instinct is aroused.
9. The acquisitive or collecting instinct with feelings of ownership or pride of possession and when carried to extremes characterized by the

impulse to hoard and the miser's unwillingness to share or contribute.

10. The instinct of construction or the impulse to build or to achieve and characterized by pride of workmanship and joy of accomplishment.
11. Self-assertion and feelings of mastery, control, and dominance.
12. Submission and feelings of self-abasement or subordination to the guidance or leadership of others.

These twelve major propensities were supplemented by some minor ones in McDougall's view. Thus he recognized such inborn tendencies as those that prompt impulses to play, to walk, to imitate, to develop habits, and a few others. He seemed to regard these as lacking the specificity of goal-directedness characteristic of hunger, disgust, and the other major ones, but he did attribute the driving force behind all human activities to this array of major and minor instincts.

There was a period following dissemination of his views when it became a rather popular and more or less accepted practice to try to account for the conduct of human beings by showing it to be a product of one or more of McDougall's instincts. Thus for a business executive to invite members of his staff to a luncheon meeting might upon analysis have been attributed to the fusion of energies stemming from activated self-assertive, gregarious, nutritive, and acquisitive instincts. This, of course, was a very different kind of motivational analysis from one the executive's psychoanalyst might have proposed in terms of the libido theory, but that's another story not to be elaborated upon at this point. It is more relevant to continue with Woodworth's critique of McDougall.

In his review of McDougall's list of major and minor instincts Woodworth noticed the omission of any reference to native capacities in the way of special talents for achievement in given fields of endeavor such as in mathematics, music, poetry, languages, scientific thinking, and other fields of creativity. In Woodworth's opinion this was a serious omission. Without recognition of such native capacities there is no way of explaining the unique accomplishments of men like Newton, Mozart, Shakespeare, Helmholtz, Faraday, Kant, and Euler. Men of such creative eminence are born rather than made. The instincts recognized by McDougall are not enough to explain their creativity. After all, such an array of instinctive equipment is common, but such genius is rare.

Woodworth did not think of native capacities as rare endowments limited to men of genius. Instead he recognized them as present in the general population in kinds and amounts varying from individual to individual. Thus, one child might have marked capacity for mathematics and little capacity for musical composition, whereas another child might have a marked capacity for literary composition or some other field of endeavor.[8] Without some such

---

[8]This allusion to a *marked* capacity is a matter of expository convenience. Woodworth recognized the existence of lesser degrees of native capacities as well. In other words,

capacity, Woodworth maintained, it is hardly likely that a child will come to experience a spontaneous and sustained interest in a particular kind of study or activity by an "appeal to his self-feeling" (1918, pp. 67–68):

> For example, a child may be induced . . . to make a start in learning to sing, but, unless he has a natural musical gift, he drops out soon, and parries the appeal to his self-feeling by deriding singing and those children who excel him. He finds some way of making this exercise appear unworthy of his effort, whereas the musical child, once started by the appeal to his self-feeling, is carried along by zeal for music itself, and puts forth great energy without requiring such extraneous stimuli to be constantly applied.

In addition, Woodworth called attention to the fact that once engaged in activity for which the child has a special gift he becomes *absorbed* in the pursuit of the activity. Such absorption requires no extrinsic sources of motivation. The activity furnishes its own drive and no outside motive is needed to keep it going. The underlying principle applies to adults as well as children. In other words, whatever we have learned to do well may become an independent source of motivation in the sense of being an absorbing interest in its own right. In the course of such learning new motives—unrelated to instinctive motives—may come into being. This generalization constitutes what Woodworth regarded as "the chief point" in his book on dynamic psychology.

THE CHIEF POINT OF WOODWORTH'S THEORY

As must be evident by this time, Woodworth never denied McDougall's contention regarding instincts as spurs or motives to activity. What he did deny was having them made the sole source of motivational goads to *all* human undertakings. Stated differently, he was objecting to having man's stock of motives or drives to action restricted to those of instinctive origin. Moreover, since the concept of instinct connotes genetic endowment, the latter kind of restriction would amount to arguing that all human motives are inherited motives, as if McDougall's instinct psychology had made no provision for *acquired* motives. This, as already indicated, constituted Wood-

---

the fact that the vast majority of school children can be taught to cipher, to sing songs, and to read and write is indicative of their possession of at least some level of the three native capacities involved. Incidentally, the role of native capacities as a factor in learning, especially the learning of language, continues to be a subject of controversy. In connection with this controversy D. O. Hebb in collaboration with two other psychologists said recently (1973, p. 56): "It is clear that man is born to talk; both *capacity* and motivation are innate. There is almost a need to learn at least his native language. It is difficult to separate what is innate from what is acquired in these circumstances" (italics added).

worth's chief criticism of McDougall's psychology. He was thus arguing for the relevance and importance of acquired motives in order to do justice to the full scope of a dynamic psychology.

It is well to realize that at the time—between 1910 and 1920—there were three dynamic psychologies in the making. There was Freud's libido psychology, McDougall's instinct psychology, and Woodworth's drive psychology. In the case of Freud the pleasure-seeking impulsiveness of the infant's libido was regarded as the instinctual matrix out of which subsequent motivational striving was to emerge. This made his psychology as much of an instinct psychology as McDougall's in the sense that both psychologies traced all motivation, desire, and wishing to the dynamics of instinct.

This was so even though, unlike McDougall, Freud never drew up a list of some ten or more specific instincts to account for distinctive modes of instinctive behavior. He had nothing to say about a gregarious instinct or about an instinct to construct or to collect or to be self-abasing or self-assertive. Even McDougall's nutritive instinct was not given explicit mention in terms of hunger, feeding, and the organism's metabolic needs. At best the nutritive instinct received implicit recognition in the libidinization of the alimentary canal with the baby's pleasure in orality at one end balanced by pleasure in anality at the other. It may also be that some of McDougall's other instincts are reflected in such libidinization. For example, with reference to orality the dependence Freud associated with longings for a return to the optimal security of the nursing infant nestled in its mother's arms is comparable to the dependence associated with McDougall's instinct of submission to the guidance of any recognized superior protective power. Similarly, Freud's anal-retentive character might be said to resemble the pride of possession McDougall attributed to the collecting instinct.

In terms of these resemblances Woodworth had as much reason to object to Freud's instinct psychology as to McDougall's. His own dynamic psychology is to be contrasted with their dynamic psychologies because of their failure to come to grips with the problem of motivation as he envisaged it.

The central issue lends itself to convenient illustration by considering the implications of what was just referred to as the collecting instinct. In Woodworth's opinion the mere existence of such an instinct taken by itself will not account for individual differences in what people come to cherish as worth collecting. As should be obvious, some are interested in collecting first editions, others in collecting coins, or art, or stamps, or autographs, or old violins, or even old jokes. Each such interest constitutes a separate desire or motive to accumulate a given class of objects. The motive of a philatelist is thus different from the motive of an art collector. Were the latter asked to explain the reason for his particular interest he might not find a ready answer. To the lover of art his interest in paintings requires no justification in the way of an appeal to reasons unrelated to aesthetics. Similarly, the avid philatelist would not account for his persistent search for a rare stamp by an appeal to an acquisitive instinct or any consideration unrelated to the world of philately.

In the language of Woodworth: the art lover has a drive to collect works of art and the philatelist has a drive to collect stamps and these drives are *sui generis.* Furthermore, as already mentioned, in his recognition of such specific acquired drives or motives his dynamic psychology provided for a much more extensive range of motives than the dynamic psychologies of either Freud or McDougall. In doing so he was recognizing the significance of what later came to be named the *functional autonomy* of motives.

CONCERNING FUNCTIONAL AUTONOMY

The new name helped to make more explicit the self-regulating or *autonomous* character of acquired drives. Recall that Woodworth had made a distinction between drives and mechanisms with the word *drive* standing for any motive and the word *mechanism* standing for any act, or process by means of which the motive could be gratified. If successful in bringing this about, then the mechanism would be transformed into a new drive in its own right and as a new drive would require different mechanisms to realize *its* objectives. The new drive or new interest was thus deemed to be liberated from its erstwhile dependence on some primal force in the way of hunger, sex, or fear. Woodworth had recognized and stressed this in 1918, but it was close to some twenty years later before Gordon Allport (1897–1967) gave it renewed and special prominence by giving it the distinctive label of *functional autonomy of motives.* By this phrase he was referring to the transition from an original or primary motive to a derived or secondary one with the latter becoming free from any dependence on the former. The derived or emergent motive was thus regarded as freed from any functional linkage to the instigating motive.[9] Allport clarified this in the following paragraphs concerned with examples of the concept of functional autonomy (1961, pp. 227–228):

> Workmanship is a good example. A good workman feels compelled to do a clean-cut job even though his income no longer depends on maintaining high standards. In fact, in a day of jerry-building his workmanlike standards may be to his economic disadvantage. Even so he cannot do a slipshod job . . .
>
> A businessman, long since secure economically, works himself into ill-health, perhaps even back into poverty, for the sake of carrying on his plans. Hard work, once a means to an end, becomes an end in itself . . .
>
> The pursuit of literature, the development of good taste in clothes, the use of cosmetics, strolls in the public park, or a winter in Miami may first serve, let us say, the interests of sex. But every one of these "instrumental" activities may become an interest in itself, held for a lifetime, even after they no longer serve the erotic motive.
>
> Some mothers bear their children unwillingly, dismayed at the thought of drudgery in the future. The "parental instinct" is wholly lacking. The

[9] Allport gave this interpretation italicized formulation in this sentence (1961, p. 229): *"Functional autonomy . . . refers to any acquired system of motivation in which the tensions involved are not of the same kind as the antecedent tensions from which the acquired system developed."*

> mother may be held to her child-tending by fear of what her critical neighbors will say, or by fear of the law, or perhaps by a dim hope that the child will provide security for her in her old age. Gross as these motives may be, they hold her to her work until gradually, through the practice of devotion, her burden becomes a joy. As her love for the child develops, her earlier practical motives are lost. In later years not one of these original motives may operate. The tenacity of the maternal sentiment is proverbial, even when, as in this case, it can be shown to be not an original but an acquired motive.

As is evident from these examples of functional autonomy, the principle is concerned with changes in motivation in the course of experience as new interests are cultivated, unwelcome habits broken, attitudes about people and things modified, and personal values transformed. Thus, as suggested by Allport, the *value* a conscientious workman places upon the ideal of a job well done has to do with motivation and so does a mother's *devotion* to her child along with her *interest* in cosmetics. Additional instances of such specificity of motivation are supplied by her husband's *desire* to spend winters in Miami, by his *liking* for detective stories, his conservative *taste* in clothes, his *disinterest* in dancing, his *worry* about investments, and also by his resigned *attitude* toward his mediocre golf.

All the foregoing italicized words are representative of the nuances of meaning to be considered in dealing with the problem of the individuality of human motives. They are descriptive of ways people differ from one another in terms of beliefs, commitments, prejudices, ideals, preferences, hopes, and intentions. They reflect ways personality traits are rooted in motivational dispositions and as such are reminiscent of the descriptive vocabulary brought into play when writing letters of reference. In brief, they reveal the broad scope and challenge of the principle of functional autonomy.

In Allport's view functional autonomy constituted a challenge to Freud's theory of motivation. On the one hand Freud appeared to trace all action back to basic motives of sex and aggression. On the other hand, according to functional autonomy, there is a multiplicity of acquired motives each one of which is free from dependence upon Freud's two basic motives. Taken strictly, each acquired motive, if genuinely autonomous, would, in the words of Woodworth, be furnishing its own drive and be divorced from any instinctive drive. Consequently, no acquired motive such as absorption in chamber music or biochemistry was to be regarded as an indirect expression of some underlying instinctive drive.

However, according to Allport, Freud would have regarded such interests in chamber music or biochemistry as sublimated manifestations of instinct. This made them disguised expressions of instinct. In other words, Freud made no provision for functional autonomy; hence the clash between his theory of motivation and Allport's theory. In fact, Allport gave succinct expression to his criticism of Freud's theory by noting that "to declare without proof that all adult interests are masquerades for what man really wants (chiefly sex and aggression) is as improbable as gargoyles" (1961, p. 244). This criticism will serve as a convenient point of departure for a brief examination of Freud's theory.

FREUD'S THEORY OF MOTIVATION

Freud approached the study of neurotic and other abnormalities of behavior from not only a medical standpoint but also a biological standpoint. The latter standpoint reflected the great interest in a Darwinian perspective so prominent in scientific circles around the turn of the century. In terms of such a perspective Freud was able to envisage man as being primarily impelled by two sets of motives, namely, the sexual and the aggressive, with the former promoting survival of his species and the latter his individual survival in competitive struggles. As interpreted by Freud, gratification of these two sets of motives turns out to be "what man really wants" once the vagaries of his behavior have been subjected to penetrating analysis. Penetrating analysis is required because, in Allport's phrase, alleged or apparent motives may be "masquerades" for the real motives. The masquerading, as Freud came to recognize it, was largely due to mechanisms like sublimation and rationalization. As a result of the operation of these mechanisms, so Freud taught, man is kept in ignorance of his real motives. This is another way of saying that he is unconscious of "what he really wants." To understand how this comes about calls for consideration of processes Freud ascribed to the unconscious—especially the process of sublimation.

The word *sublimation* is derived from the Latin *sublimare,* meaning to waft upward, as happened in the days of the alchemists when vapors streamed upward from the alembic as some substance was being distilled or refined. As a result sublimation came to suggest the notion of purifying, cleansing, or refining. This evidently commended it to Freud[10] as a satisfactory designation for a psychological process by means of which a socially unacceptable instinctual expression is changed into a socially acceptable one. As interpreted by Freud, this process takes place unconsciously and as such does not involve a change from one instinctive urge to another or from one motive to another. Only the instinct's mode of expression, not the instinct itself, is subjected to modification. Thus sublimation was not conceived of as a process resulting in the acquisition of new motives; instead it was the old motive gratified in a new way. This shift from the old to the new was a product of sublimation and since sublimation was an unconscious process it was assumed that the analyst's patient was unaware of the shift. In other words, as Freud saw it, man may often fail to recognize his real motives. In the idiom of psychoanalysis these real motives were likely to be ego-dystonic urges associated with the vicissitudes of the neurotic patient's libido.

---

[10] As noted by Jones (Vol. I, p. 317), the term *sublimation* was suggested to Freud by his friend and correspondent, the Berlin nose and throat specialist, Wilhelm Fliess (1858-1928).

In this connection it is well to call attention to a not uncommon misinterpretation of Freud's conclusion concerning such libidinal vicissitudes as causes of neurotic disturbance. On occasion Freud has been alleged to have urged sexual indulgence in order to ward off neurotic ills. Sometimes the same thought has been expressed by statements to the effect that Freud has warned against the hazards of sexual frustration. Expressed in this way one comes closer to Freud's thinking about the etiology of neuroses provided it is realized that he also taught that sublimation can circumvent such dangers. He dealt with this issue in a lecture concerned with this etiology and published in his *General Introduction to Psychoanalysis* (22nd Lecture). In the course of this lecture he made a special point of guarding against a possible misinterpretation of what he had written about the cause of neuroses. He noted that although libidinal frustration has been found to be a factor in all cases of neurosis, this does not mean that neurotic disturbance is an inevitable consequence of such frustration. His note took this form (1938, p. 302):

> In general, there are very many ways by which *it is possible to endure lack of libidinal satisfaction without falling ill. Above all we know of people who are able to take such abstinence upon themselves without injury;* they are then not happy, they suffer from unsatisfied longing, but they do not become ill. (Italics added.)

Freud then explained that failure to become ill despite sexual abstinence is due to the ease with which "the component-instincts of sexuality" can change from one means of gratification to another. In particular he noted that one such process of change serving to ward off illness is important because of its bearing on the development of culture. He described the nature of this important process in these two sentences (p. 302):

> It consists in the abandonment, on the part of the sexual impulse, of an aim previously found either in the gratification of a component-impulse or in the gratification incidental to reproduction, and the adoption of a new aim—which new aim, though genetically related to the first, can no longer be regarded as sexual, but must be called social in character. We call this process SUBLIMATION, by which we subscribe to the general standard which estimates social aims above sexual (ultimately selfish) aims.

In thus considering the sublimated aim to be genetically related to the instigating sexual motive Freud was not regarding the changed aim as a new motive. It was the old motive with a new aim. Still, this is not quite correct since, as Freud indicated, the sublimated motive "can no longer be regarded as sexual." This amounts to describing it as a desexualized sexual motive, and just how the motive continues to be sexual under the circumstances was never explained. It may be that the so-called sublimated motive is really a different one and not a disguised version of the sexual motive. If this be so, then the concept of sublimated motives may have to be discarded or drastically modified. In other words, the soundness of the concept itself is to be questioned.

CAN MOTIVES BE SUBLIMATED?

In fairness to Freud this question ought to be restricted to the sublimation of the sexual impulse and not be extended to cover other impulses. After all, Freud never suggested that the impulse to urinate could be sublimated by taking a shower or that the need for food could be sublimated by chewing gum. Nor did he ever refer to the sublimation of man's need for air. These physiologically grounded eliminative, gastric, and respiratory motives are not to be gratified by any substitute aims. This must be self-evident especially in view of their direct relationship to a distended bladder, an empty stomach, and a congested lung.

However, what may not be self-evident is the question of substitute gratification of motives unrelated to a particular visceral organ. For example, can curiosity be sublimated? To grasp the implication of this question it must be realized that we are never curious in the abstract, but always curious about definite issues. We are curious about the dentist's bill, the home team's baseball score, the content of an unopened telegram and the meaning of a strange word like *tetragrammaton.* As must be obvious, no one of these instances of curiosity can be gratified by some vicarious bit of information. The baseball score will not suffice as a substitute for the size of the dentist's bill nor will our uneasiness with reference to the telegram be dissipated by learning the meaning of *tetragrammaton.* It thus seems that the motive of curiosity is not subject to sublimation in the sense of substituting a different "aim" for the original one. However, this assumes curiosity to be a separate or distinctive motive and not a derivative of the libido.[11]

By way of exploring another facet of this issue it might prove clarifying to ask whether an acquired motive like the desire for a cigarette can be sublimated. Now that cigarettes are known to be associated with respiratory disease more and more people are thinking of continued indulgence as wrong. This renders the impulse to smoke, like illicit sex, a tabooed impulse and since sublimation as a process has been regarded as especially applicable to the tabooed sexual impulse so its applicability to another tabooed impulse merits consideration. In other words, we are raising this direct question: Can

---

[11] Freud did regard it as a derivative of the libido. Curiosity with reference to sexual matters gives rise to voyeurism. Scopophilia, as is well known, was regarded as one of the libido's component-instincts. Sexual pleasure incident to looking, or *Schaulust,* was often marked by a shift from interest in the genital region to bodily contours as such and from the latter to lines and curves in artistic expression. Such a shift from the sexual to the aesthetic constitutes an example of Freud's view of sublimation. At one time this psychoanalytic approach to artistic creativity aroused a great deal of interest. For details see the long and rather technical 1940 paper "Free Creation in the Inventive Arts" by H. B. Lee.

the desire for a cigarette be eliminated by sublimation and, if so, how is this to be accomplished?[12]

From a psychoanalytic viewpoint curbing the impulse to smoke would entail *repression* of the impulse. Precise accounts of how repression takes place are not available. It is regarded as a process by means of which ideas, wishes, worries and other mental phenomena are excluded from consciousness. The exclusion refers to expulsion from consciousness as well as to blocking or preventing any of the foregoing phenomena from becoming conscious. Moreover, the actual process of exclusion is said to occur unconsciously. This means that it is not subject to direct observation; hence the absence of any introspective accounts of repression as a process. Nevertheless, it is possible to supply introspective accounts of some instances of exclusion. These would be characterized by awareness and the process involved would be called *suppression.* Thus our hypothetical smoker might curb the impulse to reach for a cigarette by reaching for a stick of gum. In doing so he would be suppressing but not repressing the desire for a smoke. Incidentally, even though both smoking and chewing gum can be classified as oral gratifications, this does not make the latter a sublimation of the former. It is merely the substitution of a different act for the act of smoking. The same result could have been attained by non-oral substitutions such as playing the piano, typing a letter, shaving, or mowing the lawn.

As a conscious act suppression of the impulse to smoke by doing something else would not eliminate the desire for a cigarette. The motive would still be present as a craving even though response to the craving was being curbed. Such curbing of a customary response is often referred to as *inhibition.* In fact, in the present context suppression and inhibition may be regarded as synonymous terms. As every one knows, with effort a cough can be suppressed or inhibited for a time, but this does not cause the impulse to vanish. Similarly, for the smoker to turn from the cigarette case to the piano will not result in the immediate extinction of the craving for a smoke. Not until he succeeds in being absorbed in the musical score itself will he cease to be aware of his craving.

In this example we are assuming the smoker to be a musician whose need for a smoke is most acute right after a meal. In his effort to break the habit it is further assumed that he has decided to end each meal by fingering the keyboard instead of a cigarette. Should he find himself still conscious of the

---

[12]This question is being raised for the purpose of clarifying some of the implications of the concept of sublimation and not for the purpose of suggesting a psychoanalytic approach to the smoking problem. In fact, it is hardly likely that any responsible psychoanalyst would urge sublimation of the wish to smoke. As far as known, Freud himself as an inveterate smoker of cigars did not venture to sublimate his wish to smoke despite being a victim of cancer requiring oral surgery. Nor is there any reference to sublimation in current behavioral research on smoking. (For details see the eight articles in the *Special Issue* of the *Journal of Abnormal Psychology* 81 (1973): 107–198.)

ungratified craving along with a concomitant inability to concentrate on the music, he might be said to be inhibiting or suppressing his habitual response to the craving. As long as the craving continues the habit is not yet broken. However, should the time come when, following many days of such successful suppression, there is instant concentration on the musical exercises with all distracting urges in abeyance then the habit would be broken. Such an outcome would be in accord with the functionalist principle of conscious decay characterizing the shift from self-conscious preoccupation with the complexity of a problem at the beginning of learning to the stage of routine automatism once mastery has been achieved. As a principle, it will be recalled, it is the same as Helmholtz's basic process which also dealt with this shift from effortful conscious control to effortless habitual control. It might also be described as a shift from conscious to unconscious control. In this respect one might regard it as a shift from suppression to repression in the sense that the former is designated as a conscious and the latter as an unconscious process. Actually, as previously indicated, Freud referred to repression as an unconscious process, but neglected to say anything about the way such a process comes into being. Although he recognized the distinction between suppression as conscious and repression as unconscious, he did not regard the one as a prelude to the other. Repression as an unconscious affair was seemingly *sui generis* and unrelated to or independent of suppression. This left it a mystery; but, as just suggested, by equating it with the automatism of habitual control and as a derivative of suppression the mystery is brought into accord with a familiar psychological principle. In fact, there is experimental evidence in support of this interpretation of repression when treated as a technique for the control of tabooed or ego-dystonic motives.[13]

It should be noted that in thus deriving repression from antecedent suppression the unwelcome desire or motive becomes non-existent. There is no question of transforming the desire for a cigarette into a sublimated interest in music. It is just a matter of replacing one activity by another. In fact, on occasion a smoker with no intention of becoming a nonsmoker may become so absorbed in a given project as to be unaware of the unlit cigarette in his mouth and this means that the desire to smoke has vanished—at least for the time being. The situation is exemplified by the report of the business executive who when asked why he failed to eat supper answered, "I was so busy negotiating these contracts that eating never entered my mind." Under the circumstances, in the light of the foregoing interpretation, this would involve *repression* of the hunger motive by turning to an engrossing business venture. Thus there would be no mysterious sublimation of one aim into another.

This account of repression is at variance with generally accepted psychoanalytic accounts. For one reason, as already pointed out, with repression regarded as an unconscious process there is no way of observing just what is

[13] A relevant example of this sort of experimental evidence was supplied by D. V. McGranahan in his 1940 "Experimental Study of Repression."

taking place when an impulse is prevented from becoming conscious. Furthermore, in general, no provision is made for the disappearance of repressed impulses, since they are held to remain active even though concealed in the realm of the unconscious.

At one time Freud taught that the dynamics of such repressed impulses might precipitate neurotic anxiety, but later he arrived at a different conclusion. The issue is important; hence, it seems advisable to explain the nature of this issue before saying anything more about the possibility of sublimating motives.

CONCERNING ANXIETY AND REPRESSION

In his pioneering studies of neurotic disturbance Freud came to recognize the crucial part played by anxiety in the dynamics of such disturbance. In his initial thinking about the problem it seemed to him that anxiety was caused by repression. Reduced to a simple schema it is as if he had the following sequence of steps in mind: (1) a tabooed impulse; (2) repression of the impulse; (3) persistence of the impulse as an active force in the unconscious; (4) anxiety or apprehension that the latter force may overcome the ego's defensive maneuvers. According to this schema, without such antecedent repression there would not have been any consequent anxiety. In this formulation Freud was regarding the libido as menacing to the ego. This was brought out in his lecture on anxiety in his *Vorlesungen* of 1922 (originally published in 1917) in which he described repression as the equivalent of the ego's attempt to flee from a libido that it senses to be a danger.[14] In other words, according to this lecture, not until repression has taken place will anxiety be experienced.

In a lecture delivered some years later Freud revised the 1917 formulation. The revision was prompted by the need to account for the fact of repression of a tabooed impulse or wish. Why should any wish or longing be denied gratification? There must be some basis for such denial otherwise there would be no repression. With this realization Freud felt obliged to change the early schema by making repression or self-denial a *consequence* of anxiety and no longer making anxiety a consequence of repression. As he put it in his 1933 *Introductory Lectures* (p. 120), "It is not the repression that creates the anxiety, but the anxiety is there first and creates the repression!" Precisely how anxiety "creates" this was not explained. Apparently Freud was more

---

[14] This serves to convey the meaning of what he said about repression in the *Vorlesungen*, as may be noted in this sentence from the original: "Die Verdrängung entspricht einem Fluchtversuch des Ichs vor der als Gefahr empfundenen Libido" (1922, p. 434). A literal translation into idiomatic English would be difficult. To obviate the difficulty in her translation Joan Riviere combined the quoted sentence with the following one into this complex sentence: "Repression is an attempt at flight on the part of the ego from the libido which it feels to be dangerous; the phobia may be compared to a fortification against the outer danger which now stands for the dreaded libido" (1938, p. 355).

concerned with indicating what he took to be the *sequence* from anxiety to repression than he was with the *mechanism* of the sequence.[15]

In this revised formulation Freud was evidently thinking of instances in which a forbidden but alluring impulse gives rise to a wish-fulfilling daydream along with thoughts of unwelcome consequences were the daydream to become reality. Anticipation of such consequences results in anxiety and the repression follows. What Freud had in mind can be illustrated by reference to an erotic daydream.[16] Indulgence in such a daydream means that a sexual wish becomes father to the thought of its own fantasied gratification. Should the wish involve illicit or tabooed behavior, then the course of the daydream might be diverted from anticipated delights to sobering thoughts of possible disgrace, divorce, and other dire consequences incident to public exposure. The shift from anticipated pleasure to potential dire consequences marks a transition from delight to dread.

This dread or anxiety, as just mentioned, is the antecedent of repression. Unlike the old schema, which had made repression the antecedent of anxiety, this new schema reversed the sequence. Reduced to a formula this reversed sequence presupposed these four steps: (1) illicit erotic wish; (2) fantasied anticipation of what gratification might entail; (3) anxiety due to thoughts of unpleasant possibilities; (4) consequent repression of erotic desire. In Freud's view this sequence of steps is contingent upon ability to dwell upon the pros and cons of contemplated indulgence. As he made clear in his essay on "Repression," a certain level of mental development must be reached before the defense mechanism of repression can take place. He gave this italicized emphasis when he stated that it is not "present from the very beginning, and that it cannot occur until a sharp distinction has been established between what is conscious and what is unconscious: that *the essence of repression lies simply in turning something away, and keeping it at a distance, from the conscious*" (1915, p. 147).

Of course repression was not the only defense mechanism recognized by Freud. Some of the other ways of curbing strong impulses such as denial or reaction-formation, he indicated, did not require the same level of mental organization as the mechanism of repression. Not all curbed impulses were thus relegated to survival in a dynamic unconscious. This merits explicit

[15]This does not mean that Freud overlooked the question of the mechanism of repression. He dealt with it in his essay "Repression" when he wrote that "the mechanism of a repression becomes accessible to us only when we deduce it from its final results" and furthermore that "the mechanisms of repression have at least this one thing in common: *a withdrawal of energic cathexis* (or of libido, where we are dealing with sexual instincts)" (1915, pp. 154-155). However, Freud did not supply an account of a mechanism by means of which the "withdrawal" itself takes place.

[16]The selection of an erotic rather than any other kind of daydream is deliberate. It is one way of calling attention to the restricted connotation of the concept of repression as understood by Freud; for, according to Jones, he restricted the concept to the problem of coping with erotic impulses. As reported by Jones, on June 3, 1908, Freud "had told the Vienna Society that in his opinion repression affected only sexual impulses. All other effects were secondary. He never retracted this" (Vol. II, p. 320).

mention because, contrary to a common impression, Freud did not assume that ungratified motives can never die; he did not provide for the persistence of all of them in the guise of unconscious urges. On the contrary he acknowledged their mortality in the sense that they can just cease to exist. This point was brought out in his 1927 book on *Anxiety* in which he recognized "the distinction between the mere repression and the true disappearance of an old desire or impulse" (p. 82).

By thus making a distinction between impulses that disappear and those that have been repressed Freud was providing for two kinds of inhibited impulses: the one kind was inhibited by the mechanism of repression, the other kind was inhibited by some other mechanism. In terms of Freud's distinction the latter might vanish whereas the former or repressed impulses would persist. Moreover, since, as indicated in Footnote 16, "repression affected only sexual impulses," disappearance had to be restricted to nonsexual ones.

Both groups of inhibited impulses were consigned to the unconscious so that, in Freud's view, the unconscious was not just the repository for inhibited sexuality. It contained more, as was made evident in the opening paragraph of Freud's famous paper on the "Unconscious" in these sentences (1915, p. 166):

> Everything that is repressed must remain unconscious, but let us state at the very outset that the repressed does not cover everything that is unconscious. The unconscious has a wider compass: the repressed is a part of the unconscious.

This enlarged compass of the unconscious had long been part of Freud's thinking. In fact, Jones reports Freud to have conceived of the unconscious in this way as early as 1896 when he was just laying the foundations of his psychoanalytic psychology. This means, Jones held, that from the very beginning Freud had provided for the broad scope of the unconscious as a mental realm encompassing nonsexual as well as sexual ideas. It was in this connection that Jones wrote (Vol. II, p. 322): "The belief that Freud's unconscious contains only disreputable ideas that had to be repressed has not yet, however, been shaken in the popular mind."

It may also be that "the popular mind" compensated for this misinterpretation of Freud by assuming it to be possible for "disreputable ideas" to be made reputable by sublimation. As products of repression, by hypothesis, the ideas in question had to do with sexual desires and as such, again by Freud's hypothesis, were not subject to disappearance. They were presumed to persist until expressed in some mode of erotic behavior or until transposed into some desexualized sublimated activity. The question of such transposition was discussed in the previous section concerned with the possible sublimation of motives, but the discussion was curtailed in order to explain the part played by anxiety in the dynamics of repressed wishes. It is now pertinent to resume this curtailed discussion.

MORE ABOUT SUBLIMATION

On theoretic grounds it has been argued that lust can be sublimated into love for poetry, music, painting, architecture, or any other mode of creative endeavor. The argument rests upon the questionable assumption of a creative urge being common to sex and to art. According to this assumption, biologically considered, the purpose of the sex drive is to create offspring, and thus keep the species alive. In reality, at least on the conscious level, the contrary of such a purpose governs all extramarital mating behavior. Moreover, this also applies to all such behavior within the institution of marriage when the behavior is subject to contraceptive controls. To attribute biological creativity to the sexually aroused individual under such circumstances is to strain one's credulity. Furthermore, there is no evidence that childless couples—the kind who seek treatment at infertility clinics—secure vicarious relief by engaging in some kind of artistic creativity. In the words of Clarence Leuba, "There is no evidence whatsoever that creative art work—or creative work of any sort for that matter—is particularly useful for sublimating sex" (1948, p. 76).

The theory of sublimation was subjected to direct empirical investigation as reported in a monograph by W. S. Taylor in 1933. His investigation called for the cooperation of a group of "forty superior single men." They were "superior" with reference to character, to general health, to intelligence, and to aesthetic sensitivity. This made them ideal candidates for testing the sublimation theory. Nevertheless, Taylor found no support for the theory in this group of unmarried young men. Their sexual tensions gave rise to masturbatory behavior or to premarital heterosexual indulgence, but there was no sublimated release of these tensions in nonsexual creativity. Nor does any evidence indicative of such release appear to have been produced since Taylor published his report some four decades ago.[17]

Freud's concept of sublimation, as previously noted, provided for the transformation of a sexual motive into a desexualized motive. Thus sexual love might come to be expressed in love of music or love of choreography or love of country. This made the libido the matrix for the emergence of all engrossing interests, devotions, loyalties, and personal attachments. This was as if *agape*, conceived of as unselfish brotherly love or altruistic love for humanity, was a derivative of *Eros*. In fact, according to the theory of sublimation any genuinely absorbing personal value is to be construed as a desexualized derivative of Eros. Presumably a Mozart's absorption in music would be such a derivative and so would a Whitehead's absorption in mathematics. Actually Freud failed to discuss the application of sublimation theory to such specific cases of creative work in music or mathematics. There was no mention

---

[17]In his recent review of the evidence cited in support of the concept of sublimation V. W. Grant concludes that "the very reality" of sublimation "appears never to have been demonstrated" (1973, p. 648).

of the kind of evidence Woodworth had introduced when, as previously discussed, the emergence of individualized motives was attributed to the influence of native capacities. For Freud it seemed sufficient to attribute such motives to the sex impulse or libido as the fountainhead of energy. In criticism of this stand, Woodworth had this to say in his 1917 critique of Freudian psychology:

> The sex impulse is quite clearly a specialized motive, and not at all suited to be taken as the type of all motives. The "sublimation" of "libido," by which it becomes the motive force for any activity whatever, I believe to be mostly a fiction. What happens when genuine libido is aroused is either that it has its own way or, if not, that it acts as a disturbance of any other activity that is attempted. In endeavoring to distract himself from it or to resist it, indeed, the subject may get some other motive powerfully aroused and so become very active in something quite different from the natural outlet of libido. But this does not mean that the motive force for this second activity is the libido drained into another channel . . . any more than your intensified application to your book when you hear distracting noises from the athletic field, and your resulting complete absorption in the book, means that your interest in European history is a derivative of your interest in football. A plurality of motives exists within the individual, and there is no known reason for regarding them all as "transformations of the libido."

Of course a defender of the libido theory might argue that a "plurality of motives exists within" the theory itself. His argument might include references to the motivational implications of sex play, rivalry, jealousy, submissiveness, mastery, curiosity, tenderness, possessiveness, pain, longing, frustration, acceptance, rejection, and similar vicissitudes of the drama of sex. Such implications would be manifestations rather than "transformations" of the libido. The same would apply to extensions of the preceding argument by references to sex and the sale of cosmetics and perfumes, to sex and dance studios, to sex and divorce courts, to sex and literature, to sex and love songs, to sex and medical practice, to sex and the clothing industry, to sex and motion pictures, as well as to sex and the business interests of jewelers, florists, druggists, beauticians, marriage counselors, and those who promote beauty pageants. There can thus be no question about the widespread ramifications of sex as a motive. However, these ramifications are extensions and elaborations of sex. They are not sublimations of sex. Nor are they to be attributed to the vagaries of unconscious goads to behavior. Instead their association with the sex motive is conscious in the sense of being readily recognized. Often this association is as obvious as the ones introduced in advertisements in which a bathing beauty is pictured standing next to an automobile or using a given brand of tooth paste or just smiling at her dog eating the "ideal" dog food.

Nevertheless, even though obvious, might not the very multiplicity of these motivational associations with the sex drive give support to the defender of the libido theory? In opposition to Woodworth's stand, might he not be justified in regarding such associations as being the libido's expression of a plurality of individualized motives? If so, then he would also be taking a stand in opposition to Allport's concept of functional autonomy. The nature of this opposition between functional autonomy and Freud's libido theory has been discussed in an earlier section, but there are a few additional considerations that were not included. Enough background material has now been introduced to facilitate understanding of these considerations as supplementing the earlier discussion.

CONCERNING REGNANT MOTIVES

According to the principle of functional autonomy, as will be recalled, acquired motives are individualized and furnish their own drives. They are not mere derivatives of one or more instincts. As such the principle constituted a challenge to Freud's theory of motivation, for, as just outlined, his theory made virtually all motives, even so-called acquired ones, derivatives of the libido. Since sex was found to be associated with such a wide sample of individual motives, these individual motives were interpreted as manifestations of the libido's ubiquity. Stated differently, the association was regarded as a causal rather than a concomitant relationship. This was tantamount to regarding the libido as the matrix out of which a plurality of individualized motives emerges. As a theory of motivation such a view seemed to account for the ubiquity of sex interests. Furthermore, as psychoanalysts have discovered, their patients tend to confirm the theory because over and over again in the course of their free associations sexual themes emerge as key factors in what had started as an unguided stream of associations. In the light of such apparent confirmation there was no need for Freud's theory to be replaced by a theory of functional autonomy.

As might be anticipated, an advocate of functional autonomy would not be impressed by the preceding line of argument. He would point out that the ubiquity of sexual interests and their association with a multiplicity of specific motives is coincidental and not causal. By a similar line of argument, he would also point out, one might argue that all individual motives spring from the matrix of man's acquisitive or economic drive, since over and over again in the course of everyday experience the issue of money obtrudes itself as an important consideration. It even obtrudes itself in connection with sexuality as indicated by references to prostitution, alimony, dowries, and the expenses incident to marriage and parenthood. This line of argument obviously reflects a Marxist theory of motivation, since Marxists subordinate all specific motives to the regnant economic motive.

On the other hand, some sociologists might be disposed to argue in support of the gregarious drive as man's regnant motive. They would have little trouble demonstrating the dependence of the motives of the individual on interpersonal relations. This starts with the infant's dependence on Mother for gratification of the baby's needs and continues all through childhood and adulthood. Directly or indirectly all of man's desires come to involve others, as evidenced by his desires for approval, security, companionship, sexual gratification, housing, medical care, comfort, success, and recreation. As has been noted by Karen Horney, throughout life man finds himself moving with, toward, against, for, or away from others. In terms of this sociological perspective individual motives might well appear to be emergents from the matrix of gregariousness.

There is no need to add more examples. The ones just introduced suffice to show why from the viewpoint of functional autonomy no one motive is to be regarded as the fountainhead of all other motives. A given individual motive such as curiosity, it should now be evident, may be associated with sexuality or acquisitiveness or gregariousness. For this reason, as already pointed out, the association in question is coincidental rather than causal. In other words, there is no basic instinct or regnant motive that gives rise to subordinate motives and accounts for the impetus launching them as individualized drives. This conclusion is, of course, implicit in the principle of functional autonomy; for, according to the principle, the instrumental means of satisfying *any* motive–not just a single motive–may be transformed into a motive in its own right. Whether *all* individualized motives are products of the principle is a separate question involving important issues not yet considered. They call for careful examination.

FUNCTIONAL AUTONOMY RE-EXAMINED

The concept of "functional autonomy of motives" was already known a century ago,[18] but the phrase itself was unknown until Allport introduced it in a 1937 article. In succeeding years it became increasingly familiar to students of motivation as its use in books and journals became commonplace. In these writings the concept of functional autonomy was often subjected to critical analysis by some who questioned its validity, by others who called attention to its limitations, and by still others for whom it lacked usefulness. To consider all of these criticisms in any detail is out of the question. Fortunately, for present purposes it will be enough to deal with a few of the more thought-provoking ones.

---

[18]One reference to the concept is to be found in the essay *Utilitarianism* by John Stuart Mill (1806–1873). This was published in 1863 and in a section concerned with the origin of specific desires such as "cases" of desires for wealth or power or fame Mill had this to say (Lerner, p. 223):

> In these cases the means have become a part of the end, a more important part of it than any of the things which they are a means to. What was once desired as an instrument for the attainment of happiness, has come to be desired for its own sake.

Another writer who anticipated the concept is mentioned by Allport (1961, p. 229). This was Franz Brentano (1838–1917) who thought of the concept as a "well-known psychological law," stating that "what at first was desired merely as a means to something else, comes at last from habit to be desired for its own sake."

An especially provocative criticism of functional autonomy has been directed at its neglect of broad categories of motivation in favor of a multiplicity of highly individualized motives. Thus with reference to musicians one becomes a harpist, another an organist, and a third is motivated to play the oboe. Analogously, with reference to historians there is similar specificity of motivation as one man specializes in civil war battles, another in the history of Finland, and a third in the history of witchcraft. To enumerate all of the uniquely personal motives that come into existence would manifestly be an endless task; there are far too many for anybody to count, remember, or comprehend. Yet functional autonomy purports to account for their origin and their individualized specificity. The result, of course, is an unpredictable number of motives.

This result has given rise to one important criticism of functional autonomy. In connection with an extensive discussion of motivation in general in a book on personality, David McClelland (1951, pp. 383–525) had occasion to question the usefulness of Allport's principle for students of personality. In his view, as "a particularistic conception of motivation" the principle "does not promote a science of personality because one of the purposes of science is to economize in the description of a given personality in its entire richness and variety" (p. 404). In terms of this criticism, the bewildering number of "particularistic" motives existing in the world renders it difficult for the student of personality to know what to look for in his quest for understanding of individual motivation. His difficulty would be obviated were he to avail himself of a few regnant motives such as sex, security, achievement, power, or economic motives. However, to limit himself to such regnant motives would contravene a chief objective of functional autonomy as a guiding principle. Still, as McClelland saw it, application of the principle to human and animal behavior would leave the student baffled even if he were to stumble on some one "particularistic" motive. By hypothesis such a motive would be unique to the individual being studied and might not be applicable to any other individual. In other words, as a unique event it would be unrelated to any other event and thus have no bearing on any uniformities of behavior. Without such uniformities or *laws* there can be no *science* in the sense in which established sciences like chemistry and astronomy have their respective laws. This may explain why McClelland argued that functional autonomy "does not promote a science of personality."

In reply to McClelland it might first be noted that the foregoing interpretation of the unique event as being unrelated to any other is to be questioned. In a literal sense the statement would be making the unique event an *uncaused* one and this in itself would be substituting magic for science. But if the event is caused, then it *is* related to something else as an antecedent. Second, as long as the existence of unique events is acknowledged, then—as Allport contended—it is a legitimate scientific inquiry to investigate their origin. In the third place, some support for Allport's contention was provided by the geneticist T. Dobzhansky in an article that appeared in one of the psychological journals some years ago. It was almost as if he had had McClelland's objections to the "particularistic" in mind when he wrote the following rejoinder (1967, p. 41):

> One of the assertions which have gained acceptance by dint of frequent repetition is that science is competent to deal only with what recurs, returns, repeats itself. To study something scientifically, this something must be made representative of a class, group, or assemblage. A single *Drosophila* is of no interest whatsoever. A fly may merit some attention only if it is taken as a representative of its species. An individual person may, to be sure, merit attention. However, it is allegedly not in the province of science, but of insight, empathy, art, and literature to study and understand a person in his uniqueness.
>
> I wish to challenge this view. Individuality, uniqueness, is not outside the competence of science. It may, in fact it must, be understood scientifically. In particular, the science of genetics investigates individuality and its causes. The singularity of the human self becomes comprehensible in the light of genetics. You may, of course, object that what science comprehends is not really a singularity but a plurality of singularities. However, an artist, no less than a biologist, becomes aware of the plurality because he has observed some singularities.

That genetic considerations have a bearing on functional autonomy was already indicated by Woodworth's recognition of the importance of native capacities for the emergence and development of acquired motives or drives. In particular, by way of illustration, recall that Woodworth referred to the vocal artist's native capacity for singing. To account for the "singularity" of other acquired drives he might have mentioned other native capacities in the way of presumed special talents for musical composition, or literary composition, or mathematical reasoning, or achievement in athletics, dancing, chess, oratory, and other kinds of specialized endeavor.

Another objection to the Woodworth-Allport hypothesis was raised by Harlow in connection with the fact that "most derived drives . . . rapidly extinguish when the rewards which theoretically reduce the primary drives are withheld." For example, the hungry animal learns to press a bar in order to have food appear. In this situation hunger constitutes the primary drive and the derived drive of pressing the bar constitutes an instrumental act. However, this acquired drive will soon extinguish if it ceases to be a means of obtaining food. The principle involved is comparable to the moral of the fable of the boy who cried, "Wolf!" In the fable, as will be recalled, the cry as the instrumental act ceased to produce the rescuing farmers in the absence of a real wolf. It thus appears that, in terms of such examples, the instrumental acts as acquired drives can never become genuinely independent of the primary drive. In view of these observations Harlow concluded that the "hypothesis of functional autonomy of motives . . . is yet to be demonstrated experimentally" (1953, p. 25).

What appears to have been an experimental demonstration of functional autonomy was once reported by Howard Liddell. The demonstration was not directly concerned with functional autonomy, for it came to light as an unplanned incidental observation in the course of an experiment having to do with the maze learning of thyroidectomized sheep. This made the demonstration an instance of serendipity. In the experiment Liddell employed two groups of animals: normal sheep as controls, compared with the experimental sheep whose thyroids had been removed. As motives Liddell employed hunger as one motive and what might be called gregariousness or "loneliness" as the other. The latter was related to the fact that sheep huddle together in flocks. Accordingly, in some of the experiments the reward for successful traversal of the maze was return to the flock, whereas in others the reward was food. In the early stages of his experiment Liddell assumed the animals were motivated either by loneliness or by hunger. However, as the experiment progressed he "began to entertain grave suspicions about this." This was because he found his control animals, those whose thyroids were intact, acting as if running the maze was intrinsically rewarding. It was a case of running the maze for its own sake, as is evident from the following account (1954, p. 51):

> In spite of their invariable mistakes, the normal sheep seemed eager to run the maze day after day. The experimenter, on coming into the barn to start the day's work, would regularly find these animals clustered about the screen door leading to the maze, as children congregate around the ticket window for the Saturday afternoon movie. When they reached the food box at the end of the maze, they often did not tarry there. One mature ewe was always in a hurry for the next trial. At the food box she rubbed her snout along the surface of the oats perfunctorily, sometimes taking a small bite, and in one continuous wheeling motion rushed off to the starting gate again. . . . Her maze activity was completely absorbing.
>
> This sheep obviously was not motivated to exercise her defective skill in the alternating maze either for a longing for the reward of food or by the promptings of a gregarious instinct. She ordinarily ate little or nothing from the box of oats, and we found that shutting out the sight of the flock by closing the wooden storm door to the barn did not startle or disturb her. We may conclude that the running of the maze was a self-rewarding activity which was also self-perpetuating.

As reported by Liddell, this appears to be a convincing demonstration of functional autonomy: what had been a means to an end had now become an end in itself. Stated differently, what had started as a visceral motive as hunger had now been transformed into a play or recreational motive in the form of running the maze. This made running the maze for its own sake a derived or acquired motive. Unfortunately, Liddell failed to determine the nature of the animals' behavior if placed in the maze before any experience with the maze as a means of obtaining food. By so doing he could have made certain whether or not he was dealing with an acquired motive. If sheep were to run the maze as "a self-rewarding activity" right from the start, such running would not be a derivative of a visceral or any other motive. Instead it would be as much of a primary or underived motive as hunger or gregariousness.

The issue is important not only with respect to the concept of functional autonomy, but also with respect to motivation theory in general. Nor should its bearing on Freud's approach to motivation be overlooked. An excellent account of the nature and implications of this issue is to be found in a 1963 article by Seward, "The Structure of Functional Autonomy." In this article Seward introduced an impressive review[19] of a great deal of evidence to the effect that the "New Look" in motivation theory calls for a reinterpretation of functional autonomy. In particular this involved recognition of a fundamental distinction between internal and external drives or between endogenous and exogenous motives.

ENDOGENOUS VERSUS EXOGENOUS MOTIVES

Endogenous or internal motives have to do with metabolic needs and visceral tensions. The libido theory with its anchorage in the gonads and the gut is thus an endogenous theory. It accounts for all human endeavor as a direct or derived expression of visceral urges—hence oral and anal characters, Oedipal strivings, and creativity as sublimated sex. There is no recognition of the intrinsic appeal of external or exogenous stimuli in the way of games to be played, sunsets to be admired, puzzles to be solved, mountains to be climbed, pictures to paint, stories to read, skills to develop, friendships to cultivate, dances to learn, stamps to collect, or hundreds of other challenges to man's nonvisceral interests. Moreover, as incentives to learning, the latter kinds of stimuli may be more effective than endogenous or visceral tensions. Harlow had this in mind when he wrote "that learning efficiency is far better related to tensions in the brain than in the belly" (1953, p. 26).

According to the "New Look" in motivation theory, initiation of behavior also reflects Harlow's distinction between the two kinds of tensions in the sense that, as noted by Seward, "it is easier to think of responses as directed outward rather than merely pushed from within." Thus baby monkeys clutch terrycloth surfaces as if they provide comfort. Furthermore, the phenomenon of *imprinting* also shows such responsiveness to the external milieu when newly hatched birds tend to follow any moving object first brought within their field of view. In addition, it has now been demonstrated that adult chimpanzees will *play with* sticks and not, as in the case of Köhler's ape, manipulate them just as a means of obtaining food; given two sticks in the course of play, 19 out of 20 animals joined them within fifteen minutes. In other words, in addition to visceral drives behavior is instigated by sensory drives and activity drives and the latter are just as fundamental as the former. As Harlow put it, "there is no experimental literature to indicate that internal

---

[19] His review comprised close to sixty references. In considering this evidence in the next section with the exception of a few instances no bibliographic data will be included, since these data are readily available in Seward's article.

drives are ontogenetically more basic than exteroceptive motivating agencies" (1953, p. 24).

It is also well to be reminded of the fact that both animals and men without special tutelage investigate their surroundings, react to novel objects with *curiosity* not merely by visual inspection but by handling them in various ways. Such handling makes for *control* of the environment. Dogs paw soft earth and babies shake rattles. In the course of such exploration and manipulation of objects some perceptual experiences come to be preferred to others. Even at the animal level such preferences are readily observable: cats prefer to curl up on a yielding cushion to a stone floor and dogs prefer bones to bricks. Along with such preferences animals may exhibit unlearned aversions and even phobias. For example, chimpanzees become panic-stricken when confronted with the clay model of an animal's head and dogs become terrified when confronted with a horse's skin. This means that, contrary to a prevalent teaching, not all phobias are products of conditioning. Nor need all neurotic fears be attributed to the libido's vicissitudes.

The relevance and importance of exogenous stimulation has also been amply demonstrated by studies of sensory deprivation.[20] In these studies the experimental subjects had all visceral needs provided for, but were subjected to prolonged isolation in soundproof chambers with all modes of exteroceptive and kinesthetic stimulation reduced to a minimum. Even though the participants were financially rewarded for their participation in the experiments, the experience was decidedly unpleasant and some of the subjects were unable to remain until the conclusion of the study. The boredom incident to such extreme deprivation of things to do, see, hear, and touch was most acute. This suggests a cognitive need to be stimulated–for the brain to be active–and boredom may thus be listed as an unlearned motive. To cope with it victims of solitude have recourse to crossword puzzles, to doodling, to solitaire, and to any other modes of exogenous stimulation their restricted circumstances permit.

Of course, boredom is not just a consequence of stimulus deprivation. As is well known, it is also experienced by factory workers engaged in monotonous repetitive jobs, by parishioners listening to dull sermons, by students given unchallenging academic assignments, and by experts in any line of competitive endeavor when competing against manifestly inferior opponents. Under all such circumstances there is no joy of accomplishment. With nothing to be mastered, no progress to be made, and no surprise in the offing boredom is inevitable; hence, escape from boredom calls for the challenge of absorbing projects.

Man seems to require something in the way of a golden mean when it comes to the excitement of such challenge. At one extreme there can be a

---

[20] An enlightening account of these studies was presented at a symposium held at the Harvard Medical School. See *Sensory Deprivation* (Cambridge: Harvard University Press, 1971), edited by Philip Solomon et al., 3rd printing.

degree of panic or agitation too intense to tolerate and at the opposite extreme there can be the zero challenge of intolerable boredom. The one extreme calls for stimulus reduction and the other for stimulus enhancement. For smooth functioning, as noted by Seward, the organism must strike a balance between intense exogenous stimulation resulting in *emotional shock* and minimal exogenous stimulation resulting in *boredom.* The balance in question, as a golden mean, has been described as an optimal level of excitation. Presumably it is the quest for this optimal level that induces people to go to art galleries, listen to symphonies, take noncredit courses, entertain friends, play cards, listen to gossip, and read mystery stories. As an old adage has it: man lives by habit for thrills.[21]

EXOGENOUS MOTIVES AND FUNCTIONAL AUTONOMY

This old adage is actually calling attention to the importance of exogenous motivation in the life of man. His "thrills" come as a result of finding interesting things to do, to explore, to learn, and to bring under his control. This calls for ongoing transactions with his physical and social environment. In the process he comes to develop a general idea of schema or what has also been called a *cognitive map* of the world as he has come to experience it. Formation of such a schema or map renders it necessary for his brain to function as a clearing house for the myriads of bits of sensory data streaming into it as items of information to be apprehended and related to earlier items. As noted by Seward, exogenous motives are likely to emerge at critical junctures in the course of such streaming as novel patterns of stimulation require a modification of the schema. The modifications of the schema when viewed as a conspectus of his growing understanding of himself and his surroundings are thus more a product of conscious events or of external data[22] than of unconscious changes.

Now a definite change in one's schema or outlook may mean a difference in expectation, in interest, or in likes and dislikes. For example, should a

---

[21] The thrills may vary in intensity along a continuum from the incipiently pleasant to the ecstasy of peak experiences. According to circumstances the optimal level of excitation will also vary along this continuum. The greater and more absorbing one's interest in a project the higher the level of excitement. As must be obvious, absorbing interests facilitate learning. In view of this fact the drive reduction theory of learning has been rejected in favor of a drive enhancement theory. Harlow has given explicit expression to this rejection in these words (1953, p. 24):

> It is my belief that the theory which describes learning as dependent upon drive reduction is false, that internal drive as such is a variable of little importance to learning, and that this small importance steadily decreases as we ascend the phyletic scale and as we investigate problems of progressive complexity.

[22] Recognition of the importance of external data on the growing child's schemata owes a great deal to the work of Piaget. In one of his books he was particularly concerned with consideration of the "progressive involvement of the assimilatory schemata" as related to "the continuous elaboration of the external universe" (1954, p. xi).

child's first grade teacher be strict, unsympathetic, and dull, the youngster's schema with reference to school will be characterized by an expectation of unpleasant experiences. However, this schema may be modified if his second grade teacher proves to be indulgent, understanding, solicitous, and able to make the pursuit of knowledge an exciting adventure. Is this to be interpreted as the transformation of an old interest or motive in accordance with Allport's principle of functional autonomy? The principle, it will be recalled, states that what had been a means of gratifying a motive might become a motive in its own right. In the present instance the child's experience with the second teacher is not a means of coping with the first teacher; hence the exogenous motive of being eager to attend school is not a derivative of his earlier dread of school. The eagerness would have been his had he had an understanding teacher in the first place. Persistence of this eager positive attitude toward school and learning would be the equivalent of a functionally autonomous motive. This kind of persistence over long periods means resistance to extinction. With this fact in mind, as brought out in the following paragraph, Seward argued that the "properties Allport sought to embody in the concept of functional autonomy" are already embodied in the concept of exogenous motives (1963, p. 708):

> Functionally autonomous motives, as their name implies, were not subject to extinction. In this respect exogenous motives are fully qualified to take their place. Play is intrinsically rewarding; so is finding a bird's nest or solving an equation. Trips to the candy jar will cease when the jar is empty, but the desire for candy lives on. True, all the extraneous motives except boredom can be satiated to some extent as new learning reduces whatever discrepancy aroused them. So it might seem that we have merely exchanged one frailty for another. But the argument would hold only if we had exhausted the possible varieties of experience, an extremity seldom reached outside of concentration camps and zoos. Most of the earth's human inhabitants, cheerfully ignoring the specter of overpopulation, do not face psychic satiation as an immediate threat. Artists, composers, and advertisers continue to explore their media for fresh combinations to titillate or appall us. Scientists race one another into the unknown. Ordinary people find that even the companion of a lifetime is never completely predictable.

In view of considerations such as these, Seward concluded that there is no need for a *theory* of functional autonomy. He made this explicit and definite in this sentence (p. 709): "In a literal sense exogenous motives *are* functionally autonomous; since they began that way, a *theory* of functional autonomy becomes superfluous." He also realized how readily specific exogenous motives such as curiosity, play, or constructiveness are reminiscent of the concept of instinct, but he did not find this alarming. Instead, as he saw it, modern "instincts" in the form of exogenous motives might eventually help to dispel "one mystery of mind: the persistence and individuality of motives."

Although Seward found no need for a theory of functional autonomy, he did seem to need a theory of motivation. At all events, for him there was no satisfactory explanation for the fact that motives persist and are individualized. Despite years of laboratory research, clinical study, psychoanalytic probing, and philosophic theorizing this "one mystery of mind" had not yet been solved.

In his survey of the literature he found many promising clues, but none that served to dispose of the mystery. He was particularly concerned with the Woodworth-Allport theory of functional autonomy of motives because it purported to account for the individuality of motives. Incidentally, as mentioned earlier, in broad outline this theory had already been proposed about a century ago by John Stuart Mill as well as by Franz Brentano. As a theory it thus had eminent sponsorship. Furthermore, by means of some simple examples concerned with the acquisition of new interests the theory was made to appear clarifying and sound. Thus, it seemed to explain the workman's interest in doing a good job, a mother's devotion to her child, a philatelist's motive in searching for a rare stamp, and similar cases of "the persistence and individuality of motives."

Along with Seward we might ask why so eminent a theory has failed to clear up this one mystery of mind. The crux of the theory centers on the observation that often what had been desired and used as a means to achieve some goal may come to be an independent and autonomous desire—something desired for its own sake. Once again we may revert to one of Woodworth's examples: in a given school all students are required to participate in choral work with the music teacher just as they are required to take courses in algebra with the mathematics instructor. Obtaining academic credit for work in music and mathematics is thus a means of securing a high school diploma; for the vast majority of students the work has no other function. However, on occasion the teachers come across a rare student for whom the work is not just a means to an end, but an intrinsically absorbing interest. These are students for whom music or mathematics may become a career—something to be pursued for its own sake. Woodworth, it may be recalled, in effect asked why only the occasional or rare student transformed what had been a means or mechanism into a separate drive. His answer was based on the assumption that only students possessing a *native capacity* for particular subjects are the ones likely to find such subjects alluring. In the present instance the student born with a good voice may leave the music class with an operatic career as his professional goal, just as for the student with an inborn talent for mathematics high school algebra may launch him on his career as professor of mathematics.

Under the circumstances, it seems safe to say, the classroom experience *awakened* the student to his possession of a special talent, rather than *caused* the talent; hence the experience was just an occasion for self-discovery. It is thus entirely possible that independently of the classroom experience such discovery may have taken place. The future vocalist may be complimented on his voice by parents in preschool years and the future mathematician may have been fascinated by numbers from early childhood. As Seward indicated, their respective functionally autonomous interests in singing and in mathematics would consequently be of exogenous origin and not the exclusive result of a classroom experience. The ubiquity of exogenous stimuli can account for functional autonomy of motives without recourse to the Woodworth-Allport theory. As also indicated by Seward, this makes it a superfluous theory. However, this does not dispose of the problem of motivation. Even if native capacities be assumed to determine the persistence and direction of abiding motives, there is still the mystery of the origin and nature of such capacities. We still do not know why one child is born with a special aptitude for aesthetic appreciation, another with capacity to become a great theoretic physicist, a third with talent for medical research, and other children with no special talents at all. To find answers to this mystery of mind psychologists must turn to geneticists for help. Once some answers are placed at their disposal not only will their understanding of motivation be enhanced, but so will their recognition of possible unconscious sources of motivation. However, the nature and implications of such enhancement will be seen in clearer perspective after a retrospective summary of the salient issues introduced in the present chapter.

SUMMARY REVIEW

The present chapter took the historic meeting of James and Freud at Clark University as its point of departure. In particular it was noted that the one lecture James attended stressed the central themes of this chapter, namely, the unconscious and the problem of motivation. It was also pointed out that the lecture was being delivered by a leading champion of the unconscious in the presence of a leading critic of the unconscious. At the time, Freud was seemingly unfamiliar with James's objections to the notion of unconscious mental processes.[23] This resulted in consideration of the following topics:

1. Freud's interpretation of James's encouraging remark.

---

[23] At a later time, during the 1920s, Freud did have his attention called to James's views. This was in a book on the unconscious by an English author, Israel Levine, in which among other incidental references to the views of James he included the following summary statement (1923, p. 44):

> Thus the concept of an Unconscious seems superfluous to James. The facts on which Hartmann and the others rely only prove; for James, "either that conscious ideas were present which the next instant were forgotten, or they prove that certain results, *similar* to results of reasoning, may be wrought out by rapid brain-processes to which no ideation seems attached." They do not prove the existence of mental processes which are unconscious.

Levine's book with its explicit account of James's rejection of the concept of an unconscious was known to Freud. In fact, the book was translated into German by Anna Freud and published in 1926. The preceding quotation from Levine's book is to be found on pages 38–39 of the translation.

2. James's hopes for some phases of psychoanalytic work but misgivings about others.
3. Acceptance of some psychoanalytic teachings and rejections of others discussed in the light of the science-orthodoxy antithesis.
4. Ernest Jones and the three essential characteristics of psychoanalysis.
5. Hidden motives and Spinoza's teaching concerning man's ignorance of the causes of his desires.
6. The distinction between a scientific determinism of means as contrasted with an unscientific determinism of ends.
7. Freud's failure to differentiate between motivation and causation.
8. Spinoza's concept of desire incompatible with the concept of unconscious motivation.
9. Freud's regarding it as impossible for emotions and feelings to be unconscious.
10. How James conceived of instinct and the difference between impelled and motivated behavior.
11. Woodworth's distinction between (*a*) drives and mechanisms and (*b*) native capacities and instincts.
12. Woodworth's theory of motivation as related to his (*a*) defense of instinct; (*b*) dynamic functionalism; (*c*) critique of McDougall; and (*d*) views regarding the individuality of human motives.
13. Allport's theory of the functional autonomy of motives.
14. The contrast between Allport's theory of motivation and Freud's libido theory.
15. A critique of the concept of sublimation.
16. Anxiety as related to repression and the concept of desexualized erotic motives.
17. No basic instinct or regnant motive generates individualized motives.
18. Can the study of individualized motives be made congruent with the scientist's quest for *laws* underlying uniformities of behavior?
19. The possible experimental demonstration of functional autonomy.
20. Seward's critique of functional autonomy with specific reference to (*a*) the distinction between endogenous and exogenous motives; (*b*) responses pulled from without rather than pushed from within; (*c*) the impact of sensory deprivation; (*d*) the question of a golden mean between *emotional shock* on the one hand and *boredom* on the other; and finally (*e*) no need for a *theory* of functional autonomy.

THE CHAPTER IN RETROSPECT

Functional autonomy was found to be a provocative but superflous theory. It was provocative because it called attention to the problem of accounting for the persistence and individuality of human motives. However, its suggested disposition of the problem in terms of the Woodworth-Allport thesis proved questionable and unnecessary. The latter thesis held that any means of achieving a goal may become a drive in its own right and thus come to function as an autonomous individualized motive. By implication this made acquired or individual motives derivatives of some antecedent goal-directed behavior, as exemplified by Liddell's sheep, whose joyous maze-running as an independent quasi-avocational pursuit was interpreted as a product of the original serious business of running the maze in order to be fed. This suggested that the serious business was the *cause* of the emergence of the quasi-avocational pursuit. There was no explanation for the fact that this alleged cause failed to influence all the sheep in the same way. After all, running the maze for its own sake was unique for the one ewe mentioned by Liddell; hence the antecedent running for food could not have been the *cause* of the subsequent running for fun. At best it might be regarded as the *occasion* for the discovery of the fun in question. But this discovery might have been made had the sheep been confronted with a maze initially as a neutral object unassociated with any extraneous reward. Of course, Liddell failed to provide for this kind of arrangement. Had he done so and had the animal responded as if maze-running were its own reward, then there would have been no need to invoke the theory of functional autonomy. However, assuming that this response to the maze had been unique to this one animal, then the response in question might be attributed to a *native capacity.* The presence of a maze as an exogenous stimulus plus the existence of such a native capacity would thus suffice to account for this example of a nonvisceral drive.

According to the preceding example, native capacities combined with the pull of exogenous stimuli can account for the individuality of motives. As illustrated in terms of human behavior mention might be made of Mozart's spontaneous interest in music. He was drawn to the piano from early childhood and was already composing minuets and other musical compositions by the age of five. In this instance there can be no question about Mozart's possession of a native capacity for music; even as a child he took music seriously. In fact, his father once wrote that when still a child his son would be so absorbed in music that "no one dared to have the slightest jest" with the boy. There was no need to attribute Mozart's musical creativity to sublimated sex. For a Mozart, absorption in music is intrinsically wish-fulfilling and not an indirect expression of a visceral craving.

As brought out in this chapter, visceral cravings in the form of endogenous motives may be thought of as internal goads to action. They contrast with exogenous motives conceived of as external incentives to action. The descriptive vocabulary is new, but the underlying thought is of ancient vintage. It goes back to Aristotle's *De Anima* and his discussion of appetite as "a kind of movement" involving pushes and pulls, since "everything is moved by pushing and pulling" (R. McKeon, ed., 1947, p. 230). Incidentally, the centrality of the wish in Freud's psychology may also have Aristotelian roots as shown in this passage from the same discussion (pp. 228–229):

> As it is, mind is never found producing movement without appetite (for

> *wish* is a form of appetite, and when movement is produced according to calculation it is also according to *wish*), but appetite can originate movement contrary to calculation, for desire is a form of appetite. (Italics added.)

Desire as potential wish-fulfillment is also reflected in Aristotle's definition of desire as "just the appetition of what is pleasant." In fact, this emphasis upon desires and wishes is a recurrent theme in psychology's history. Spinoza recognized it in this sentence: "Desire is the very essence of man." It is also implicit in the intentionalism of Brentano in the sense that to desire something is to purpose or intend its realization. Accordingly, for Brentano mental events were presented as dynamic processes; hence his psychology was known as act psychology. This is worth noting because in his student days Freud had studied with Brentano and thus Brentano's intentional act may have been a forerunner of the Freudian wish. It is also worth noting in the present context that both James and Wundt, more or less independently of one another, had stressed the dynamics of mental life. In the case of James, by way of reminder, it will suffice to quote the following from his famous chapter on "Will" (Vol. II, p. 526):

> The first point to start from in understanding voluntary action . . . is the fact that consciousness is *in its very nature impulsive.* We do not have a sensation or a thought and then have to *add* something dynamic to it to get movement.

Wundt's basic interest in the dynamics of mental life is indicated by the fact that, systematically considered, his psychology was a *voluntaristic* psychology. In his analysis of volitional acts he called attention to a distinction between the *impelling* force of a given act and its *moving reason.* He clarified this by writing (1897, pp. 185-186): "The reason for a criminal murder may be theft, removal of an enemy, or some such idea, the impelling force the feeling of want, hate, revenge or envy." The latter feelings reflect the murderer's desires or wishes or what he willed to do. In this connection it is relevant to note that one of the root meanings of volition has to do with wishing since it is derived from the Latin *velle,* meaning to wish, to want, to be willing; hence the Latin *volo* may be translated "I wish." However, this does not mean that the Wundtian wish was a forerunner of the Freudian wish. But it does mean that psychology's interest in the problem of motivation is not a derivative of Freud's dynamic psychiatry. As just reviewed, academic psychology in its dynamic orientation may be traced back to Aristotle's recognition of the wish as a form of appetite, to Spinoza's omnipotence of desire as a basic conatus, to Brentano's intentional acts, to James's impulsive consciousness, and to Wundt's voluntarism.

The foregoing psychologies of motivation differ from Freud's in their recognition of motives as experienced or conscious phenomena. In other words, unlike Freud, not one of them endorsed the concept of mind as unconscious. James, as has been amply demonstrated by this time, was definitely critical of the concept. Furthermore, as once noted by Titchener in writing about respects in which Brentano and Wundt were in agreement: "They reject the unconscious as a principle of psychological explanation" (1929, p. 6).

Finally, as pointed out earlier in the present chapter, Spinoza also provided for the role of consciousness in our experience of motivated behavior. He made this explicit when he wrote, "we are conscious of our actions and desires, but ignorant of the causes by which we are determined to desire anything." Thus, the exhausted man is conscious of his fatigue and his desire to sleep, but unless he chances to be a physiologist he will be ignorant of the chemistry of fatigue and the neurology of sleep. Similarly, the talented poet is cognizant of his literary desires, but would be nonplussed were he to be asked to account for the causation of his talent.

Moreover, most of us would be nonplussed were we to be asked to explain just what causes us to prefer justice to injustice, beauty to ugliness, approval to disapproval, kindness to viciousness, and success to failure. We tend to take such preferences or desires so much for granted that very few of us feel impelled to inquiry into their causation. Consequently, in Spinoza's phrase, most of us remain "ignorant of the causes by which we are determined to desire anything." Whether such ignorance is to be described as unconscious causation or as unconscious motivation will depend on recognition of a distinction between motives and causes. As brought out in an earlier section, the distinction involves a generalization to the effect that all motives are causes, but not all causes are motives. By regarding all behavior as motivated Freud may be said to have overlooked this distinction. He conceived of the unconscious as replete with concealed motives in the form of wishes and repressed desires inaccessible to direct conscious recognition. In accordance with his principle of psychic determinism as elaborated upon in his discussion of the psychopathology of everyday life all behavior, even seemingly accidental or unintentional behavior, is motivated behavior with the motives buried in the unconscious.

Now, Spinoza's view of mind was just as deterministic as Freud's. However, with specific reference to the concept of motivation he differed from Freud not only with respect to his recognition of the distinction between motives and their causes, but also with respect to his recognition of the difference between endogenous and exogenous motives. Without going into detail by considering what he had to say about "desire of sexual intercourse" and "whether it be held within bounds or not," for present purposes it is enough to note his inclusion of both kinds of motives in this single sentence (Ratner, p. 276):

> It is the part of the wise man, I say, to refresh and invigorate himself with moderate and pleasant eating and drinking, with sweet scents and the beauty of green plants, with ornament, with music, with sports,

with the theatre, and with all things of this kind which one man can enjoy without hurting another.

With reference to man's readiness to avail himself of this array of visceral and nonvisceral sources of refreshment and invigoration Spinoza may be interpreted to have arrived at this conclusion: man is conscious of his motives but ignorant or unconscious of the causes of his motives. This use of the word *unconscious* as applied to the causation of motives is obviously different from Freud's unconscious and constitutes one of the many ways in which the word has been employed. In fact, as noted in the first chapter, the word has been employed in so many different ways that it is virtually impossible to incorporate their different meanings into one comprehensive definition.

The many meanings associated with the word *unconscious* and its consequent ambiguity have a direct bearing on the use of the word in the phrase *unconscious mind.* Without suitable qualification the meaning of the phrase will be vague and uncertain. As a result of this uncertainty the notion of mind as unconscious may turn out to be unconfirmed hypothesis rather than established fact. Discussion of the nature and significance of these ambiguous and hypothetical aspects of the unconscious are reserved for the next chapter.

REFERENCES

Allport, G. W. 1937. "The Functional Autonomy of Motives." *American Journal of Psychology* 50: 141–156.

——. 1961. *Pattern and Growth in Personality.* New York: Holt, Rinehart and Winston, Inc.

Birney, R. C., and Teevan, R. C., eds. 1961. *Instinct–An Enduring Problem in Psychology.* New York: D. Van Nostrand Company, Inc.

Cannon, W. B. 1929. *Bodily Changes in Pain, Hunger, Fear, and Rage.* New York: D. Appleton-Century Company.

Darwin, C. 1965. *The Expression of the Emotions in Men and Animals.* Chicago: The University of Chicago Press. (First published in 1872.)

Dobzhansky, T. 1967. "Of Flies and Men." *American Psychologist* 22: 41–48.

Eidelberg, L., ed. 1968. *Encyclopedia of Psychoanalysis.* New York: The Free Press.

English, H. B., and English, A. C. 1958. *A Comprehensive Dictionary of Psychological and Psychoanalytical Terms.* New York: Longmans, Green and Co.

Freud, S. 1910. *Über Psychoanalyse–Fünf Vorlesungen Gehalten zur 20Jährigen Gründungsfeier der Clark University in Worcester, Mass. September 1909.* Leipzig und Wien: Franz Deuticke.

——. 1912. "A Note on the Unconscious in Psycho-Analysis." In *The Standard Edition of the Complete Psychological Works of Sigmund Freud,* translated by James Strachey, Vol. XII, pp. 260-266. London: The Hogarth Press.

——. 1915. "Repression." In *The Standard Edition of Sigmund Freud,* Vol. XIV, pp. 141-185. London: The Hogarth Press.

——. 1915. "The Unconscious." In *The Standard Edition of Sigmund Freud,* Vol. XIV, pp. 159-215. London: The Hogarth Press.

——. 1922. *Vorlesungen zur Einführung in die Psychoanalyse.* 2nd edition. Leipzig: Internationaler Psychoanalytischer Verlag. (First published in 1917.)

——. 1927. *The Problem of Anxiety.* New York: W.W. Norton & Co.

——. 1933. *New Introductory Lectures in Psycho-Analysis.* New York: W.W. Norton & Co.

——. 1938. *A General Introduction to Psychoanalysis.* Translated by Joan Riviere. New York: Garden City Publishing Company, Inc.

——. 1938. "Some Elementary Lessons in Psycho-Analysis." In *The Standard Edition of Sigmund Freud,* Vol. XXIII, pp. 279-286. London: The Hogarth Press. (Freud's last paper.)

Funkenstein, D. H. 1955. "The Physiology of Fear and Anger." *Scientific American* 192: 74–80.

Grant, V. W. 1973. "Love, Sexual." In *The Encyclopedia of Sexual Behavior,* edited by A. Ellis and A. Abarbanell, pp. 646–656. New York: Jason Aronson, Inc.

Harlow, H. F. 1953. "Mice, Monkeys, Men, and Motives." *Psychological Review* 60: 23–32.

Hebb, D. O., Lambert, W. E., and Tucker, G. R. 1973. "A DMZ in the Language War." *Psychology Today* 6: 55–62.

Hilgard, E. R. 1956. *Theories of Learning.* 2nd edition. New York: Appleton-Century-Crofts.

James, W. 1890. *The Principles of Psychology,* Vols. I and II. New York: Henry Holt and Company.

Jones, E. 1946. "A Valedictory Address." *International Journal of Psychoanalysis* 27: 7–12.

Jones, E. 1953, 1955, 1959. *The Life and Work of Sigmund Freud,* Vol. I, Vol. II, and Vol. III (respectively). New York: Basic Books, Inc.

Lee, H. B. 1940. "A Theory Concerning Free Creation in the Inventive Arts." *Psychiatry* 3: 229–293.

Lerner, M., ed. 1961. *Essential Works of John Stuart Mill.* New York: Bantam Books.

Leuba, C. 1948. *Ethics in Sex Conduct.* New York: Association Press.

Levine, I. 1923. *The Unconscious–An Introduction to Freudian Psychology.* New York: The Macmillan Company.

——. 1926. *Das Unbewusste.* Translated by Anna Freud. Leipzig: Internationaler Psychoanalytischer Verlag.

Liddell, H. S. 1954. "Conditioning and Emotions." *Scientific American* 190: 48–56.

Marmor, J. 1949. "Psychoanalysis." In *Philosophy for the Future,* edited by R. W. Sellars, V. J. McGill, and M. Farber, pp. 317–339. New York: The Macmillan Company.

McClelland, D. C. 1951. *Personality.* New York: William Sloan Associates.

McDougall, W. 1908. *An Introduction to Social Psychology.* London: Methuen and Company.

McGranahan, D. V. 1940. "A Critical and Experimental Study of Repression." *Journal of Abnormal and Social Psychology* 35: 212–225.

McKeon, R., ed. 1947. *Introduction to Aristotle.* New York: Random House, The Modern Library.

Munroe, R. L. 1955. *Schools of Psychoanalytic Thought.* New York: Henry Holt and Company, Inc.

Murphy, G., and Ballou, R. O. 1960. *William James on Psychical Research.* New York: The Viking Press.

Piaget, J. 1954. *The Construction of Reality in the Child.* Translated by Margaret Cook. New York: Basic Books, Inc.

Rabkin, R. 1969. "Is the Unconscious Necessary?" *International Journal of Psychiatry* 8: 570–578.

Ratner, J., ed. 1927. *The Philosophy of Spinoza–Selected from His Chief Works.* New York: Random House, The Modern Library.

Seward, J. P. 1963. "The Structure of Functional Autonomy." *American Psychologist* 18: 703–710.

Skinner, B. F. 1972. "Humanism and Behaviorism." *The Humanist* 32: 18–20.

Taylor, W. S. 1933. "A Critique of Sublimation in Males." *Genetic Psychology Monographs* 13: 1–115.

Thorpe, W. H. 1969. *Learning and Instinct in Animals.* Cambridge: Harvard University Press.

Titchener, E. B. 1929. *Systematic Psychology: Prolegomena.* New York: The Macmillan Company.

Wolfson, H. A. 1934. *The Philosophy of Spinoza,* Vols. I and II. Cambridge: Harvard University Press.

Woodworth, R. S. 1917. "Some Criticisms of the Freudian Psychology." *Journal of Abnormal Psychology* 12: 174–194.

——. 1918. *Dynamic Psychology.* New York: Columbia University Press.

——. 1927. "A Justification of the Concept of Instinct." *Journal of Abnormal and Social Psychology* 22: 3–7.

——. 1932. "Autobiography." In *A History of Psychology in Autobiography,* edited by C. Murchison, Vol. II, pp. 359–380. Worcester, Mass.: Clark University Press.

Wundt, W. 1897. *Outlines of Psychology.* Translated with the cooperation of the author by C. H. Judd. Leipzig: Wilhelm Engelmann.

6

The Unconscious: Ambiguous and Hypothetical Aspects

The title of this chapter indicates that there are both ambiguous and hypothetical characteristics implicit in the concept of mind as unconscious. They can be made explicit by first considering the ambiguity of the concept and only later considering the question of its possible hypothetical status. In some ways the latter is dependent upon or emerges from the former; hence the need for prior consideration of the ambiguity.

As mentioned in the first chapter, the word *unconscious* has so many different meanings that its connotation varies from context to context and from writer to writer. Even when employed with the definite article by referring to "*the* unconscious," as in the present chapter title, ambiguity has not been eliminated. As a phrase "the unconscious" might be understood to stand for the sum total of autonomous bodily processes functioning independently of cognitive control; digestion, circulation, and respiration are unconscious in this sense. On the other hand the phrase might be taken to stand for a *system* of cognitive or mental processes regarded as not amenable to direct observational inspection in the way sights, sounds, and other sensory impressions are amenable to such observation. It is this notion of a *system* of unconscious processes that is implicit in a phrase like *unconscious mind.* However, even this usage is not free from ambiguity. Without suitable qualification there is no way of knowing whether the reference is to an unconscious mind as understood by Freud or by Jung or by Stekel or by Horney or by some other proponent of mind as unconscious.

Another possible source of ambiguity depends upon the way the concept of an unconscious mind is to be interpreted. Descriptively, as a concept, it is contrasted with the concept of a conscious mind. In terms of this contrast does this mean that man is equipped with two minds, one conscious and the other unconscious? If so, this interpretation would be in conflict with the concept of the *unity* of mental life for one thing and with the concept of the *integrated* action of the nervous system for another. It should thus be obvious that both the word *unconscious* and the phrase *unconscious mind* have multiple meanings. Some of these ought to be surveyed before undertaking a reinterpretation of the unconscious.

CONCERNING THE MEANINGS OF THE WORD *UNCONSCIOUS*

Some of the meanings of the word *unconscious* have been noted incidentally from time to time in the preceding chapters. For purposes of the present chapter it will prove helpful to subject certain of these multiple meanings to less incidental and more systematic presentation. In each instance the meaning in question will be introduced by a single descriptive word or phrase to suggest its relationship to the unconscious as a concept.

Ignorance

This factor was recognized by Spinoza when he wrote that we are conscious of our desires but ignorant or unconscious of their cause or causes. In terms of food preferences, for example, we may be aware of a desire for something sweet or salty and be ignorant of metabolic reasons for the desire in question. Similarly, after exertion we desire rest even though unconscious of the biochemistry of fatigue. Furthermore, in a non-Spinozistic sense the factor of ignorance explains why one might be said to be unconscious of what has never been learned. In this sense most of us are unconscious of Sanskrit, of topology, and of the history of Borneo.

Inattention

It is virtually a truism to equate being conscious with being attentive and hence being inattentive with being unconscious. As Boring once noted, attention is "the criterion of consciousness" so that consciousness and attention are "almost" synonymous (1963, p. 231). When absorbed in an exciting game the child fails to attend to or is unconscious of his mother's call to dinner, just as his father, a surgeon, is unconscious of outside traffic noises and his own aching muscles when engaged in a difficult operation demanding intense concentration. The broader implications of this state of affairs were well summarized by James Miller in this statement (1942, p. 33):

> When *unconscious* is used in the sense of *unattended,* one's actions, ideas, emotions, needs, drives, etc., are *unconscious* not because one cannot think of them since they are kept from consciousness, as psycho-

analysts insist, but simply because one is thinking of something else. This is an important theoretical difference.

Subliminal Unconscious

In some respects this is the obverse of the factor of inattention. As a factor it has to do with subtle, unobtrusive modes of stimulation presumed to influence behavior even though one is unconscious of the influence. In the area of sales promotion these modes of stimulation have been regarded as "hidden persuaders." Whether they ought to be classified as subconscious rather than unconscious influences is a moot point. As subthreshold modes of stimulation they may be classified as subconscious, but as influences eluding awareness they might be classified as being unconscious. Incidentally, in his essay "The Unconscious" Freud rejected the concept of subconsciousness "as incorrect and misleading" (p. 170).

Conditioning

To promote favorable attitudes toward given commercial products advertisers sometimes employ conditioning techniques. For example, a beverage may be pictured in the hand of a ruggedly healthy, successful man of affairs. The objective is to foster an association or a conditioned reaction between the product and the admired man of distinction. Should there be no awareness of the formation of this association, the resulting conditioned reaction might be regarded as an instance of unconscious conditioning. Obviously, not all such instances need be unconscious in this sense, but in other instances it appears to be possible to employ techniques of conditioning under laboratory control for the purpose of investigating some phases of unconscious processes.

An informative survey of such instances has been supplied by Gregory Razran (1901-1973) in a long monograph concerned with "the observable unconscious." As one of the leading American students of the work of Soviet psychologists, he surveyed the results of their work through the first six decades of the present century. In fact, he estimated that there have been about 5,000 experimental reports of investigations concerned with conditioning in the Russian laboratories since the turn of the century. In his survey Razran cited instances of such studies as involving different animal species as well as human beings. His coverage is so detailed, technical, and comprehensive in scope as to preclude adequate summary review. For present purposes it will suffice to explain the nature of the procedures involved in the demonstration of the "observable unconscious" in the case of human subjects.

In one series of experiments patients afflicted with urinary disease volunteered to serve as subjects. An abnormal opening or fistula made it possible to introduce measured amounts of fluid into the bladder with the resulting distention giving rise to an urge to urinate. Recording devices such as manometers "equipped with conspicuous dials" registered the degree of intravesical pressure as the urge was being experienced. These dials were placed so that the patients could observe changes in the readings as they occurred. In addition to the manometers other recording devices registered respiratory and other physiological changes as concomitants of the urinary urge. After the patients had come to associate the urge with a given manometer reading the manometer was detached from the fistula, but the patient was kept in ignorance of the detachment. Now the experimenter proceeded to control the dials of the detached manometer to determine whether the urinary urge could be conditioned to these artificial or sham readings with the following results (p. 91):

> Conditioning to the sham readings was effected readily in all cases. The patients began reporting intense urinary urges, *accompanied by all or most of the . . . objective changes,* when the manometer readings were high . . . even though the inflows were minimal or totally omitted. On the other hand, low or zero readings failed to produce the urge *and its accompaniments,* even if the inflow was considerably above that which normally produced it; much increased, sometimes double, inflows were now needed to be fully effective. (Italics added.)

The sham readings thus resulted not only in urinary impulses, but also, as indicated by the italicized phrases, in the normal physiological concomitants of such impulses. These concomitants in terms of blood pressure and other metabolic changes are autonomic functions taking place spontaneously just as breathing and digestion do under normal conditions. In this sense they are *unconscious* processes. As described by Razran, in subjecting these concomitants to instrumental observation the Russian experimenters were dealing with the *observable unconscious.* But this is very different from the Freudian unconscious. In fact, Razran (p. 121) refers to "the fact of the Russians' wholesale rejection of the views . . . of Freud" and also to the fact that "while Soviet psychophysiologists and psychologists grant some status and force to unconscious psychic mechanisms, they are by no means willing to accord these mechanisms Freudian ubiquity and potency–and contents."

The kind of conditioning experiments reviewed by Razran may be regarded as forerunners of contemporary studies of instrumental autonomic conditioning frequently described as biofeedback studies. As noted by Schwartz, there are more than 250 articles dealing with the use of biofeedback techniques "and four volumes reprinting much of this work are now available" (1973, p. 666). To the extent that these techniques are successful they too, in Razran's phrase, would be revealing "the observable unconscious."

Failure to Discriminate

Another phase of conditioning experiments has involved investigations of the organism's capacity to detect differences or to differentiate between one and a closely related mode of stimulation. Thus, the experimental subject–man or animal–might be conditioned to respond positively to the sight of a circle and negatively to an ellipse. Once this discrimination has been established the experimenter then proceeds to make the ellipse increasingly circular until there is failure to differentiate between the geometric figures. At this stage the subject might be said to be *unconscious* of the difference. This also means that in the preceding stages when discrimination was taking place there was consciousness of the difference. In fact, capacity to make discriminations has sometimes been regarded as one of the criteria of consciousness. For example, Boring made this quite explicit: "Consciousness is *discriminative,* and discrimination is the symptom of consciousness" (1963, p. 234). Accordingly, failure to discriminate becomes one more meaning of the word *unconscious.*

Gender as a Factor

In some circles it is taught that gender identity is an important factor among the attributes of the unconscious. Followers of Jung, for example, regard man's unconscious as characterized by the "anima" or feminine factor. Jung noted, "every man carries a woman within himself," and then added (1964, p. 31):

> It is this female element in every male that I have called the "anima." This "feminine" aspect is essentially a certain inferior kind of relatedness to the surroundings and particularly to women, which is kept carefully concealed from others as well as from oneself. In other words, though an individual's visible personality may seem quite normal, he may well be concealing from others—or even from himself—the deplorable condition of "the woman within."

As is well known, followers of Adler also recognize the importance of gender, as reflected in the Adlerian concept of "the masculine protest" or the tendency for many to interpret sexuality as a "protest" against feminine submissiveness or alleged inferiority as well as against masculine domination or alleged superiority. According to Adler, this need to dominate and be superior is a compensatory reaction to feelings of inferiority—especially organ inferiority. By way of illustration, in one of his case reports he mentioned a patient's statement to the effect that "I have imperfect genitalia." In reacting against this conviction he "reached the thought, I too wish to possess my mother as my father and brother possess her." The patient then proceeded to test his mother's devotion to him by various maneuvers such as having spells of illness to see if she would nurse him as she had nursed his brother. Adler recognized the patient's behavior as a product of Oedipal strivings, but differed from Freud in what he attributed to the patient's "tests" of the mother's devotion by writing as follows (1916, p. 207):

> These tests he carried out with a genuine neurotic instability, and thus we see in this case that the Oedipus-complex is of the nature of an especially arranged fiction, utilized as a means of expression for the masculine protest against a feeling of uncertainty and inferiority, and dependent upon the neurotic craving for security, the desire to possess everything.

Seemingly, even with reference to their Oedipal strivings, the unconscious of Adler's patients had different goals from the unconscious of Freud's patients.

The Phylogenetic Unconscious

Carl Jung's analytic psychology has provided for an inherited predisposition or *Anlage* of the unconscious in the form of *archetypes* or *primordial images.* The latter stem from experiences of remote ancestors in coping with recurrent situations of crucial biological significance. These would be experiences directly related to survival in the history of the human race and thus have to do with themes of universal appeal. The resulting racial memory or collective unconscious is presumed to render mankind sensitive to thoughts of spirits, gods, storms, motherhood, birth, mother earth, monsters, sunshine and whatever else may have impressed preliterate man as a force for good or evil. Implicit in this concept of the collective unconscious was endorsement of the now outmoded Lamarckian belief in the inheritance of acquired characteristics. At all events, Jung taught that the effect of experience on the neurology of memory in one generation of men is somehow genetically transmitted to later generations. In his own formulation of this teaching he stated that (1953, p. 61):

> . . . although our inheritance consists in physiological paths, still it was mental processes in our ancestors that created the paths. If these traces come to consciousness again in the individual, they can do so only in the form of mental processes; and if these processes can become conscious only through individual experience and thus appear as individual acquisitions, they are none the less pre-existing traces, which are merely "filled out" by the individual experience. Every "impressive" experience is such an impression, in an ancient but unconscious stream bed.

Jung made much of archetypes and primordial images in his interpretation of the symbolism of dreams. In this respect the Jungian unconscious differed from the Freudian unconscious, but this is not to say that Freud had also differed from Jung with respect to belief in phylogenetic inheritance.[1] As a matter of fact, he once mentioned his full agreement with Jung with respect to this belief in the following passage from his "History of an Infantile Neurosis" (p. 97):

> I should myself be glad to know whether the primal scene in my present patient's case was a phantasy or a real experience; but taking other similar cases into account, I must admit that the answer to this question is not in reality a matter of very great importance. The scenes of observing parental intercourse in childhood and of being threatened with castration are unquestionably *an inherited endowment, a phylogenetic*

---

[1]This belief implies endorsement of Lamarckianism and, as reported by Jones (Vol. I, p. 347), "Freud early cherished the Lamarckian belief to which he adhered throughout his life."

> *inheritance,* but they may just as easily be acquired by personal experience. . . .
>
> All that we find in the prehistory of neuroses is that a child catches hold of this *phylogenetic experience* where his own experience fails him. He fills in the gaps in individual truth with prehistoric truth; he replaces occurrences in his own life by occurrences in the life of his ancestors. *I fully agree with Jung*[2] *in recognizing the existence of this phylogenetic inheritance;* but I regard it as a methodological error to seize upon a phylogenetic explanation before the ontogenetic possibilities have been exhausted. (Italics added.)

This subordination of phylogenetic to ontogenetic explanation is, as Freud indicated, in accord with sound scientific procedure. It accords with the scientific principle of parsimony, since the assumption of the inheritance of racial experience entails more unconfirmed hypotheses than are involved in belief in the results of individual experience. This is so obvious that it seems safe to guess that Jung would have agreed with Freud had the issue been presented to him. After all, it places a greater strain on one's credulity to account for a gymnast's exquisite muscular control by the tree-swinging practices of his remote biological ancestors than by the results of his own years of practice in the gymnasium.

Still, there is a more important issue connected with this recognition of phylogenetic inheritance by both Freud and Jung; namely, the attribution of this inheritance to "physiological paths." This places the racial unconscious in the nervous system or, more definitely, in the "paths" or fiber tracts of the brain. If this holds true for the hypothetical racial unconscious, does it not also hold true for the less hypothetical ontogenetic individual unconscious? If so, then the concept of unconscious mental processes has to do with modifications of brain tissue[3] rather than with a psychic being or concealed thinker or ghost scheming schemes while we sleep. Of course, with the concept subject to so many meanings it is difficult to be confident of the precise meaning of particular references to *the* unconscious as employed by different writers. Very likely all those affiliated with medical schools or universities

---

[2]It is of more than passing interest to find this agreement with Jung mentioned in this essay. At the time Freud was already at odds with both Jung and Adler, as is clear from this footnote Freud introduced by way of introduction to the essay (1918, p. 7):

> This case history was written down shortly after the termination of the treatment, in the winter of 1914–1915. At that time I was still freshly under the impression of the twisted re-interpretations which C. G. Jung and Alfred Adler were endeavouring to give to the findings of psycho-analysis.

[3]That Freud was prepared to think of unconscious mental processes as involving such modifications is indicated, as pointed out by Jones (Vol. I, p. 368), by his having once written:

> Perhaps it might be more correct to say: these processes are not of a psychical nature at all, but are *physical processes* the psychical consequences of which are represented as if what is expressed by the words 'detachment of the idea from its affect and false connection of the latter' had really happened. (Italics added.)

would bristle at the suggestion of the unconscious being a ghost in the bodily machine. But precisely how each of them, especially as affiliates of rival psychoanalytic and related institutes, conceives of the intrinsic nature or mechanism of the unconscious is rarely if ever made clear.

A Numerical or Depth Factor

Another issue that is not made clear involves the possible existence of more than one unconscious; it might be more accurate to speak of the unconsciouses than of the unconscious. The plural suggests layers or levels of the unconscious and is in accord with the concept of a *depth* psychology.[4] By implication this concept suggests that the unconscious is deeper than the conscious. In one of his books Freud called attention to the crudity of such a spatial metaphor when with reference to the relation between the conscious "system" and that of the unconscious he wrote (1938, p. 260): "The crudest conception of these systems is the one we shall find most convenient, a spatial one." He then suggested thinking of the unconscious as akin to "a large ante-room, in which the various mental excitations are crowding upon one another," while consciousness was to be thought of as residing in a smaller "reception-room" next to the ante-room.

The notion of mental excitations belonging to the unconscious system "crowding upon one another" is also implicit in one passage of Freud's essay on "The Unconscious," in which he had this to say with reference to those of his critics who had thought of the unconscious system as "a second consciousness" (p. 170):

> We must be prepared . . . to assume the existence in us not only of a second consciousness, but of a third, fourth, perhaps of an unlimited number of states of consciousness, all unknown to us and to one another. In the third place . . . we have to take into account that analytic investigation reveals some of these latent processes as having characteristics and peculiarities which seem alien to us, or even incredible, and which run directly counter to the attributes of consciousness with which we are familiar. Thus we have grounds for modifying our inference about ourselves and saying that what is proved is not the existence of a second consciousness in us, but the existence of psychical acts which lack consciousness.

In answer to his critics Freud appears to have recognized the existence

[4]According to Jones (Vol. I, p. 269), Bleuler was the first to have called psychoanalysis "depth psychology." However, even before Bleuler had introduced the phrase, Jones also noted, Freud had already begun to regard study of the neuroses as providing "access to deep layers" of man's mind. Incidentally, the spatial characteristics thus ascribed to mental processes by these references to "depth" and "layers" may be regarded as part of commonsense psychology. Long before Freud it was not unusual to hear about some deep thinker as contrasted with some shallow thinker. The characterization in question even goes back to Biblical times, for the Psalmist evidently thought of God as a deep thinker when he wrote in Psalm 92:6, "How great are Thy works, O Lord! Thy thoughts are very deep."

"not only of a second" but also "of a third and fourth" and possibly "of an infinite series" of "certain mental operations lacking in the quality of consciousness." Each member of the series was presumed to be "unknown to us and to one another," hence making a plurality of segregated unconscious mental operations. This changed *the* unconscious from a single unified system into a multiplicity of autonomous systems. However, neither Freud nor his followers ever made the term *unconsciouses* a constituent of the psychoanalytic everyday working vocabulary. Indirectly, of course, the concept of a plurality of levels of unconsciousness became such a constituent, as references to the spatial metaphor of *depth psychology* became increasingly common as a synonym for psychoanalytic psychology. Just how this metaphor was to be interpreted was not spelled out, that is, the figure of speech was never replaced by a literal description. Thus, there was no way of deciding in what respect psychoanalytic psychology was *deeper* than other psychologies or whether, by implication and in what way, other psychologies were shallower than the psychoanalytic ones. It serves as one more example of the differing meanings and connotations that have come to be associated with the concept of unconscious mental life.

There is no need to introduce additional examples. The ones supplied suffice as reminders and elaborations of the fact mentioned in the first chapter, that what is attributed to the unconscious by one writer may be very different from and even in opposition to what is attributed to it by another writer. Even those who identify themselves as psychoanalysts may not agree in what they attribute to the Freudian unconscious. This lack of agreement accounts in part for the existence of separate psychoanalytic institutes and societies reflecting the cleavage between the orientation of so-called classical Freudians on the one hand and the so-called neo-Freudians on the other. Of course, the cleavage is not an absolute one in the sense of being indicative of disagreement with respect to all Freudian teachings.

Actually, they all share a common appreciation of Freud as the founder of psychoanalysis. All, including the most radical of the neo-Freudians, continue to think of Freud as a genius. They all continue to endorse many of his insights, suggestions, and beliefs, and all continue to avail themselves of Freud's distinctive psychoanalytic vocabulary. Whether any psychoanalyst is so loyal to the memory and prestige of Freud as to be prepared to endorse *all* that Freud taught is another issue. Such blind loyalty obviously would presuppose abrogation of critical thinking and replacement of the scientist's outlook by the faith of a zealot. It is hard to believe that any devotee of Freudian teachings would claim such uncritical faith in the soundness or validity of these teachings. Some of the implications of this issue were already considered in the previous chapter in connection with a discussion of the essentials of psychoanalysis, but there are a few additional implications which ought to be brought out now in view of their bearing on the chief objectives of the present chapter.

ON SEEING FREUD IN PERSPECTIVE

Freud's writings covered a period of more than sixty years: he was 21 when his first paper was published in 1877 and 82 when his last paper was published. The vast scope of his literary output is a product of study and reflection through the intervening decades and its range is reflected in the fact that the standard edition of his *Collected Works* comprises twenty-four volumes. Under the circumstances one might raise this question: Is it likely that one man who wrote so much over so many decades was either invariably right in his reports and judgments or consistently in error? The obvious answer to this rhetorical question means that recognition of Freud's genius does not justify automatic endorsement of whatever he chanced to espouse. Each teaching or conclusion ought to be evaluated in terms of supporting evidence rather than in terms of a Freudian *ipse dixit.*

To entertain the latter kind of confidence in Freud as an authority would be to follow the example of scholars of old who settled questions of fact by consulting Aristotle without considering the possibility of Aristotelian error. Sometimes, of course, Aristotle had even been wrong about matters as mundane as counting ribs or teeth. For example, he taught that man has sixteen ribs and that women have fewer teeth than men. This is not to suggest that Freud was a poor observer of such obvious anatomic fact; but it is to suggest that just as the genius of Aristotle was no guarantee against error neither does the genius of Freud supply such a guarantee. By way of illustration it will be enough to call attention to just a few of Freud's errors.

Freud's endorsement of Lamarckianism serves as one instance of acceptance of an erroneous belief. Other instances are to be found in the chapter on occultism in the Jones biography (Vol. III, Ch. 14). For example, Jones mentions Freud's "apotropaeic acts," or acts carried out as quasi-magical maneuvers to ward off trouble. Knocking on wood is a common example of an apotropaeic act. Freud, according to Jones, has cited acts of this kind he himself has "unconsciously carried out with the aim of averting disaster." At one time when his daughter was critically ill he smashed a small marble statue of Venus, in the nature of "a sacrificial offering to preserve his child's life." Jones also gives several instances of Freud's belief in numerology as well as in clairvoyance. In a different context Jones mentions another of Freud's questionable beliefs, one having to do with the laying on of hands. As reported by Jones (Vol. I, p. 243), when a patient was blocked in her associations "Freud would press her forehead with his hand" while assuring her that additional memories would occur to her. Obviously, there is no basis for assuming a relationship between activated recall and such pressure on the patient's forehead. However, this erroneous belief is not as manifestly wrong as the one introduced in Freud's report of one of his famous cases.

The case in question was reported under the title of "A Case of Paranoia Running Counter to the Psycho-Analytic Theory of the Disease." Without going into great detail it is enough to note just one episode in this case. This had to do with a patient's report of having heard "a noise like a click or beat"[5] while indulging in an amorous embrace with her lover. At the time she was unable to account for the noise, but later as she was leaving she saw two men carrying what appeared to be a box resembling the shape of a camera. In retrospect she then accounted for the noise as having been the click of the camera as the men in obedience to orders from her lover had surreptitiously taken a picture of the amorous scene. In Freud's opinion there was no external source of the noise at all. To quote him exactly (1957, p. 270): "I do not believe . . . that there was any noise to be heard at all. The woman's situation justified a sensation of a *knock or beat in her clitoris*" (italics added).

Freud appears to have been convinced of the reality of this phenomenon of an audible clitoris, for he mentioned it again in connection with another of his patients who suffered from an obsession which, among other symptoms, was marked by the need to remove all clocks and watches from the bedroom before she could prepare for sleep. In commenting on this symptom Freud wrote (1938, p. 236):

> Now this patient's special fear was that the ticking of the clocks would disturb her during sleep. The ticking of a clock is comparable to the throbbing of the clitoris in sexual excitation. This sensation, which was distressing to her, had actually on several occasions wakened her from sleep; and now her fear of an erection of the clitoris expressed itself by the imposition of a rule to remove all going clocks and watches far away from her during the night.

Unfortunately, Freud failed to cite any evidence in support of this gynecological interpretation of the ticking and clicking noises reported by these two patients. There does not appear to be any such evidence in the relevant literature.[6] At best the interpretation is to be relegated to science fiction, for to consider it as possibly factual is to place an intolerable strain on one's credulity.

Once again it is well to mention the chief reason for thus calling attention to Freud's mistakes, namely, to avoid confusing what he merely claimed or believed with what he had actually proved or demonstrated. This amounts to a platitudinous reminder of the fact that scientific questions are to be settled

---

[5]To check on the accuracy of this translated phrase the original German was consulted in the *Gesammelte Werke* and it was found that Freud had employed three rather than just two kinds of noise. The original reads (1946, p. 241): "ein Geräusch wie ein Ticken, Klopfen, Pochen" meaning "noise like a ticking, knocking, beating." In the italicized sentence in the next quoted excerpt from the case history Freud just referred to two kinds of noise in this formulation (1946, p. 244): "Die Situation, in der sie sich befand, rechtfertigte eine Empfindung von Pochen oder Klopfen an der Klitoris."

[6]When Dr. W. H. Masters of the Reproductive Biology Research Foundation was asked whether he knew of any factual basis for Freud's interpretation he replied, "While we have no concept of where the woman Freud counselled felt the knock or heard the clock ticking, we can assure you it was not in the clitoris."

by appeals to evidence rather than by appeals to authority—even the authority of a Freud. After all, there is always the danger of being overawed by the voice of authority.

However, this word of caution is not to be construed as blindness to or disparagement of Freud's place in the history of psychology. As a seminal thinker he belongs in psychology's hall of fame along with James, Wundt, Helmholtz, Fechner, Bain, Binet, and other stars of the first magnitude. As pioneer investigator he explored phases of human behavior his psychological predecessors had either avoided or ignored as taboo territory. The scope of his influence can be glimpsed by a hasty review of salient theories and concepts he introduced for consideration as important psychological topics: defense dynamisms such as projection and reaction-formation, psychosexual development, oral characters, penis envy, regression, repression, dream symbolism, latent content, death instinct, wish-fulfillment, and kindred Freudian additions to the psychologist's professional vocabulary.

It is also well to realize that even when Freud's conclusions met with adverse criticism they were not necessarily devoid of scientific value, especially if they stimulated new avenues of investigation. To stimulate this kind of investigation is often to contribute to the progress of science. Accordingly, if and when those whose thinking has diverged from Freud's have thereby enhanced understanding of man's psychology then, as instigator of such divergent thinking, Freud merits some credit for the resulting enhancement. From this viewpoint the heads of rival schools of psychoanalytic thought such as Adler, Jung, and Rank are indebted to Freud. This also applies to those who have reinterpreted or even rejected some of Freud's teachings, such as Horney, Fromm, Sullivan, and others. In brief, had there been no Freud, there never would have been classical Freudians, anti-Freudians, and neo-Freudians.

ON THE TESTING OF FREUD'S HYPOTHESES

The emergence of these three different kinds of reactions to Freud's teachings is indicative of their provocative nature, and of the fact that many of them are subject to more than one interpretation. Furthermore, the evidence cited in their support is not based upon laboratory observations, field studies, or statistical data. Much of it, at best, is more conjectural than coercive. Under the circumstances neither wholesale endorsement nor wholesale rejection of these teachings is justified. Instead, it might be preferable to be governed by the following "word of warning" with which Ernest Hilgard once concluded an appreciative chapter concerned with Freud's psychodynamics (1956, p. 324):

> Psychoanalytic thinking is very complex and loosely formulated, so that it is not easy to find out what is essential, what is dispensable, and what internal contradictions there are in it. We need a careful, critical

> systematization of what appears to be best substantiated through clinical experience and through other sources of scientific evidence, so that irrelevancies and contradictions are either discarded or stated in form for decisive testing. We need to locate the most pertinent issues, and then do our best to get adequate evidence to resolve these issues. There is much in Freud that nearly everyone will reject, such as the inheritance of acquired characteristics, and some metaphorical statements about localization of function in the brain. The problem is not to guess what Freud "really" meant and then to defend or refute him. The problem is to find out what is true, regardless of who said it. Freud uncovered some interesting hypotheses. We need to state them as carefully as we can, and then put them to the test.

Some attempts have been made to subject various Freudian hypotheses to scientific test. Those undertaken by the 1940s were reviewed by Robert R. Sears and, in general, he found the results discouraging. He concluded that he doubted "whether the sheer testing of psychoanalytic theory is an appropriate task for experimental psychology" (p. 329). In the 1950s J. R. Sewell conducted a careful test of the validity of psychoanalytic teachings concerning experiences of early infancy on subsequent personality development. The experiences had to do with nursing, weaning, toilet training, and sleeping "alone during the first year of life" as contrasted with those babies who had "slept with mother during the first year of life." The findings failed to confirm the hypotheses under investigation. Similarly, in his review of studies concerned with the Freudian hypothesis of the forgetting or repression of unpleasant experiences Charles E. Osgood also failed to obtain confirmation of the hypothesis. Other psychoanalytic hypotheses have been subjected to experimental check, many of which are reviewed in considerable detail in Eysenck and Wilson's *The Experimental Study of Freudian Theories.* After critical examination of each of them they had this to say (p. 392):

> What, then, is our main conclusion? We would say that the studies looked at in this volume give little if any support to Freudian concepts and theories; . . . that several of the studies dealing in particular with treatment and with 'single case' investigations give results powerfully challenging Freudian hypotheses; and that the quality of the studies allegedly supporting psychoanalytic views is so poor that very little of interest can in fact be gathered from the results reported.

Whether the negative outcome of these experimental studies deprives psychoanalysis of scientific status is a moot issue. According to one psychoanalyst, Harley C. Shands, if the methodology of science be identified with the process of subjecting anticipated consequences of specific hypotheses to experimental check, then "psychoanalysis is the antithesis of science" (p. 96). This, as Sands indicates, reflects a principle sponsored by students of the philosophy of science. Consequently, as he also indicates, if psychoanalysis is to be classified as a science, it will be "necessary to change the traditional definition of science" (p. 97). Furthermore, if it is not a science in this traditional sense of the concept, then there is still a need to check on the "reliability of its insights."

By implication, such checking would call for examination of the evidence cited in support of given insights. Even nonlaboratory fields of investigation may be presumed to be guided by evidence in reaching "insights" or conclusions, and to the extent that such evidence is available it may be possible to bring such fields within the orbit of science provided the conclusions reached are justified by the evidence. In this sense nonlaboratory fields of study like linguistics, topology, economics, and comparative jurisprudence come to be classified as sciences. The scientific or nonscientific status of any subject or topic is thus to be judged in terms of this criterion, even a restricted topic like the unconscious. This amounts to asking, "What is the scientific status of the concept of mind as unconscious?"

THE UNCONSCIOUS AS A SCIENTIFIC CONCEPT

The criterion under consideration has been implicit in many of the discussions of the unconscious in previous chapters; however, it will facilitate critical evaluation of the subject to render it explicit. This requires examination of statements made about the nature of the unconscious in the light of a deliberate search for evidence cited in support of or as proof for the statements. In other words, according to the criterion just mentioned, the scientific status of the unconscious is contingent upon the existence of such evidence.

As a matter of fact, some few years ago, as alluded to in the previous chapter, the psychiatrist Richard Rabkin subjected the unconscious to this kind of examination. He was unable to find the kind of evidence required by the criterion, and as a consequence he had misgivings about the scientific status of the unconscious. In this connection he wrote (1969, pp. 571–572):

> It is therefore appropriate to treat the unconscious as nonscientific, as a basic assumption that cannot be proved but must be accepted as a given. In so doing I am following Freud himself; in his General Introduction, among other places, he says he must be given this assumption or nothing satisfying can be made out of dreams and parapraxes. In a similar, more general argument Jones quotes Freud: "What speaks against the physiological conception is its unfruitfulness; for the psychoanalytic one it can be claimed that it has been able to make intelligible interpretation of thousands of dreams and has used them to achieve a knowledge of intimate mental life."
>
> Thus Freud's argument is not in the form of a scientific proof; his point is that such an assumption is practical in its consequences. It is also clear from this excerpt that Freud set his theory against organic ("physiologic") theory. In this formulation Freud argues not that dream interpretation leads to the unconscious, but the reverse—that the assumption of an unconscious leads to an interpretation of a dream. In modern terminology, Freud's argument runs that the concept of an unconscious is a condition of the psychoanalytic game; if you are to

> interpret a dream you must grant this hypothesis. As such it cannot be tested but rather is a general *program* by which such activity is designed to proceed—a map, or a topography.

From the context it is evident that Rabkin's reference to "the concept of an unconscious" is a reference to the Freudian unconscious. In designating this concept as the *hypothesis* of an unconscious he was not really clashing with Freud's interpretation, as might appear at first impression. This is so because in his last paper, "Some Elementary Lessons in Psycho-Analysis," Freud had written "our science involves a number of hypotheses—it is hard to say whether they should be regarded as postulates or as products of our researches" (1938, p. 282). Furthermore, in his subsequent discussion of the statement Freud linked these hypotheses to mental functions he attributed to the unconscious. It is well to note that at the close of his life Freud himself in retrospect was seemingly unsure about the scientific status of the unconscious. He found it hard to decide whether his researches had confirmed the hypothesis of an unconscious mind or whether it was still an assumption or postulate not yet supported by his researches.

It ought to be stressed that Rabkin was not *denying* the concept of a Freudian unconscious. He recognized it as an assumption, but reported that in his clinical work he found the concept to be unimportant. This, of course, is not the same as denying the assumption. Nevertheless, one of his critics, Benjamin Brody, writing in the same journal, charged him with having registered a "denial of the unconscious" and he called such denial "a great leap backward."[7] In his view the success of psychoanalysis "in effecting improvement or cure" of neuroses "has seemed a proof of the theory of unconscious processes" (p. 593). The fact that Rabkin was also able to help his patients was not regarded as being in conflict with the latter kind of proof. Instead, Brody suggested that "Rabkin's techniques work" because it is possible "that Rabkin, by virtue of his special authority as a therapist, his power of suggestion, and his personality, is utilizing the unconscious without knowing it" (p. 595).

---

[7] A phrase like "a great leap backward" suggests consternation at the very thought of questioning Freud. Brody is not alone in this. There are other contemporary writers who view such questioning with equivalent or even more intense consternation. For example, Irving Sarnoff has referred to those who "had the temerity to question and to depart from the basic tenets of psychoanalytic theory or therapy" as "rebels" and as "petty, carping, and ungrateful heirs" of Freud's "priceless legacy." Moreover, "Freud himself so regarded those who, like Jung and Adler, had the presumption to compare alternate versions of the phenomena he had sought to illuminate" (1971, pp. 3–4).

The defections of Jung and Adler were also deplored by Reuben Fine, but in less flamboyant language. In his view Freud's original favorable judgment of these men was to be attributed to Freud's being a poor judge of character or *Menschenkenner*—his deficient "insight into the petty grievances and malices that make up so much of many people's lives." Indeed, "his choice of Adler as president of the Vienna group . . . and of Jung as president of the International Psychoanalytical Association, demonstrated the high hopes he had placed in these men, their subsequent behavior how completely he had misjudged them" (1973, p. 169).

In terms of the argument advanced by Brody it becomes impossible to subject the hypothesis of an unconscious to the test of clinical success. By implication, Brody attributes *all* psychotherapeutic success to utilization of the unconscious whether or not therapists are cognizant of such utilization. If this be so, then there is no way to provide for a test of the therapeutic efficacy under consideration, since even those therapists who report finding reliance upon the unconscious unnecessary would have their reports questioned. It would be held that unwittingly they were relying upon the unconscious. This means inevitable confirmation of the hypothesis with all negative evidence interpreted as unrecognized positive evidence. Such logic renders it impossible to treat the hypothesis of unconscious mental life as a testable hypothesis or as one theoretically capable of being confirmed in terms of anticipated consequences.[8]

At one time it was argued that even though the factual status of the unconscious continued to elude confirmation its acceptance as a working hypothesis might nevertheless be justified because of its value for dealing with phenomena of psychopathology. This argument was mentioned back in the 1920s by G. C. Field in a paper he contributed to a British symposium concerned with the concept of the unconscious. Actually, the symposium was restricted to this question: "Is the Conception of the Unconscious of Value in Psychology?" Before dealing directly with this question Field alluded to the possibility of belief in "unconscious mental processes" having "a certain value as a provisional working hypothesis" for the limited field of psychotherapy. However, he did not elaborate upon this since, as he explained, the symposium was concerned with the value of the unconscious for psychology as contrasted with its possible value for psychoanalysis. In fact, he contrasted his own answer to the question with an answer supplied by Ernest Jones. In his view, sponsors of the unconscious are really unable to supply a meaningful characterization of the concept. He added that the concept comes close to being "a confession of ignorance" when it is alluded to in negative terms as something neither physical nor conscious and hence as a mysterious *X* or "an unknown cause" of dreams, conflicts, and behavior. After giving expression to this opinion he elaborated upon it as follows (p. 414):

> This, of course, would not be admitted by the advocates of the claims of the Unconscious. And we find them, accordingly, continually speaking of the activities of the unconscious mind in exactly the same terms as of the activities of the conscious mind, so that we hear of unconscious desires, emotions, wishes, fears, or of unconscious thoughts or

---

[8]It is well to note that, as Wesley Salmon has put it in a recent article, it is an "oversimplification" to describe the testing of hypotheses as a simple process of having them confirmed or disconfirmed in the light of anticipated consequences. In fact, with particular reference to the consequences derived from inductive anticipation of consequences, as is common in empirical investigations, Salmon demonstrates the complexities involved. Even the underlying logical processes are still subject to debate. For this reason Salmon concludes, "There is more to scientific confirmation than merely finding true consequences" (1973, p. 77).

> memories. These unconscious mental processes as Dr. Ernest Jones tells us "present all the attributes of mental ones, except that the subject is not aware of them." And consciousness thus becomes, he says, "merely one attribute of mentality, and not an indispensable one." I have searched in vain for a clear statement of what the other attributes of mentality are which these processes do possess. And when I reflect on what I mean by a wish or an emotion or a feeling, I can only find that I know and think of them simply as different forms of consciousness. . . . And to ask us to think of something which has all the characteristics of a wish or a feeling except that it is not conscious seems to me like asking us to think of something that has all the attributes of red or green except that it is not a colour.

Field and other participants in the symposium referred to "the New Psychology" in their discussions of the value of the concept of an unconscious mind for scientific psychology. From the context it was obvious they were identifying "the New Psychology" with Freud's psychology. However, there was no direct quotation from any of Freud's writings in the published accounts of the symposium. Instead, as in the cited excerpt from Field's account, Jones was quoted as a spokesman for Freud's psychology. In terms of the Jones quotation it was as if Freud had regarded man as equipped with two minds—one conscious and the other unconscious—and the latter mind was endowed with "all the attributes" of the former mind "except that the subject is not aware of them." This struck one of the symposium's speakers just as "preposterous" as if savages were to be described as being "cannibals in all respects except the act of devouring the flesh of the victims."

Whether Freud's understanding of the unconscious justified this kind of *reductio ad absurdum* is to be questioned. At all events, the brief Jones quotation failed to include several beliefs about the unconscious to which Freud had given expression from time to time. These beliefs rendered Freud's conception of the unconscious more complex than could be compressed within the succinct Jones formulation.

It is unfortunate that the symposium's discussion neglected to deal with Freud's own formulation of the subject. Had this taken place there would have been a more comprehensive analysis of the possible value for psychology of the meaning of unconscious mental processes as understood by Freud himself. What this issue entails is sufficiently important to merit separate consideration, apart from its possible retrospective bearing on this symposium of long ago.

CONCERNING FREUD'S UNDERSTANDING OF THE UNCONSCIOUS

In addition to his paper "The Unconscious" Freud had occasion to introduce incidental and less systematic references to the subject in his other papers and books. To find and collate all these references would call for a separate volume. Consequently, the present account will be much more modest in scope, limited to consideration of some salient but often overlooked attributes of the unconscious as described by Freud. Many of these were mentioned in previous chapters in the form of verbatim citations from Freud's writings.[9] These, along with a few others, will now be reviewed in summary fashion in preparation for their later reinterpretation.

As may be recalled, Freud was explicit in objecting to having the word *psychical* employed as a synonym for the word *conscious.* As he contended, because these two words have different meanings it is *not* "palpable nonsense" for the psychoanalyst to talk about "unconscious psychical processes." However, in elaborating upon this contention Freud neglected to specify in what precise respect or respects psychical differ from conscious processes. Stated differently, he failed to show what made the psychical a *mental* process even though, by hypothesis, it was divested of all attributes characteristic of conscious processes. The one mental attribute he ascribed to the unconscious had to do with thinking. He did this when he wrote that "a single analysis of a dream" will suffice to demonstrate "that the most complicated and most rational thought-processes, which can surely not be denied the name of psychical processes, can occur without exciting the subject's consciousness."

Note that Freud was implicitly appealing to the reader's knowledge of the nature of thinking in thus equating "rational thought-processes" with psychical ones. In doing so he was assigning what had been learned as a conscious experience as a characteristic of the unconscious. Similarly, a phrase like *unconscious wish* presupposes knowledge of wishing as a conscious experience. In other words, the descriptive vocabulary employed by Freud with reference to the unconscious is a derivative of the vocabulary of consciousness. There is no independent, underived nonconscious descriptive vocabulary. A chief reason for calling attention to this rather obvious point is that Freud would have objected to it, basing his objection on what he regarded as the error of deriving the unconscious from the conscious. For him the unconscious constituted "the true psychical reality" conceived of as vast enough to encompass the phenomena of consciousness. He deemed "everything conscious" to be the outcome of "an unconscious preliminary stage." In this connection he introduced the following italicized sentence in his *Interpretation of Dreams* (p. 613):

> The unconscious is the true psychical reality; *in its innermost nature it is as much unknown to us as the reality of the external world, and it is as incompletely presented by the data of consciousness as is the external world by the communications of our sense organs.*

In thus venturing to derive the conscious from the unconscious Freud appears to have disregarded the conventional maxim governing scientific explanations—that the known may explain the unknown and not vice versa.

---

[9]The sections in Chapter 4 concerned with Freud's interest in the unconscious contain the more immediately relevant verbatim citations.

In other words, in saying that the unconscious is "unknown to us" but at the same time making it the fountainhead of mind he was virtually accounting for knowledge by appealing to ignorance. This is one possible interpretation; but careful reading of the italicized sentence suggests a different one. The distinction between "data of consciousness" and ignorance of the "reality of the external world" suggests Kant's metaphysics and the distinction between phenomenal and noumenal worlds. Both in the *Traumdeutung* as well as in his later writings Freud revealed familiarity with Kant's philosophy. Thus, in different contexts Freud mentioned such characteristic Kantian concepts as the categorical imperative, the a priori, and the categories of understanding.

In terms of this Kantian perspective Freud made the unconscious "the true psychical reality" just as Kant had made the noumenal world or thing-in-itself the true physical reality. Furthermore, just as Kant had acknowledged our inability to get to know the noumenal world in its intrinsic nature so Freud acknowledged the inaccessibility of the "innermost nature" of the unconscious. The following sentence from "The Unconscious" (p. 171) will serve as a reminder of this Kantian influence on Freud's thinking:

> Just as Kant warned us not to overlook the fact that our perceptions are subjectively conditioned and must not be regarded as identical with what is perceived though unknowable, so psycho-analysis warns us not to equate perception by means of consciousness with the unconscious mental processes which are their object. Like the physical, the psychical is not necessarily in reality just what it appears to us to be.

Although, as just suggested, Freud seems to have had Kant's concept of phenomenal and noumenal realms in mind in his concept of a distinction to be made between conscious and unconscious mental activity, he did not make the unconscious the precise equivalent of the Kantian noumenon. The latter realm, as treated by Kant, was merely assumed to exist as the inaccessible antecedent of phenomenal events. Being inaccessible there was nothing more to be said about it. However, in the case of Freud's unconscious even though it too was deemed to be inaccessible in its "innermost nature" there was a great deal that Freud was able to say about it. This made it analogous to the noumenon only with respect to its "innermost nature" and not with reference to its more peripheral nature.

At all events, in different sections of "The Unconscious" Freud called attention to certain aspects or characteristics of the unconscious. For example, he endowed the kernel of the unconscious with "wish-impulses" and thus placed it under the sway of *primary processes* of instinct-gratification. It was also described as being divorced from identity with notions of past or future, so "timelessness" was another of its characteristics. Moreover, it was limited in its mental processes by inability to entertain negative attitudes, feelings of doubt, and gradations of personal conviction. As formulated by Freud, in the unconscious system there is "no negation, no dubiety, no varying degree of certainty." Furthermore, in his conceptualization of the conscious as contrasted with the unconscious system Freud refused to speculate about the "anatomical locations" of these systems. He was not willing to localize consciousness "in the cortex and to localize the unconscious processes in the subcortical parts of the brain." In his view it was not "one of the tasks of psychology" to settle such neurophysiological issues–his "mental topography" was not "concerned with anatomical locations, but with regions in the mental apparatus, irrespective of their possible situation in the body."

ON PROOF FOR "THE ASSUMPTION OF THE UNCONSCIOUS"

Freud made the unconscious an essential constituent of man's "mental apparatus." In doing so he recognized the need for proof or justification of what he called "the assumption of the unconscious." This was in his 1915 essay "The Unconscious"; years later, in his essay of 1938, he dealt with the same issue by referring to the "hypothesis" of the unconscious. In the 1915 essay he supplied what he regarded as proof for this hypothesis or assumption by writing as follows (p. 167):

> When . . . it turns out that the *assumption* of there being an unconscious enables us to construct a successful procedure by which we can exert an effective influence upon the course of conscious processes, this success will have given us an *incontrovertible proof* of the existence of what we have assumed. (Italics added.)

This is questionable proof. It is not the equivalent of confirmation of a scientific hypothesis by means of relevant controls, the quest for negative instances, and examination of alternative assumptions. In accordance with such a "proof" revivalists might claim "useful influence upon the course of the conscious processes" of "sinners" following prayer to God, but such influence would not constitute "incontrovertible proof of the existence" of God. Nor was the existence of phlogiston or of the luminiferous aether established by "the useful influence" of these concepts on the "conscious processes" of those who had entertained them as working hypotheses.

There is a possibility that Freud was not unmindful of the weakness of his alleged proof. This may be so because, as will be recalled, in his 1938 essay he found it "hard to say" whether the unconscious and a number of other hypotheses "should be regarded as postulates or as products of our researches." Nevertheless, despite such uncertainty, he was never in doubt about the actual existence of unconscious mental processes.

His conviction concerning the existence of the unconscious was already evident in his *Interpretation of Dreams.* In it he attributed different functions to conscious as contrasted with unconscious processes. In fact, he gave italicized expression to the difference. For example, on the one hand he noted that "*the most complicated achievements of thought are possible without the assistance of consciousness*" (p. 593). On the other hand, with reference to the question of the part "to be played in our scheme by consciousness" he offered this reply: "*Only that of a sense-organ for the perception of psychical qualities*" (p. 615). These two italicized conclusions involve an important distinction having important implications, some of which appear to have been overlooked by Freud. At least he failed to mention them.

It may be that no mention was made of them because they are not directly related to the subject of dream interpretation. Of course, the fact that Freud employed italics is indicative of the importance he attached to these conclusions, but this had to do with his need to justify belief in mental processes as unconscious. This is different from the importance of certain broad implications of these conclusions when viewed from the standpoint of systematic psychology. This is different also from the standpoint of psychoanalysis and may thus account for Freud's neglect of these implications. Furthermore, as will be brought out in the next chapter, one possible outcome of these implications is a rapprochement between what otherwise would be an irreconcilable conflict between academic psychology and psychoanalytic psychology with specific reference to the concept of unconscious thinking.

A CONCLUDING COMMENT

The present chapter was directly concerned with the many shifts in meaning of the word *unconscious.* Many of these shifts have nothing to do with *the* unconscious conceived of as an autonomous mental agency or unconscious mind in the sense of an independent entity over which its possessor has no control. Thus, there is no question of an unconscious mind being involved when a daydreaming schoolboy is unconscious of his teacher's explanation of the difference between a participle and a gerund. Nor was there a question of activation of an unconscious mind in Razran's report of the Russian studies of "the observable unconscious." However, there was such a question with respect to Freud's "assumption of the unconscious." In fact, in his book of 1938 (p. 377) he had referred to this assumption as one among several "hazardous hypotheses." As indicated in the present chapter, this hypothesis has not yet received experimental confirmation. It continues to be a *postulate* in the sense in which Freud stated by writing that he had difficulty deciding whether this and some other hypotheses "should be regarded as postulates or as products of our researches."

In reality, Freud does not appear to have entertained serious question about the validity of this postulate. For him the lack of experimental confirmation was not disturbing. He evidently found certain clinical observations along with his dream interpretations sufficiently reassuring so that mind as unconscious became more conviction than hypothesis. Thus for him the unconscious mind was fact and not fiction. When it was conceived of as hitherto unknown psychological territory, he came to be thought of as the *discoverer* of the unconscious and his written reports came to be regarded as a discoverer's accounts of explorations of new territory. Moreover, in the course of writing the *Traumdeutung* during the 1890s he was already writing as this kind of discoverer. In other words, the postulate or conviction of mind as unconscious was already his at the start of his professional career. This was definitely reflected in the two italicized sentences toward the end of the *Traumdeutung* as just quoted at the close of the previous section. Their implications are important enough to be elaborated upon in the next chapter.

REFERENCES

Adler, A. 1916. *The Neurotic Constitution–Outlines of a Comparative Individualistic Psychology and Psychotherapy.* Translated by Bernard Glueck and John E. Lind. New York: Moffat, Yard and Company.

Boring, E. G. 1963. *The Physical Dimensions of Consciousness.* New York: Dover Publications, Inc. (First published in 1933.)

Brody, B. 1969. "The Denial of the Unconscious: A Great Leap Backward." *International Journal of Psychiatry* 8: 590–595.

Eysenck, H. J., and Wilson, G. D. 1973. *The Experimental Study of Freudian Theories.* London: Methuen & Co., Ltd.

Field, G. C. 1922. "Is the Conception of the Unconscious of Value in Psychology?" *Mind* 31: 414–423.

Fine, R. 1973. *The Development of Freud's Thought.* New York: Jason Aronson, Inc.

Freud, S. *The Interpretation of Dreams.* Translated by James Strachey. New York: Basic Books, Inc.

——. 1915. "The Unconscious." In *The Standard Edition of the Complete Psychological Works of Sigmund Freud,* translated by James Strachey, Vol. XIV, pp. 159-215. London: The Hogarth Press.

——. 1918. "From the History of an Infantile Neurosis." In *The Standard Edition of Sigmund Freud,* Vol. XVII, pp. 7-122. London: The Hogarth Press.

——. 1938. *A General Introduction to Psychoanalysis.* Translated by Joan Riviere. New York: Garden City Publishing Company, Inc.

——. 1938. "Some Elementary Lessons in Psycho-Analysis." In *The Standard Edition of Sigmund Freud,* Vol. XXIII, pp. 279-286. London: The Hogarth Press.

——. 1946. "Mitteilung Eines der Psychoanalytischen Theorie Widersprechenden Falles von Paranoia." *Gesammelte Werke,* Vol. X. S. Fischer Verlag.

——. 1957. "A Case of Paranoia Running Counter to the Psycho-Analytic Theory of the Disease." In *The Standard Edition of Sigmund Freud,* Vol. XIV, pp. 263–272. London: The Hogarth Press.

Hilgard, E. R. 1956. *Theories of Learning,* 2nd Edition. New York: Appleton-Century-Crofts, Inc.

Jones, E. 1953, 1957. *The Life and Work of Sigmund Freud,* Vol. I and Vol. III (respectively). New York: Basic Books, Inc.

Jung, C. G. 1953. "On Psychical Energy." In *Collected Works,* Vol. VIII. New York: Pantheon Press.

——. 1964. *Man and His Symbols.* Garden City, New York: Doubleday & Company, Inc.

Miller, J. G. 1942. *Unconsciousness.* New York: John Wiley & Sons, Inc.

Osgood, C. E. 1953. *Method and Theory in Experimental Psychology.* New York: Oxford University Press.

Rabkin, R. 1969. "Is the Unconscious Necessary?" *International Journal of Psychiatry* 8: 570–578.

Razran, G. 1961. "The Observable Unconscious and the Inferable Conscious in Current Soviet Psychophysiology: Interoceptive Conditioning, Semantic Conditioning, and the Orienting Reflex." *Psychological Review* 68: 81-147.

Salmon, W. C. 1973. "Confirmation." *Scientific American* 228: 75–83.

Sarnoff, I. 1971. *Testing Freudian Concepts–An Experimental Social Approach.* New York: Springer Publishing Company, Inc.

Schwartz, G. E. 1973. "Biofeedback as Therapy–Some Theoretical and Practical Issues." *American Psychologist* 28: 666–673.

Sears, R. R. 1944. "Experimental Analysis of Psychoanalytic Phenomena." In *Personality and the Behavior Disorders,* Vol. I, edited by J. McV. Hunt, pp. 306–332. New York: The Ronald Press Company.

Sewell, J. R. 1952. "Infant Training and the Personality of the Child." *American Journal of Sociology* 58: 150–159.

Shands, H. C. 1968. "Psychoanalysis and the Twentieth-Century Revolution in Communication." In *Modern Psychoanalysis–New Directions and Perspectives,* edited by Judd Marmor, pp. 82–113. New York: Basic Books, Inc.

7

The Unconscious as Implicit Non-Sensory Ideation

As may be recalled, in the last section of *The Interpretation of Dreams* (pp. 610-621) Freud wrote about the clash between academic and medical psychology with specific reference to the concept of "unconscious psychical processes." He did this by contrasting the opposition to such a concept on the part of "professors" with ready endorsement on the part of "physicians" familiar with the nature of "abnormal mental states." In his view a concept dismissed as "palpable nonsense" by the professors was welcomed as "a solidly established fact" by the physicians. Under the circumstances, Freud added, "the physician can only shrug his shoulders" upon being reminded that "consciousness is an indispensable characteristic of what is psychical." By implication, the physician in question was Freud himself, for in this connection he also added that analysis of a single dream suffices to show that complicated thinking "can occur without exciting the subject's consciousness."

Since the *Traumdeutung* was published in 1899, the foregoing final section of the book must have been written late in that decade.[1] Accordingly, Freud's reference to "professors" as being antagonistic to the medical view of the unconscious had to do with views expressed before the 1890s. Actually, he failed to name any of the professors, nor did he name any of the endorsing physicians. Furthermore, since the book had not yet been published, the professors could not have been objecting to Freud's distinctive concept of the

---

[1]According to Jones (Vol. I, p. 351), Freud himself had once written: *"The Interpretation of Dreams* . . . was finished in all essentials at the beginning of 1896 but was not written down until the summer of 1899."

unconscious as reflected in the light of dream interpretation. In other words, Freud appears to have been dealing with *anticipated* objections to the unconscious by those who made consciousness an indispensable criterion of mind. If so, then he was dealing with imaginary rather than actual professors; hence his failure to list any of them by name. This is one possible interpretation. An alternative interpretation would be that Freud had reference to writings of professors who had registered opposition to belief in unconscious mental processes. In terms of this alternative the opposition would have been directed at the pre-Freudian unconscious. A third possibility might be that Freud was thinking both of published objections to the doctrine of the unconscious sponsored by his predecessors as well of anticipated objections to his own version of the doctrine. There is no assured way of deciding among these three possibilities. It is well to suspend judgment with respect to this issue and to rest content with the assured fact of Freud's role as ardent defender of belief in mind as unconscious. In the idiom of psychoanalysis, professorial questioning of that belief had aroused his resistance.

PRE-FREUDIAN OBJECTIONS TO THE UNCONSCIOUS

It is important to note that such questioning had taken place in the pre-Freudian era. The pros and cons of belief in mind as unconscious had been debated by scholars long before Freud had become its champion; taken in the abstract, evaluation of the belief as a technical scientific issue had thus arisen independently of Freud. As already mentioned in Chapter 4, in the generation before Freud there had been opposition to the belief by both professors and physicians. By way of reminder, among professors it will be enough to recall Wilhelm Wundt (1832–1920) of the University of Leipzig and William James (1842–1910) of Harvard University. And among physicians it will suffice to recall Hughlings Jackson (1835-1911) who had called attention to the contradiction involved in the concept of "unconscious states of mind" and Henry Maudsley (1835-1918) who had voiced his objection to the latter concept by writing about the *physiology* rather than the *psychology* of mind.[2] For Maudsley, mental diseases were conceived of as brain diseases. Incidentally, both Jackson and Maudsley had dealt with "abnormal mental states" in the course of their routine clinical experience as physicians. Quite manifestly Freud was not thinking of them when he suggested that physicians with such experience, unlike the professors, would have been ready to endorse the concept of "unconscious psychical processes."

---

[2]This merits explicit mention because, as noted in Chapter 4, Freud had once been misled into regarding Maudsley as one who had recognized the importance of the unconscious. Similarly, Whyte also appears to have misunderstood Maudsley, for he lists him among those who dealt with the influence of unconscious mental factors in pre-Freudian days. He even quotes Maudsley as the author of this sentence: "The most important part of mental action, the essential process on which thinking depends, is unconscious mental activity" (Whyte, 1960, p. 162).

Thus it is evident that even before Freud had appeared on the scientific scene *both* professors and physicians were to be found among critics of the unconscious. Of course, this was the pre-Freudian unconscious. Whether they would have been just as opposed to the Freudian unconscious is a separate question, the answer to which might give rise to endless and possibly fruitless speculation.

Instead of indulging in such speculation it will be more fruitful to revert to consideration of the Freudian unconscious in terms of the two key sentences Freud had introduced toward the end of his *Interpretation of Dreams* and which are quoted at the close of the previous chapter. Their importance for Freud is indicated by the fact that he had them printed in italics. It was his way of calling attention to what he regarded as a chief difference between consciousness on the one hand and the unconscious on the other. In the case of the unconscious, as shown in the following passage, he noted that thoughts incident to the occurrence of a dream need not have *originated* while the dreamer was asleep (p. 393):

> On the contrary, these thoughts may very well have originated from the previous day, they may have proceeded unobserved by our consciousness from their start, and may already have been completed at the onset of sleep. The most that we can conclude from this is that it proves that *the most complicated achievements of thought are possible without the assistance of consciousness*—a fact which we could not fail to learn in any case from every psycho-analysis of a patient suffering from hysteria or from obsessional ideas.

The italicized words thus reveal the unconscious to be an organ of thought. Then, by way of contrast, on a later page Freud raised the question of the function of consciousness in the psychoanalytic scheme of psychology. His question and answer took this form (p. 615):

> But what part is there left to be played in our scheme by consciousness, which was once so omnipotent and hid all else from view? *Only that of a sense-organ for the perception of psychical qualities.*

According to the two italicized passages, the unconscious stands revealed as the organ of thought and consciousness stands revealed as the organ of sensation and perception. The division of labor suggested by this differentiation or distinction has rather widespread systematic implications Freud either failed to notice or disregarded; but they are too important to be overlooked. Freud, either wittingly or unwittingly, had introduced an important distinction.

AN IMPORTANT DISTINCTION

Actually, the distinction in question was already alluded to in Chapter 4 in connection with this Kantian maxim: "The understanding cannot see. The senses cannot think. Only by their union can knowledge be produced." As a result, one might say that it was in accordance with this maxim that Freud had allocated thinking to one division of mind and sensation to a second division. Having attributed sensation and perception to the *conscious* division he, in effect, then attributed thinking and reasoning to a *nonconscious* division; hence, the two Freudian mental realms of conscious and unconscious.

Recognition of a duality of mental functions was not unique either to Kant or to Freud. It was already evident to Aristotle.[3] Among man's "psychic powers" he mentioned the "sensory" and "the power of thinking" with the former shared by man and animals and the latter as the "rational soul" being unique to man. Incidentally, Freud's distinction between perceiving and thinking had already been made by Aristotle in the following passage from the *De Anima* in which he had this to say about "opining" or thinking (McKeon ed., p. 176):

> We have no evidence as yet about mind or the power to think; it seems to be a widely different kind of soul, . . . it alone is capable of existence in isolation from all the other psychic powers. All the other parts of the soul . . . are . . . incapable of separate existence though, of course, distinguishable by definition. If opining is distinct from perceiving, to be capable of opining and to be capable of perceiving must be distinct.

Aristotle's distinction between these two mental functions was known to and elaborated upon by John Locke (1632–1704) in his famous *Essay Concerning Human Understanding.* His main purpose in writing the essay was to account for the origin of our ideas and he defined *idea* (p. 16) as "whatever is the *object* of the understanding when a man thinks." Without defining thinking he made it a constituent of the process of *reflection* as defined in the course of presenting his basic thesis to the effect that *all our ideas originate from sensation or reflection.* He first explained sensation to be the fountain of "ideas we have of yellow, white, heat, cold, soft, hard, bitter, sweet, and all those which we call sensible qualities." Then, by way of explaining the nature of reflection, he wrote (pp. 18–19):

> Secondly, the other fountain, from which experience furnisheth the understanding with ideas, is the perception of the operations of our own mind, within us, as it is employed about the ideas it has got; which operations when the soul comes to reflect on and consider, do furnish the understanding with another set of ideas which could not be had from things without; and such are perception, thinking, doubting, believing, reasoning, knowing, willing, and all the different actings of our own minds, which we, being conscious of, and observing in our-

---

[3]Freud was not unfamiliar with Aristotle. He had occasion to be introduced to Aristotle's thought in his student days when enrolled in Brentano's courses, since Brentano was deeply immersed in Aristotle as brought out at the close of Chapter 5. As there indicated, Aristotle had anticipated Freud in stressing the place of appetite and *wishing* in the dynamics of mental life. Freud's familiarity with Aristotle is also suggested by some explicit references to Aristotle in the *Traumdeutung.*

> selves, do from these receive into our understanding as distinct ideas, as we do from bodies affecting our senses. This source of ideas every man has wholly in himself; and though it be not sense as having nothing to do with external objects, yet it is very like it, and might properly be called *internal sense.* But as I call the other *sensation,* so I call this *reflection,* the ideas it affords being such only as the mind gets by reflecting on its own operations within itself.

Reduced to bare essentials, Locke made knowledge or human understanding a result of the conjoint operation of sensation and reflection. Kant's later formula also reduced the acquisition of knowledge to a conjoint operation of a somewhat different sort with the difference having to do with the question of the origin of man's intellect or understanding. Locke appears to have based his disposition of the question upon a sentence in Aristotle's *De Anima* reading (McKeon ed., p. 225): "No one can learn or understand anything in the absence of sense." This makes both knowledge and understanding a function of sensation. The Latin equivalent of this formulation as known to and endorsed by medieval scholars became this famous text: *Nihil est in intellectu, quod non prius fuerit in sensu,* meaning, "There is nothing in the intellect that had not first involved the sensorium." As understood by Locke this made mind or understanding a product of sensory experience and made Locke a champion of *empiricism* in the history of psychology. In opposition to this stand, the philosopher Leibnitz (1646–1716) modified the Latin text by appending the phrase *nisi intellectus ipse* so that the translation now reads, "There is nothing in the intellect that had not first involved the sensorium, *except the intellect itself.*" This made Leibnitz a champion of *rationalism* in the history of psychology.

It thus became evident that Locke's empiricism was not altogether devoid of rationalistic factors. His concept of reflection involving, in his words, "the operations of our own minds" implied the prior existence of mind or intellect to be affected by sensory experience. Intellect was affected by but not produced by experience. This was made explicit in Kant's maxim when modified to read: "The understanding or intellect cannot see and the senses cannot think." Kant's famous categories of understanding were not products of experience but ways of dealing with experience. His rationalism was thus not altogether devoid of empiristic factors. In other words, the Lockean and Kantian views regarding the acquisition of knowledge did not constitute radically antithetic or irreconcilable orientations. In broad perspective their views were more alike than different.

In terms of this broad perspective Freud might appear to have been following this philosophic precedent when he contrasted the effects of sensory stimulation with the "achievements of thought." As had Aristotle, Locke, and Kant he was calling attention to a duality of cognitive functions, namely, those having to do with sensation and those involved in thinking. However, he differed from these three philosophic predecessors by making thinking an unconscious function. Had they known about this difference, they might not have known what to make of it; to relegate thinking and reasoning to an unconscious realm was altogether alien to their conceptual outlook. In their perplexity they might even have asked whether he was relegating intellect and understanding to the unconscious.

CONCERNING THE "VOICE OF THE INTELLECT"

This brings up an issue already considered in Chapter 4 in connection with discussion of Freud's recognition of what he had called "the primacy of the intellect." In reply to those who had come to think of psychoanalytic psychology as an anti-intellectualistic instinct psychology he had this to say (1934, p. 93):

> We may insist as much as we like that the human intellect is weak in comparison with human instincts and be right in doing so. But, nevertheless, there is something peculiar about this weakness. The voice of the intellect is a soft one, but it does not rest until it has gained a hearing. Ultimately, after endlessly repeated rebuffs, it succeeds.

Recall that this quotation was written some thirty years after Freud had introduced his distinction between the contrasting functions of conscious and unconscious processes. Consequently, he may have overlooked the need to reconcile what he was writing in the 1930s with what he had written in the 1890s. At all events, when "the voice of the intellect" succeeds in gaining a hearing the cognitive experience in question is not an unconscious happening, but a conscious process.

Such a conscious process is experienced by the neurotic patient as *insight* or recognition of irrational, maladaptive impulses and the need to bring them under control by intelligent planning. Resolution of his neurotic conflict is thus contingent upon the acquisition of insight; hence the success of his psychoanalysis depends upon this acquisition. To paraphrase Freud: with each moment of insight there is concomitant arousal of intellect's soft voice so that eventually after many such moments its call will be heeded.

If viewed as the culmination of successful analysis, insight appears as the equivalent of an *"Aha" experience.* This is the experience of sudden intellectual illumination taking place when, after persistent effortful thought, there is sudden understanding of and resolution of a felt difficulty. It is the kind of experience associated with Archimedes and his triumphant *"Eureka!"* His cry of triumph meant that he had insight into his problem; as an "Aha" experience he knew that he knew the solution. This made his moment of insight a conscious experience. Accordingly, Freud's notion of insight as implicit in "the primacy of intellect" amounts to recognition of thinking as a conscious process. This, as previously indicated, is at variance with his earlier teaching to the effect that sensation is a conscious process whereas thinking per se is a function of the unconscious.

Freud does not seem to have noted any inconsistency in his two views of thinking. When he was writing about the primacy of the intellect he could view thinking as a conscious process and be unmindful of what he had written some thirty years before about the role of consciousness as that of a sense organ and about thinking as an unconscious process. Moreover, he had never declared thinking to be an *exclusively* unconscious process. He had merely contended that "the most complicated achievements of thought are possible without the assistance of consciousness." The inconsistency may be more paradoxical than contradictory. This calls for examination of what might be meant by the concept of unconscious thought.

THE PARADOX OF UNCONSCIOUS THOUGHT

In developing his concept of the unconscious, it will be recalled, Freud had asked what justifies belief in the unconscious as being *psychical.* He found the answer by attributing capacity to think to what he had come to call the unconscious. This answer was worded in various ways in Freud's different writings. A particularly definite formulation was this previously quoted one from the *Traumdeutung:* "The most complicated achievements of thought are possible without the assistance of consciousness." In effect, when it came to thinking as a distinctive process, the unconscious was played up and consciousness was played down. Moreover, by limiting the function of consciousness to that of "a sense-organ for the perception of psychical qualities" this contrast was made more drastic and definite. It amounted to making consciousness responsible for sensation and the unconscious responsible for thought, and when expressed in this way it made for a rather striking dichotomy.

By means of this dichotomy Freud hoped to dispose of those critics of psychoanalysis among the "philosophers" who deemed the concept of unconscious mind to be absurd. According to them, consciousness is the *sine qua non* of mind, so Freud's concept became the equivalent of belief in unconscious consciousness. Such a belief, so they indicated, is as self-contradictory and absurd as belief in illegible legibility or finite infinity. However, by making thought and not consciousness the *sine qua non* of mind Freud tried to meet the philosophers' challenge. In terms of his dichotomy the concept of mind as unconscious was no longer the same as the self-contradictory concept of unconscious consciousness. At least so Freud seemed to argue.

Freud's argument was a *tour de force* to justify belief in the reality of unconscious thought. As previously quoted, this made the unconscious the "true psychical reality." Furthermore, since he had equated the psychical with thought and not with consciousness, this meant that consciousness could not be the "true psychical reality." In arguing this way he wrote as if he expected all readers to understand the meaning of the words *thought* and *consciousness.* No formal definitions of the words or illustrative explanations were introduced; their meaning was assumed to be self-evident and hence *conscious.* Under the circumstances these meanings were not being regarded as derivatives of the unconscious. They were conscious in their own right and as such illustrated this previous observation: had Freud never been conscious of thinking, he could never have entertained the notion of unconscious thought, just as his idea of an unconscious wish was contingent upon prior acquaintance with conscious wishes.

The priority of the conscious to whatever is ascribed to the unconscious seems so obvious that it is hard to believe it had eluded Freud's psychological probing. Still the fact remains that he never called attention to it. This is puzzling. In other words, how could he argue that conscious thinking is a derivative of unconscious thinking even though in doing so he was obliged to employ descriptive vocabulary stemming from conscious thinking? How is this seeming oversight to be explained?

It may be that what, in retrospect, appears to have been an oversight was not an oversight at all. Unless the question of the priority of consciousness comes up for consideration, there would be little need to be concerned about the source of descriptive vocabulary employed in discussing presumed psychological processes. To understand Freud's neglect of this question it is advisable to recall his interpretation of the concept of consciousness. By restricting it to data ordinarily classified as sensations and perceptions he, in effect, was excluding all psychological data not so classifiable. Having called the sense-organ data *conscious* he then called all other data *unconscious.* Taken literally the latter word was thus a designation for non-sensory events deemed to be "psychic" or mental. However, the word *unconscious* is also used to designate events of whose existence one is unaware. This makes them unknown or unobservable events. In terms of the latter designation Freud equated the non-sensory "psychic" events with concealed or unknowable events. Moreover, as already mentioned, since for Freud the word *psychic* in this context had to do with the process of thinking, the non-sensory events were taken to be unconscious thoughts.

Actually, Freud did not employ the word *non-sensory* in his discussions of the unconscious. We have introduced it for expository purposes in order to highlight Freud's contrast between conscious sensations and unconscious thoughts. Although he recognized the former as sensory, he failed to describe the latter as non-sensory. Instead he described them as unconscious as if they were not amenable to direct observation. In brief, he treated them as *unknowable* even though the concept of non-sensory data, considered in the abstract, does not mean *unknowable.* This should be evident once it is realized that the contrast between sensory and non-sensory data is another way of referring to the venerable philosophical contrast between the data of sensation and those of thinking. By way of reminder, this contrast was already implicit in Aristotle's distinction between sentience and "the power of thinking," as well as in Locke's sensation-reflection antithesis and in Kant's recognition of a difference between the non-sensory "understanding" and the noncognitive "senses." As reflected in this philosophical tradition, terms pertaining to thinking, to reflection, and to understanding had to do with Aristotle's "opining" as a knowable experience and not as an unobservable or unconscious process. This means that upholders of the tradition would have been mystified by Freud's notion of unconscious thought.

As a matter of fact, neither they nor Freud had studied the psychology of thinking by obtaining reports of thought processes as experienced by different thinkers under controlled laboratory conditions. As will be explained on a later page, this was not done until the early decades of the present century under the aegis of Oswald Külpe (1862-1915) of the University of Würzburg. As briefly noted in Chapter 3 when dealing with mental sets, he and his students reported discovery of a difference between two kinds of thoughts: (1) those characterized by conventional conscious content in the form of sensations and images and (2) those devoid of such content and hence called *imageless* thoughts. This raises a possible alternative to the paradox of unconscious thoughts. In other words, are unconscious thoughts the same as imageless thoughts? This is a provocative question. Viewed in historical perspective it may shed light on Freud's attitude toward academic psychology. Consequently, before dealing with it this attitude merits a few words by way of introduction to the broader implications of the question.

FREUD'S VIEW OF ACADEMIC PSYCHOLOGY

If what Freud had called unconscious thoughts can be shown to be the equivalent of what academic psychologists had called imageless thoughts and had Freud realized this, it might have enabled him to glimpse a possible rapprochement between psychoanalysis and psychology. Actually, this never took place. As a matter of fact, even as early as the 1890s he viewed his espousal of the unconscious to be a challenge to psychology's espousal of the conscious. Moreover, despite his warm reception at the 1909 Clark University celebration, he continued to entertain this view. For example, as late as 1933 he dealt with this issue in a letter to the head of a university in connection with the question of providing for instruction in psychoanalysis at the university. Evidently, the university head had believed such instruction should be postponed until after provision had been made for the teaching of psychology. To this suggestion Freud had replied as follows (E. L. Freud ed., p. 414):

> The view that it is premature to create a chair for psychoanalysis so long as none for psychology exists invites a discussion of the relationship between the two sciences. My opinion is as follows: psychoanalysis is also psychology in the sense that it is a science of the *unconscious* psychic processes, whereas what is taught as academic psychology is confined to dealing with *conscious* phenomena. There need be no contradiction between the two; psychoanalysis could be presented as an introduction to psychology; in reality, however, the contradiction is produced by the fact that the academic circles don't want to have anything to do with psychoanalysis.

It is to be noted that Freud referred to psychoanalysis as "a psychology" and not as a branch of medicine. As a psychology, in contradistinction to academic psychology, it was described as being concerned with unconscious *psychic* processes. In this connection it is also to be noted that the word *psychic* was not used with reference to the teachings of academic psychology. These were described as being limited to phenomena of consciousness. Failure to designate the latter phenomena as psychic or mental was probably not an oversight. It reflected the same point he had raised more than thirty years earlier in the *Traumdeutung* in his answer to those who had deemed it absurd to believe in unconscious thought on the ground that it was the same as believing in unconscious consciousness.

His answer, as previously explained, took the form of restricting consciousness to sensory processes and thus reserving the allegedly distinctive *psychical* processes of thinking to the non-sensory unconscious. By implication, his letter of 1933 showed his disappointment in what he regarded as academic psychology's neglect of or indifference to this kind of defense for his belief in unconscious psychical processes. His disappointment might have been less acute had his attention been called to the concept of imageless thinking as developed by some psychologists in the preceding decades. At least he might have regarded the concept as possibly giving promise of recognition by academic psychology of his contention to the effect that thinking may be independent of sensory consciousness. Furthermore, he might also have been heartened by learning that the concept included acknowledgment of the existence of cognitive processes whose nature and influence may elude the thinker's observation. In terms of one meaning of the word *unconscious* these would be unconscious cognitive processes. At all events, had Freud known about them, he might have been less despairing of the promise of academic psychology. As previously suggested, he might have perceived a relationship between unconscious thinking and imageless thinking and thus between psychoanalytic and academic psychology.

UNCONSCIOUS THINKING AS IMAGELESS THINKING

Taken in the abstract the meaning of the psychoanalytic concept of unconscious thinking is not immediately obvious. The same statement applies to the psychological concept of imageless thinking. Consequently, before considering their possible relationship to one another it will be necessary to review and elaborate upon what has already been said about each of these concepts on previous pages. As a matter of expository convenience the topic of imageless thinking will be taken up first.

Although the concept of imageless thought was introduced shortly after the turn of the century at Würzburg in Germany, it soon won the endorsement of psychologists in other countries, including Binet in France and Woodworth in the United States. All those concerned with the concept were ready to grant that thinking is often, if not usually, characterized by symbolic expression in the forms of words, gestures, diagrams, and images belonging to any sense modality. Thus, they were not questioning the occurrence and relevance of such a direct relationship between thinking and conscious content, but rather the need for activation of conscious content in *all* instances of thinking. In figurative language, they were contending that not all thoughts had to be dressed in the garb of mental images. Some could be experienced as naked thoughts. In this sense they were *imageless* or devoid of any conscious content; hence, they might conceivably be described as unconscious thoughts. This would be consistent with one of the many meanings of the word *unconscious*. The degree to which this interpretation approximates Freud's concept of unconscious thinking is a separate question to be considered later.

To avoid misunderstanding it is advisable to realize that the term *imageless* was not used in a restricted sense. It was not limited to visual images, but was extended to include *all* modes of imagery so that in the context of the Würzburg teachings the word *imageless* meant absence of tactual, auditory, olfactory, visual, thermal, and other kinds of images. As a matter of fact, the German originators of these teachings never referred to imageless *thinking*. Instead they referred to *unanschauliches Denken,* meaning thinking that does not lend itself to direct observation or inspection. There is no precise English equivalent for the adjective *unanschaulich* just as there is no precise German equivalent for the English word *imageless*. The latter word came to be used as the closest approximation to the meaning of the German original word. Similarly, the French alluded to imageless thinking as *pensee sans images*. Moreover, since the underlying meaning had to do with thinking that is independent of sensory content, Woodworth suggested *non-sensory thinking* as a more accurate descriptive phrase. This was a clarifying suggestion. Accordingly, in reading works concerned with the Würzburg doctrine of imageless thought one would be well advised to regard the word *imageless* as meaning non-sensory or non-sensuous. There is no reason to avoid using the term *imageless* provided it is interpreted in accordance with Woodworth's suggestion. In fact, Woodworth employed both terms in discussing the work of the Würzburg psychologists.

WOODWORTH'S CONCEPT OF IMAGELESS THOUGHT

Woodworth and other students of imageless thinking based their reports on observations of their own thinking and also, and more commonly and more systematically, on data supplied by observations of their experimental subjects. These were either colleagues or graduate students with special training in this kind of self-observation. Representative instances of such reports of non-sensory thinking are to be found in the following excerpts from Woodworth's article "Imageless Thought" (1939, pp. 75–76):

> A few instances may be cited. First, one from a subject who usually . . . reports visual or verbal imagery at moments of effective thinking. To the question, What substances are more costly than gold? she answered promptly, 'Diamonds,' and reported as follows: 'I had no visual image of the diamond; the thought of diamonds was there before the sound of the word.'
>
> The following instances are from my own introspection. I introduce them for two reasons; because of my meager imagery and because, since becoming interested in the problem, I have sought to catch myself at the moments of most effective thought, and have succeeded a number of times, with always the same result—clear consciousness of a particular thought, and no images.
>
> I quote from my notes made at the time: 'While reading, I heard some one playing on the piano a piece which I felt at once to be familiar, but which I did not at first identify. My first attempt at identification was felt to be wrong, and immediately afterward I identified it properly and with confidence. . . . Resting satisfied with my identification, I was about to turn to other things, when it occurred to me to ask whether, in identifying the piece, I had had its name present in the form of verbal imagery, and I found that I certainly had not; in fact, it required a moment's further thought to recall the sound of the composer's name and the name of the piece. . . . I regard the example as a good one, since the thought was perfectly overt, conscious, and definite, though it not only began but was completed without any image.'

Woodworth introduced other specific instances of such imageless thinking and then arrived at this conclusion (p. 77):

> It seems impossible to describe these facts without admitting the existence of other than sensorial contents of consciousness. *I would suggest that in addition to sensorial elements, thought contains elements which are wholly irreducible to sensory terms* [italics added]. Each such element is *sui generis,* being nothing else than the particular feeling of the thought in question. Each is a quality, as red and sweet are qualities; not syntheses of sensory qualities, but simply and purely the qualities of particular thoughts. They are not to be elevated, as "activities," into another dimension of existence; they lie in the plane of content. There is a specific and unanalyzable conscious quale for every individual and general notion, for every judgment and supposition.

BÜHLER ON "WHAT IS THINKING?"

A year after publication of the foregoing Woodworth article Karl Bühler (1879-1963), an active member of the Würzburg group, published the first of a series of reports of his investigations of thinking as a psychological process. Fortunately, David Rapaport[4] has supplied a translation of a portion of

---

[4]Rapaport's text entitled *Organization and Pathology of Thought* contains translations and notes on the work of two members of the Würzburg group, namely, Narciss Ach and

this first of Bühler's reports entitled "On Thought Connections." As Woodworth had, so Bühler confronted his subjects with questions calculated to provoke thought with the request that they be prepared to report on the way answers to the questions came to them. The time required for arousal of each answer was duly noted along with a verbatim account of the answer itself. Bühler then followed this by questioning the subject concerning specific details of the reported cognitive experience. Such detailed questioning of introspective reports, as introduced by Bühler, came to be known as the *Ausfragemethode.* As a question-answer type of probing it once reminded Boring of the verbal interchange between psychoanalyst and patient (1950, p. 406). For Bühler, the procedure was for the purpose of getting an answer to this question: "What are the constituents of the experience of thinking?" In fact, all those concerned with the Würzburg studies were dealing with this question or a variant of it. In essence, they were asking, "What takes place when we have a thought?"[5] In this connection Bühler noted (Rapaport, p. 39):

> There is probably no other specific scientific question to which so many different answers are given as, What is thinking? Thinking is connecting; thinking is analyzing; thinking is judging; thinking is apperceiving; the essence of thinking is abstraction; thinking is relating; thinking is activity—a voluntary process.

This list is by no means exhaustive. Roget's *Thesaurus* lists more than thirty designations for the verb *to think.* Furthermore, some psychologists have described thinking in a way that fails to be included in any list. Watson, for example, as may be recalled, described thinking as a laryngeal mechanism in the form of subvocal speech. And H. L. Hollingworth (1880–1957), to cite another example, identified thinking with the process of *redintegration,* in

---

Karl Bühler. These translations are the only English accounts of Ach's studies of determining tendencies as well as of non-sensory "awareness" (Ch. 1) and of Bühler's studies of thinking (Ch. 2).

[5]It is unfortunate that this basic question has so frequently been taken to mean that they were solely interested in the possible occurrence of thoughts without images. Their work is then dismissed as relatively inconsequential. Not many years ago, for example, in the book *The Psychology of Consciousness,* in discussing the "limitations" of introspection the author introduced this disparaging comment (Ornstein, 1972, pp. 4–5):

> This and other limitations soon led to a sterility in the contents of psychology. Controversies of only academic import (in the worst sense of the term) arose, due to the limitations placed on inquiry. One, for instance, concerned whether "thoughts without images" could or could not occur. The concerns of psychologists drifted further and further away from the original ones.

A comment like this fails to indicate that the imageless thought question was subordinate to the broader question of the nature of the thought process as such. As a result there is complete neglect of significant findings reported by the Würzburg psychologists, such as the directive influence of mental sets or *Aufgaben,* the control exercised by determining tendencies, the phenomenon of the Aha experience, and the varied concomitants of thinking in the form of *Bewusstseinslagen* or "conscious attitudes." All such findings, as manifest in the consciousness of the thinker, merit consideration in a volume having to do with the psychology of consciousness.

which any part or fragment of a previous experience may substitute for or symbolize the antecedent experience so that thoughts can be defined as "events of any sort whatsoever that function for larger antecedent contexts" (1926, p. 208).

Having recognized the large number of psychological factors subsumed under the concept of thinking, Bühler did not venture to bring all of them within the scope of a single comprehensive definition, as if he realized the difficulty of reducing the complexity of the thought process and its concomitants to a formal definition. He was especially concerned with the concomitants of thinking both because of their importance and because their nature had often been overlooked. These had been called *Bewusstseinslagen* or *conscious attitudes* by some of his Würzburg colleagues and what they meant by these attitudes was brought out by Bühler in the following account of their directive influence on thinking as a *psychological* and not just a logical process (1951, pp. 39-40):

> Besides thoughts, yet other knowledge is present in our thinking. For instance, we know whether or not we are on the right track; whether or not we are approaching our goal; whether the thought occurs to us for the first time or derives from our memory; we may know even where we have picked it up; we know how it is related to the one preceding. This knowledge only rarely becomes an independent psychic act; we do not specifically focus on its content. It lies, so to say, in between thoughts. Subjects will actually report: 'In the meanwhile I was also aware of this and that.'

Non-sensory thinking as viewed by Bühler is illustrated by these verbatim excerpts from his laboratory protocols (pp. 41, 51, 49):

> 1. (Do you understand?) "We depreciate everything that can be explained."—Yes (5 sec.)—"Immediately upon hearing it, I thought of a fanatical realist. Then I thought of certain esthetics and immediately said, 'Yes.' It would be difficult to reproduce the thought exactly. . . . The connection of these thoughts to the task was clearly conscious. . . . It is marvelous, *how we can know something without actually thinking it; I mean that there are in our knowledge conscious relationships which have no objects of their own.*"
>
> 2. (Do you understand?) "Where is an ocean one still can drown in?—that is the slogan of our times"—Yes (11 sec.)—"First, reverberation of the words, then a pause. Then a thought emerged linked to the internally spoken word 'depth'; something, a great powerful idea to which one can give one's whole soul, and with that I understood it (the words are explications of originally wordless thoughts.)"
>
> 3. (Do you understand?) "The most glowing colors in which the virtues shine are the inventions of those who lack them." Yes (21 sec.)—"First, again helplessness; I was unable to bring the possession and lack of virtues into the required contrast. There was a search connected with this (perceptually represented only by eye movements, as though shifting

> back and forth on a surface), interrupted by occasional reverberations of the words, now of the first, now of the second part of the sentence. Then comprehension came suddenly with an affect like 'Aha!'[6] (not spoken); *the basis of comprehension was the farfetched analogy,* or as I would prefer to put it, a superordinate relationship: one prizes most highly what one lacks. Comprehension was tied in with this, and I said yes."

SOME KEY OBSERVATIONS

For Bühler and other members of the Würzburg group the foregoing kinds of introspective reports obtained under controlled conditions constituted *experimental* studies of thinking, just as Ach's investigation of determining tendencies constituted *experimental* studies of volition. This point or observation was stressed by Bühler in a book he wrote during the 1920s on the then contemporary status of psychology.[7] In it he noted that around the turn of the century "a group of younger psychologists associated with Külpe in Würzburg had broadened the scope of experimental research to include the subjects of thought and volition" (1929, p. 12). He interpreted their activities as marking an advance over efforts to account for thinking in terms of "classical association theory."

The process of thinking, he explained, is unique and is governed by its own laws and not just the law of association. As he put it: "In well-regulated disciplined thinking the thoughts are something more than images under the sway of the law of association. Instead they are governed by the demands of the objects to which the thoughts apply." Thinking is characterized by "operations" of definite form. Thus, Bühler, in obvious allusion to the Würzburg discoverery of *Aufgaben,* observed that dealing with numbers is not solely a function of associations aroused by the digits as such, but more importantly by the "operations" symbolized by signs calling for subtraction, multiplication, extracting the square root, or some other arithmetic maneuver. Analogously, with reference to "thoughts" involved in reading it is obvious that

---

[6]As pointed out by Rapaport, this is very likely "the first mention of the often-quoted aha-phenomenon" (p. 49). Aha as an interjection is of ancient vintage; but its use as a designation for a distinctive cognitive phenomenon was due to this work by Bühler. Recognition of this Aha experience may thus be included in any list of positive outcomes stemming from the imageless thought controversy.

[7]The book's title, *Die Krise der Psychologie,* as Bühler explained in a foreword, was chosen deliberately to give prominence to the concepts both of crisis and of critic. He noted that in terms of the Greek verb *krinō*, meaning "I separate," the latter two concepts come together, since as a critic of the critical status of psychology at that time he hoped to be able to effect a reconciliation between *separate* rival systems of psychology responsible for the crisis. Among the systems he discussed there are those of classical associationism, behaviorism, Gestalt psychology, psychoanalysis, and act psychology. It was broad in scope and encompassed the ideas of thinkers as different as Darwin, Dilthey, Mach, Jennings, Spranger, Brentano, Husserl, and many others. Although now almost fifty years old, Bühler's presentation and critique of their ideas is still informative and thought-provoking.

different "operations" determine the kind of thought emerging. The same text may be read to check on the spelling of each word, to translate the sentences into French, to evaluate its stylistic excellence, or for some other purpose. The same manuscript will call for different operations in a lawyer, in a book publisher, in an English teacher, in a lexicographer, in a translator, and in the author's mother. The resulting thoughts aroused in each of the readers will be more a function of each distinctive operation or controlling *Aufgabe* than of chance associations or images. This makes thinking an *active* process and not the consequence of a passive associationism. As such it may be viewed as one of Bühler's key observations.

Another of Bühler's observations centered on the difference between psychological and psychoanalytic research. In his words, "their methods are very different." In the case of psychology, as shown by investigations of the nature of thinking, there is marked emphasis placed on the value of the laboratory "protocols" and on "the careful establishment of an inventory of what is experienced in the very process of thinking." On the other hand in the case of psychoanalysis,[8] Bühler pointed out, there is no such interest in laboratory protocols. Instead the chief interest of the psychoanalyst is in his patient's unconscious wishes or libidinal urges. This results in reliance on *Indizienbeweise* or "circumstantial evidence and on more or less astute detective work." In saying this Bühler was undoubtedly having reference to Freud's mode of procedure in tracking down latent dream thoughts from the evidence of manifest dream content and tracking down *real* thoughts and intentions from the evidence of lapses in speech and behavior. In contrast to Bühler's *Ausfragemethode* this was a very different approach to the psychology of thinking.

FREUD'S PSYCHOLOGY OF THINKING

Freud never wrote a separate chapter or treatise on the subject of thinking as a psychological process. His comments on the subject are scattered through his writings in incidental fashion. There are no "protocols" of the kind Bühler had introduced to show what his subjects had described as the experience of thinking. Instead there are accounts of experienced dreams and Freud's interpretation of the unconscious thoughts or wishes of which the dreams were presumed to be a disguised expression. Furthermore, he was emphatic in holding *unconscious* wishes in contradistinction to conscious ones as the instigators of the dream thoughts. He gave the following italicized expression to this conviction in the *Traumdeutung* (p. 553): *"My supposition is that a conscious wish can only become a dream-instigator if it succeeds in*

---

[8]Bühler devoted the last section of his book (pp. 162–212) to a critique of psychoanalysis. In fact, of the sixteen chapters in the book three are concerned with this critique.

awakening an unconscious wish with the same tenor and in obtaining reinforcement from it." As indicated by the word *supposition,* this conviction is more assumption than established fact; but it serves as a reminder of the great importance Freud attributed to what he regarded as the reality of unconscious mental life.

His entire theory of dreaming was contingent upon the actual occurrence of unconscious thinking. This can be demonstrated by almost any one of the many dreams cited in the *Traumdeutung.* For present purposes it will suffice to illustrate this by a dream Freud had called a "model dream." Incidentally, it will also serve to illustrate what Bühler had described as Freud's reliance on circumstantial evidence. Freud evidently had regarded it as an important dream because he referred to it some five times (pp. 590-511, 533-534, 542, 550, 571) in various contexts.

FREUD'S "MODEL DREAM"

The dream had been reported to Freud by a woman patient who had first heard about it in a lecture on the subject of dreaming. The identity of the original dreamer was never established, but the account of the dream had so impressed the woman that, as Freud indicated, she was able to "re-dream" it and thus "to repeat some of its elements in a dream of her own." In the subsequent description of the dream Freud did not make any distinction between the lecturer's version of the dream and the patient's own dream as instigated by the latter version. It was really impossible to find out the precise nature of the original dream.

The original report constituted one version of the dream and the lecturer's account constituted a second version. The woman's recollection of the lecture gave rise to a third version and her own dream of the reported dream made for a fourth version. Freud ignored consideration of possible changes in the original dream incident to these four versions. Instead he presented what must have been a composite or generalized outcome of the impression he received from his patient's story of the dream heard at the lecture and her own "re-dreaming" of the dream. In place of a fifth version based upon a paraphrase of Freud, to avoid misunderstanding, it will be preferable to introduce the following verbatim account of Freud's version of the dream (p. 509):

> The preliminaries to this model dream were as follows. A father had been watching beside his child's sickbed for days and nights on end. After the child had died, he went into the next room to lie down, but left the door open so that he could see from his bedroom into the room in which his child's body was laid out, with tall candles standing round it. An old man had been engaged to keep watch over it, and sat beside the body murmuring prayers. After a few hour's sleep, the father had a dream that *his child was standing beside his bed, caught him by the arm and whispered to him reproachfully: 'Father, don't you see I'm burning?'* He woke up, noticed a bright glare of light from the next room, hurried into it and found that the old watchman had dropped off to

> sleep and that the wrappings and one of the arms of his beloved child's dead body had been burned by a lighted candle that had fallen on them.

The lecturer's explanation of the dream, as reported by his patient, centered on the fact that light from the candles in the next room must have been shining on the sleeping father's eyes and thus gave rise to the idea of something burning. The latter conclusion, Freud noted, is one the father would have arrived at under comparable circumstances had he been awake. In general, Freud regarded this as a correct explanation. He even added to its plausibility by suggesting that the father prior to falling asleep might possibly have been apprehensive about the old man's reliability as a watchman. It also seemed likely to Freud that words spoken by the child in the dream were repetitions of remarks once actually made. The phrase *"I'm burning,"* Freud suggested by way of example, might have been spoken by the child during a seige of fever. Of course, under the circumstances there was no way for Freud to determine the factual basis for these suggestions. It was impossible to find out what the father thought about the old man's reliability or what the boy said when he had a fever or even whether he ever had had a fever. At best the suggestions are to be classified as supposititious circumstantial evidence.

As might be expected, Freud did not rest content with the foregoing explanation of the dream. In accordance with his central thesis there was still need to establish the nature of the instigating wish responsible for the dream. The lighted candle as a stimulus explained causation but not motivation, and for Freud interpretation of a dream was contingent upon discovery of the motive of which the dream itself is an expression. In the present instance, like a diligent detective, Freud proceeded to search for the underlying motive in order to get at the *meaning* of the dream. In reality, Freud observed, since the fallen candle was starting a fire, the father should have rushed into the next room at once. The dream delayed emergency action; hence the crucial question: Why the delay? To this Freud answered (p. 510):

> And here we shall observe that this dream . . . contained fulfillment of a wish. The dead child behaved in the dream like a living one: he himself warned his father, came to his bed, and caught him by the arm, just as he had probably done on the occasion from the memory of which the first part of the child's words in the dream were derived. For the sake of the fulfillment of this wish the father prolonged his sleep by one moment. The dream was preferred to a waking reflection because it was able to show the child as once more alive. If the father had woken up first and then made the inference that led him to go into the next room, he would, as it were, have shortened the chld's life by that moment of time.

Some might object to this as a model Freudian dream because of the absence of sexual content, but Freud himself disposed of this kind of objection in a letter written in 1927 (E. L. Freud ed., p. 376):

> So please allow me a correction which can easily be confirmed in my various writings. I have never maintained that all dreams have a sexual content, nor that sexual impulses are the mainspring of all dreams. On the contrary, I have always forcefully contradicted this opinion whenever it has been ascribed to me. So I have reason to be dissatisfied when you too repeat this error.

For Freud the dream under consideration was a *model* dream because in terms of the foregoing interpretation a *wish* had been revealed as the instigator of the dream. However, he failed to demonstrate the wish in question to have been an unconscious wish and, as previously quoted, he held that "a wish can only become a dream-instigator if it succeeds in awakening an unconscious wish." In the present instance the wish attributed to the grieving father amounted to a longing for the life of the child and concomitant undoing of the death. A wish of this kind is a common experience following personal tragedy and is altogether congruent with associated thoughts of survival of bodily death. As a common experience it is conscious rather than unconscious and thus there does not appear to be any reason for regarding the father's hypothesized wish as an unconscious wish. Consequently, in this respect the father's dream was not a flawless model of Freud's dream theory. It might also be said to have other shortcomings as a model,[9] but their consideration would constitute too much of a digression from consideration of Freud's own thought processes.

The episode of the father's model dream was introduced primarily by way of illustrating Freud's own thinking. Notice that in his quest for the instigating wish he proceeded to marshall bits of evidence or thoughts pointing to the possible existence of such a wish. These appear to have been *conscious* thoughts just as Conan Doyle's Sherlock Holmes did his successful detective work by *conscious* evaluation of the significance of fragments of evidence. This means that what Freud came to attribute to the unconscious had initially been conscious. Nevertheless, as may be recalled, toward the end of the *Traumdeutung* (pp. 612-613) he made "everything conscious" the outcome of "an unconscious preliminary stage" so that "the unconscious is the true psychical reality." Moreover, on a later page (p. 615) in connection with the question of the role of consciousness in psychoanalytic psychology, Freud supplied this answer: *Only that of a sense-organ for the perception of psychical qualities.* It is hard to reconcile this notion of consciousness as a sense organ with the kind of thinking of which Freud himself seems to have been conscious in connection with the analysis of the father's dream. In fact, it is hard to square the reasoning and subtle distinctions characteristic of all of Freud's

---

[9]As a model the dream failed to illustrate the difference between manifest and latent dream content. Consequently, the interpretation was not based upon the dreamer's associations to individual details of the dream. Nor did it illustrate secondary elaboration, the "fractional" method, condensation, displacement, and other characteristics of dream-work.

writings with this notion of consciousness as an organ of sensation rather than an organ of thought.

Whether Freud intended the latter distinction to be taken literally is difficult to determine. It appears to be contradicted by some statements he made in other passages. For instance, in one (p. 550) he states that "daytime thinking produces psychical acts of such various sorts–judgments, inferences, denials, expectations, intentions, and so on" and in another (p. 613) he refers to "the conscious character of intellectual and artistic production." In a third passage concerned with the nature of sleep he noted that when "our thought-processes are able to become conscious in the normal way at night, we are simply not asleep" (p. 555). Such passages appear to contradict the thesis in terms of which the unconscious becomes the organ of thought and consciousness the organ of sensation. As a possible contradiction it has important implications.

AN APPARENT CONTRADICTION AND ITS IMPLICATIONS

To appreciate the nature of this seeming contradiction it is well to recall the circumstances that prompted Freud's disparagement of consciousness. As he saw it, the "professors" had made consciousness the hallmark or indispensable criterion of mind or the psychical. For this reason they regarded the notion of unconscious mind as absurd and made it the equivalent of belief in the contradictory notion of unconscious consciousness. In defense of the unconscious Freud challenged the latter belief by rejecting its underlying premise. In fact, he mentioned such rejection once again in his very last paper when he stated that "being conscious cannot be the essence of what is mental" (1938, p. 283). He evidently regarded the process of thinking as "the essence of what is mental"; for, as previously mentioned, he never listed any other process as justification for regarding the unconscious as mental or psychical. This was evident in what he wrote about "the most complicated achievements of thought" being "possible without the assistance of consciousness." Since he had restricted the function of consciousness to "that of a sense-organ," he was not regarding sensation as a criterion of the psychical. Having made thought the criterion of the psychical it seems that he was regarding sensation either as less psychical than thought or possibly as more nearly physical than thought.[10]

There is no way of finding out just how Freud interpreted his distinction between thought and sensation. He failed to elaborate upon the foregoing few

[10]One psychologist who did classify sensation as physical was Franz Brentano (1838–1917). Incidentally, the only nonmedical courses taken by Freud were those taught by Brentano, over a two-year period from 1874 to 1876. Since Brentano was steeped in Aristotle's philosophy, it is altogether likely that Freud was introduced to that philosophy as interpreted by Brentano. With reference to this question about the classification of sensation it is well to note that, as reported by Titchener, for Brentano mental con-

key statements concerned with the distinction. There was no discussion of thinking as a process, nor any detailed consideration of sensations as conscious phenomena. No space was devoted to theories of color vision, to auditory theory, or to any specific receptor characteristics. Instead Freud rested content with the implicit statement to the effect that sensations per se, even though conscious, are not criteria of mind. There is nothing mental or psychical about sensations taken in the abstract. Freud wrote as if he expected this to be readily understood without special explanation. After all, cows and hogs are endowed with capacity for sensation, but this does not make them *thoughtful* creatures. In the language of Aristotle they possess a sentient soul, but not man's rational soul. Reason is thus obviously more indicative of mind than sensation. It should also be obvious as instanced by Helen Keller that loss of sensation does not mean loss of reason. Conversely, despite unimpaired sense organs there may nevertheless be loss of reason. These statements come close to being truisms and when viewed as truisms they may explain why Freud deemed it unnecessary to elaborate upon the difference between thoughts and sensations.

What is not so easy to explain is Freud's contradictory treatment of the difference. In some contexts he made thought a function of the unconscious and sensation a function of consciousness, but in other contexts he had thought-processes becoming conscious. Actually he appears to have been unaware of any contradiction involved[11] in such shifts of opinion from context to context. Something akin to compartmentalized thinking seems to have been operative here. When opposing the "professors" who had ridiculed the concept of unconscious thinking as the equivalent of unconscious consciousness he questioned their belief in consciousness as the criterion of mind. As previously stated, by a *tour de force* he met their challenge by refusing to regard consciousness as "the essence of what is mental" and also by declaring that "the unconscious is the true psychical reality." This constituted disposition of the problem as a defense of unconscious thinking. However, in other situations unrelated to the need for such a defense, the problem of thinking was disposed of in a different way. Thus when considering the outcome of

---

tent in the form of sensation is "physical" (1929, p. 245). The same point is made by a direct quotation from Brentano's writing by Rancurello in his more recent study of Brentano (1968, p. 33 and pp. 54–57). There is no way of knowing whether Freud recalled this point twenty years later when he was writing about consciousness as a sense organ. Nor is there any way of determining whether he had Brentano in mind when referring to "professors" who reject the notion of unconscious mental processes; for, as also reported by Titchener, Brentano belonged to those who "reject the unconscious as a principle of psychological explanation" (1929, p. 6).

[11] Another instance of his seeming indifference to or lack of awareness of a contradiction is to be found toward the end of the *Traumdeutung* when discussing retentiveness in the unconscious. Thus on one page (p. 577) Freud states: "In the unconscious nothing can be brought to an end, nothing is past or *forgotten.*" But on the next page (p. 578) the objective of psychotherapeutic intervention results in this statement: "Its task is to make it possible for the unconscious processes to be dealt with finally and *forgotten*" (italics added).

psychoanalytic treatment Freud did not attribute "insight" and the "primacy of the intellect" to the workings of the unconscious. Instead these terms were used as descriptive of the patient's enlightenment. They had to do with the patient's ego and not with his id and as such would have been regarded as conscious rather than unconscious.

With insight and intellect so regarded, consciousness was no longer just "a sense-organ for the perception of psychical qualities." The very concept of intellect connotes active rather than passive mental processes and suggests not just having sensory impressions but reacting to them. It is a complex concept involving a tremendous number of factors.[12] To consider them in detail would call for a separate volume. Nor did Freud have them in mind when he wrote about the "primacy of the intellect," for he was using the word *intellect* as a popular rather than a technical term. He supplied no formal definition or explanation of the word as if he expected an everyday connotation to suffice. Such a connotation would be replete with reminders of such conscious cognitive activities as finding the right word, trying to understand a text, recalling the past in order to deal with the present, locating the weakness in an argument, planning a trip, deciding on an investment, judging a person's character, and so on and on.

From this viewpoint it would seem that Freud, at least by implication, was no longer restricting consciousness to awareness of sights, sounds, smells, and other sensory impressions, but had expanded the scope of its influence to include the active intellect. In effect he was now regarding both sensation and thought as conscious. This amounted to recognition of two aspects of mind: one pertaining to sensory and the other to cognitive processes. It was recognition of a venerable tradition already mentioned in this and earlier chapters, the tradition that included such dichotomies as Aristotle's sentient and rational souls, the *res extensa* and *res cogitans* of Descartes, Locke's sensation and reflection, Kant's senses and understanding, Brentano's sensory and noetic consciousness, and then early in the present century the Würzburg sensory processes on the one hand and the imageless or nonsensory processes on the other.

What made these non-sensory processes *mental* was not so much their status as conscious happenings as their processing of information.[13] Possibly

---

[12]As brought out by J. P. Guilford and his collaborators, there may be as many as 120 factors in "the structure of intellect." The studies in question are based upon the results of factor analysis. For details and references to these studies see Guilford's 1956 article "The Structure of the Intellect," and the 1963 article by J. R. Royce. As studies of intelligence these investigations had to do with logical thinking, creative thinking, symbolic thinking, thinking about people and social relations, and kindred dimensions of cognition. Although numerous hitherto overlooked or unknown factors were brought to light in the course of these investigations, this did not make factor analysis a technique for learning more about the Freudian unconscious. Instead, as a technique it made the "soft" words of the "voice of intellect" more audible.

[13]Such processing of information has important implications for systematic psychology, as J. P. Guilford has brought out in his 1973 paper dealing with Operational-Informational Psychology. Furthermore, in an earlier paper entitled "Executive Functions and a

Freud had reference to this when he objected to making consciousness rather than thought the hallmark of mind. As already pointed out, he gave undue emphasis to this objection by relegating thought to the unconscious as an unobservable, esoteric, concealed, or nonconscious mental realm. Nevertheless, as also pointed out previously, when discussing the primacy of the intellect all this was changed. Now the voice of intellect was given a hearing and its culmination in the patient's "insight" made thinking a conscious process. As a conscious process it was a non-sensory consciousness and thus different from the paradox of unconscious thinking with its connotation of unconscious consciousness. This is tantamount to denial of The Unconscious as a separate mental realm and its replacement by a less mysterious and more readily verifiable non-sensory consciousness. Moreover, the latter phrase is not to be construed as another name for the former realm. More than a shift in descriptive vocabulary is involved. Actually, there is a drastic difference in meaning with important implications.

WHAT NON-SENSORY IDEATION IMPLIES

The concept of non-sensory ideation as a synonym for reflection, thinking, judging, and other cognitive processes suggests the unity of mental life. It does away with the notion of man being endowed with *two* minds, namely a conscious mind and an unconscious mind. It also dispenses with a not uncommon tendency to personify or reify the unconscious into some sort of spectral homunculus or psychic entity controlling the content of dreams, initiating blunders of speech and action, and even solving problems while the conscious mind is asleep. A tendency of this kind was not alien to Freud's view of the unconscious. In his 1915 paper "The Unconscious" he endowed the unconscious with life by writing (p. 190): "It would certainly be wrong to imagine" that the unconscious is like an inert "vestigial organ" since it "is *alive* and capable of development" (italics added).

The concept of non-sensory ideation dispenses with belief in one mind located within another mind. This eliminates a possible complication and resulting mystification implicit in the concept of *depth* psychology. With the unconscious mind patterned after what is known of the conscious mind the latter is presumed to relegate ego-dystonic impulses into the former by

---

Model of Behavior" Guilford noted the following relationship between this concept of information and the concept of consciousness as developed by the functional psychologists (1972, p. 285):

> An important feature of the model for behavior is the large amount of short-circuiting that it recognizes. Following William James' early treatment of habit formation, functional psychologists frequently held to the principle that in the early stages of learning there is considerable conscious content, which progressively drops out as a habit becomes more automatized. The model makes one important conceptual gain by substituting "information" for "consciousness." Information is a much more specifiable and manageable concept, in step with much current thinking.

repression. There may then be a troubled unconscious mind having to get rid of *its* unwelcome impulses by repressing them into a sub-unconscious mind. With a whole series of successively deeper levels of the unconscious in the offing the world of scientific fact would have to yield to the world of science fiction. Furthermore, recognition of the non-sensory character of thinking as a cognitive enterprise renders it unnecessary to entertain the fiction or paradox of unconscious consciousness.

In some respects this concept of cognition might be reminiscent of Locke's concept of reflection. As noted early in the chapter, for Locke reflection has to do with "operations of our own mind" including "thinking, doubting, believing, reasoning, knowing, willing, and all the different actings of our own minds." In the later idiom of William James, all these "actings" were brought into the current of the stream of consciousness. This made reflection or the streaming of man's thought processes so complex as to render full knowledge of the details of this complexity a never-ending quest. This is so because it entails research into such diverse areas as mental retardation, creative thinking, aesthetic sensitivity, mathematical aptitude, social intelligence, dreaming, paranoid thinking, intolerance of ambiguity, rationalization, ideational flexibility versus rigidity, and many additional components of intellect now being subjected to factor-analytic investigations. In the light of the latter investigations all that Locke subsumed under reflection is now revealed as far more complex than he suspected. At the risk of begging the question it might be said that he was unconscious of this complexity just as most of us are unconscious of the complexity of what is subsumed under the concept of intellect. Employed in this way the word *unconscious* means being unaware, failing to realize or notice, or failing to appreciate. In what follows the word will be used in this sense.

It might also be said that until the Würzburg investigations were undertaken most of us were unconscious of imageless or non-sensory thinking, of conscious attitudes, of mental sets, of determining tendencies, and of the "Aha" experience. However, the thinking, attitudes, tendencies, and experiences designated by these terms had existed as cognitive occurrences prior to their Würzburg discovery. Once noted, described, and given distinctive names it became possible for such occurrences to be detected and observed by others. Under the circumstances such detection and observation is the equivalent of making the unconscious conscious. Another way to put this is to say that it results in making the unobserved observable, the implicit explicit, the unknown known, the concealed exposed, or—in general—making the latent manifest.

All these ways of becoming increasingly aware of what lies within the drift of one's thinking facilitate insight and self-discovery. As such they constitute discovery of unconscious attributes or components of one's stream of thinking. But this is not the same as discovery of a separate or segregated mental realm in the form of an unconscious mind conceived of as divorced from another mental realm in the form of a conscious mind. There is only one mind or one intellect for each individual to explore and to get to know.

The *know thyself* of the Greek adage was an allusion to such exploration. As an admonition it suggested that self-knowledge is contingent upon discovery of hitherto ignored or unknown phases of one's being as a thinking being. Moreover, with thinking equated with non-sensory consciousness the increase in self-knowledge will be dependent upon discovery of such previously overlooked constituent features of one's thinking. As features these are concomitants of thinking ignored by or unknown to the thinker and as such may be described as non-sensory *unconscious processes.* Obviously, the latter phrase does not refer to a segregated mental agency in the form of a reified unconscious.

As a matter of fact, such unconscious processes are the same as the conscious attitudes of the Würzburg studies as previously mentioned in connection with Bühler's investigation of thinking. To Bühler's brief examples of such attitudes it will prove clarifying to introduce a familiar instance from everyday life. Known to almost all students is the complex of changing attitudes they are apt to entertain when taking examinations. They note the ease or difficulty of the questions. As the answers are being written the student may be doubtful of some, confident of others, and frustrated by still others. There may be feelings of impending success or failure as the last question is being answered. All such processes or feelings of doubt, confidence, frustration, success, or failure are concomitants of the thoughts aroused by the questions. As comcomitants they surround or accompany the ideation or reasoning concerned with the answers per se. This is what makes them conscious attitudes. As such they do not constitute part of the answers even though, psychologically considered, they are constituents of the totality of thinking leading to the answers. Some of them may influence the direction of the thinking. This would be the case when a given idea is rejected as too irrelevant or as being in conflict with the examiner's favorite theory. Still other ideas may be rejected as too hard to explain or too weak as arguments. Far more goes on in the student's mind than gets to be recorded in his written answers, and in some respects this means that conscious attitudes may be regarded as surplus ideation from the viewpoint of the final outcome of successful thinking. This renders the problem solving of human beings different from that of digital computers—which is obvious once it is called to our attention.

ON MAKING THE UNCONSCIOUS CONSCIOUS

In connection with human problem solving it is well to elaborate upon what was previously referred to as making the unconscious conscious or the latent manifest. As noted, psychologists had been unaware of conscious attitudes until the Würzburg investigators had called attention to them by giving them a distinctive name. After that their fellow psychologists were alerted to the existence and variety of conscious attitudes. This is a reminder of the fact that knowing what to look for often makes the difference between being conscious or unconscious of something. A stock instance of this is supplied by the case of the child who, upon being told how prose differs from poetry, was excited to discover that he was talking prose.

Similarly, even in the case of adults, recognition of specific concomitants of thinking may fail to occur until somebody calls attention to their existence by giving them a definite label. For example, psychologists had overlooked the nature of some fixed social attitudes until the early 1920s when Walter Lippmann called attention to them in his book *Public Opinion.* His term *social stereotypes* then became an accepted designation for the fixed and biased attitudes implicit in references to the Scottish as penurious, to blondes as fickle, to atheists as immoral, to politicians as crooked, and to Nordics as superior. Before Lippmann's term had been introduced, even though such biased attitudes were commonplace, neither sociologists nor social psychologists devoted space to them in their textbooks. However, once they and journalists gave currency to the term more and more educated people came to recognize social stereotypes in others and sometimes even in themselves. They had now become an addition to their stock of *Bewusstseinslagen* or conscious attitudes.

A variant and elaboration of such stereotypes came to be recognized a generation later in the 1950s as a result of the studies by Adorno and associates of antidemocratic, ethnocentric attitudes associated with the *authoritarian* personality. In these studies hundreds of subjects answered carefully prepared questionnaires and many submitted to personal interviews. In the course of such interviews some of the investigators introduced questions related to the libido theory. As one of them wrote (Adorno, p. 316): "An attempt was also made to probe into pre-Oedipal fixations, that is, to pay attention to the 'orality' and 'anality' of the subject and especially to the defense mechanisms with which these and other instinctual problems had been handled." This sentence suggests that what came to be attributed to the authoritarian personality had some roots in psychoanalytic theory and also in the investigator's clinical experience.

This suggestion is also reflected in the reference to defense mechanisms. In other words, having learned about the concept of defense mechanisms the examiner could probe for them and be on the watch for them during the interviews. They were constituents of his conscious attitudes and influenced his thinking accordingly. Being identified with conscious attitudes this made the thinking non-sensory thinking, thinking about an array of defense mechanisms such as denial, projection, and others. To the extent that the examiner recognized any of these mechanisms in the person being examined then he, as examiner, would be conscious of them while the examinee would be unconscious of them. In other words, the examinee would unwittingly be projecting or rationalizing and thus be ignorant or unconscious of their occurrence as defense mechanisms; they would then be constituents of his non-sensory unconscious. However, were he to learn about them and then recognize them in himself and in others, they would cease to be unconscious and as conscious attitudes would become constituents of his non-sensory consciousness.

This cognitive process holds true for all kinds of thinking. For example, if one has never heard about ethnocentrism, there is little likelihood of spontaneous recognition of the bias underlying one's exaltation of the in-group and corresponding disparagement of those belonging to out-groups. Analogously, the rationalizer will be oblivious of his rationalizing until his thinking comes to include both the word and the concept of rationalization. Similarly, neither therapists nor their patients were cognizant of their wishful thinking until Freud had called attention to the process. The same statement can be made about clinicians and their failure to note the nature and existence of emotional complexes and introversive attitudes prior to Jung's introduction of the words *complex* and *introversion* as psychiatric terms. It is also true that not until Bleuler supplied them with the term and description of autistic thinking were they likely to detect such thinking in their patients. Nor should their indebtedness to Adler for recognition of the mechanism of overcompensation be overlooked in this connection.

The list could be extended to include paranoid attitudes, schizophrenic apathy, somatic compliance, screen memories, glove anesthesia, and other manifestations of psychopathology that had eluded the observation and thinking of clinicians until the technical terms in question had first been invented. Prior to becoming clinicians they can be said to have been unconscious of such clinical manifestations, but with completion of a psychiatric residency such manifestations are noticed, named, and evaluated so that what had once been unconscious is now conscious.

Another way to put this is to say that when he is examining a patient the significance of such manifestations now falls within the scope of the clinician's professional thinking. It is in accordance with such thinking and all it connotes that he arrives at a diagnosis and decides upon appropriate treatment. Usually in the case of mental patients the treatment will center on psychotherapy and this, of course, will entail changes in the patient's thinking or outlook. It might even occur to the clinician that in some respects the cognitive changes he had undergone in the course of professional training will resemble those to be experienced by his patient in the course of psychotherapy. At all events, both kinds of changes have to do with making the unconscious conscious. As cognitive changes they have to do with what Freud had called the primacy of the intellect, which suggests the intellect's involvement in psychotherapy and the unconscious.

PSYCHOTHERAPY AND THE UNCONSCIOUS

In the interest of historical accuracy it is well to note that Freud did not write about the primacy of the intellect in connection with the subject of psychotherapy. Instead he introduced the phrase in his volume *The Future of an Illusion.* This work was first published in 1927 and dealt with Freud's views of religion. As indicated by the title, he regarded religion as an *illusion.* However, in doing so, as Ernest Jones has explained (1957, Vol. III, p. 356), Freud was not contending "that religious beliefs are untrue, illusory in the sense of their being non-existent." Freud had written that an illusion does not necessarily refer to an error but that what constitutes an illusion is any belief resulting from a wish to believe. As an instance of such wish-fulfillment Freud cited the belief or illusion of the peasant girl who anticipates the arrival of a rescuing prince. Obviously this is as unrealistic as belief in divine intervention to save one from academic failure or bankruptcy. In Freud's view religion conceived of as an expression of such wish-fulfilling hopes is an illusion. It was with reference to the possibility of dispensing with such an illusion that he mentioned the primacy of the intellect. After months and months of futile waiting for the rescuing prince the voice of the peasant girl's intellect tells her the prince is an imaginary prince and, accordingly, her illusory wishful thinking is replaced by realistic thinking. And such realistic thinking is conscious and not unconscious thinking.

In large measure the goal of psychotherapy is also concerned with having unrealistic thinking replaced by realistic thinking. This is so to the extent that the thinking of psychiatric patients reflects mistaken, illusory ideas about themselves and others. In the course of successful psychotherapy such warped ideation is replaced by straight thinking. According to modern views, the interaction between therapist and patient is a learning experience, as erroneous beliefs are exposed, novel insights brought to light, anxiety reduced, self-respect enhanced, and personal values restructured. This makes psychotherapy an educational procedure with the therapist acting as teacher and his patient in the role of student. The lessons can be taxing for both teacher and student. Often what seems obvious to the therapist meets with the patient's incredulity or stubborn resistance, and sometimes the nature of a patient's fixed belief may perplex his therapist. As is evident in the following quotation from one of Freud's lectures, the task of overcoming such resistances and fixed beliefs was described as being in "the nature of an *education*" (1938, p. 392):

> Analytic treatment makes as great demands for efforts on the part of the patient as on the physician, efforts to abolish the inner resistances. The patient's mental life is permanently changed by overcoming these resistances, is lifted to a higher level of development, and remains proof against fresh possibilities of illness. The labour of overcoming the resistances is the essential achievement of the analytic treatment; the patient has to accomplish it and the physician makes it possible for him to do this by suggestions which are in the nature of an *education.* It has been truly said therefore, that psycho-analytic treatment is a kind of *re-education.*[14]

[14] This passage occurs in the last lecture comprising the series in the *General Introduction to Psycho-Analysis.* The concept of re-education does not seem to be in keeping with the general drift of the thoughts developed in these lectures. Upon consulting the original

PSYCHOTHERAPY AS EDUCATION

This view of psychoanalytic treatment was also stressed in another of Freud's lectures, namely, his 1904 lecture to a group of physicians in Vienna—the one entitled "On Psychotherapy." In it he noted that suitability for psychotherapy depends upon various factors. Among others to be considered he mentioned education under two sets of circumstances (p. 258). In one set the therapist wonders "whether the patient is educable" and in the other he wonders whether the patient is too old since "old people are no longer educable." A minimum level of intelligence along with a certain degree of intellectual flexibility were thus prerequisites for successful psychotherapy. They made it possible for problems to be solved by taking thought or by what Freud once called "rational mental effort."[15]

Since thought and rational mental effort presuppose activation of conscious processes, the patient's psychoanalytic "education" was more conscious than unconscious. In effect Freud was saying that without such activation the patient will not succeed in recognizing and coping with unconscious influences responsible for his personality difficulties. Coming to grips with these influences was envisaged as a function of conscious thought. Consequently, when discussing psychoanalytic treatment as a form of education Freud was no longer regarding "consciousness as a sense organ which perceives data that arise elsewhere." Instead, as should now be evident, in the context of psychotherapy consciousness was regarded as an organ of thought sensitive to "the voice of the intellect." This made it an organ of reason, reflection, and whatever else pertains to the structure of intellect.

Freud was the first to recognize intellect and psychoanalytic therapy as related to educational procedures. However, he did not supply a detailed account of the procedures to guide the educational therapist. In fact, few if any of the early psychoanalysts and their immediate successors ever thought of themselves as educational therapists in the special sense of being engaged in promoting the education of their patients. Neither did they dwell upon psychotherapy as related to various theories of learning. Not until very

---

German it was found that the sentence in question reads: "Man hat darum auch mit Recht gesagt, die psychoanalytische Behandlung sei eine Art von *Nacherziehung*." Now the word *Nacherziehung* does not mean re-education, but rather supplementary education. The word for re-education would have to be *Wiedererziehung*. To illustrate the difference in meaning between these two terms it may suffice to note that having to repeat a course because of failure exemplifies re-education, whereas having to enroll for an advanced course in order to round out one's preparation for a given undertaking exemplifies supplementary education.

[15] This phrase occurs on page 77 of *The Future of an Illusion* in a section concerned with control of impulses in which Freud wrote that "the time has probably come to replace the consequence of repression by the results of rational mental effort." It should be recalled that in Freud's view repression had to do with the sexual etiology of neuroses. In fact, as mentioned in Chapter 5, according to Jones (Vol. II, p. 320), "Freud had told the Vienna Society that in his opinion repression affected only sexual impulses. All other effects were secondary. He never retracted this."

recent decades did Freud's original insight into the educational implications of psychotherapy arouse the active interest of psychoanalysts.

A representative example of such active interest is to be found in two chapters of a contemporary (1974) volume, *Psychiatry in Transition,* by the psychoanalyst Judd Marmor. This interest is revealed in the chapter titles, one being "Psychoanalytic Therapy as an Educational Process" and the other being "Psychoanalytic Therapy and Theories of Learning." They reflect the accumulation of more than fifty years of clinical experience dating back to Freud's first reference to such aspects of psychotherapy. They also reflect more than fifty years of laboratory studies of the learning process by experimental psychologists. The result is a sophisticated elaboration of Freud's pioneering insight far in excess of what Freud could have had in mind, the nature of which is made especially clear in the following paragraph. Here Marmor subjects the concept of insight itself to critical examination (pp. 198–199):

> But what *is* insight? To a Freudian it means one thing, to a Jungian another, and to a Rankian, a Horneyite, an Adlerian or a Sullivanian, still another. Each school gives its own particular brand of insight. Whose are the correct insights? The fact is that patients treated by analysts of all these schools may not only respond favorably, but also believe strongly in the insights which they have been given. . . . Moreover, the problem is even more complicated than this; for, depending upon the point of view of the analyst, the patients of each school seem to bring up precisely the kind of phenomenological data which confirm the theories and interpretations of their analysts! Thus each theory tends to be self-validating. Freudians elicit material about the Oedipus complex and castration anxiety, Adlerians about masculine strivings and feelings of inferiority, Horneyites about idealized images, Sullivanians about disturbed interpersonal relationships, etc. The fact is that in so complex a transaction as the psychoanalytic therapeutic process, the impact of patient and therapist upon each other, and particularly of the latter upon the former, is an unusually profound one. What the analyst shows interest in, the kinds of questions he asks, the kind of data he chooses to react to or ignore, and the interpretations he makes, all exert a subtle but significant suggestive impact upon the patient to bring forth certain kinds of data in preference to others. . . . I should like to suggest that *what we call insight is essentially the conceptual framework by means of which a therapist establishes, or attempts to establish, a logical relationship between events, feelings, or experience that seem unrelated in the mind of the patient.*

This view of insight is limited to the therapist-patient interaction, and it is different from the view of insight associated with animal experimentation. By way of reminder, in the famous study of the chimpanzee insight was said to have been revealed on the occasion when he fitted two sticks together in order to retrieve a distant banana. In the same way a young child might be said to have insight were it to fit the pieces of a formboard into place immediately on the first attempt and with no prior contact with formboards. In such nonclinical settings the word *insight* is employed as meaning possession of requisite understanding or knowing what to do to solve a problem. An expert garage mechanic exhibits this kind of insight when confronted with a stalled motor. This is different from Marmor's use of insight as a clinical term.

An illuminating example of this clinical meaning of insight is supplied by an incident involving Rank's concept of the trauma of birth. Freud had questioned the soundness of Rank's theory, but Ferenczi had endorsed it. Nevertheless, according to Jones (Vol. III, p. 68), Freud tried to test the theory over a period of several weeks "by interpreting the associations whenever possible in terms of birth, but he got no response from his patients, nor had the interpretations any other effect on them. Ferenczi, on the other hand, had had wonderful results by applying the same method and could not do without it in a single case."

Incidentally, Freud and Ferenczi had another difference of opinion. This had to do with astrology and the fact that despite Freud's remonstrations Ferenczi continued to take horoscopes seriously. Presumably Ferenczi had some "insight" into his patient's unconscious just by learning the date of his birth. On the other hand, even though Freud disavowed astrology, he did take telepathy seriously and, as brought out by Jones (Vol. III, p. 381), he thought of it as opening "the door to endless possibilities," one of which might be mental processes operative "independent of the human body." On a more personal note, Jones reports, Freud "fancied" having received telepathic messages from his son on military duty during the war. On another page (p. xii) Jones referred to telepathy as one of many matters Freud "regarded as fundamental" but upon which he and Jones differed. What Freud accepted as fact Jones rejected as myth and in this respect their clinical interpretations could not be in agreement. Moreover, another of Freud's early associates, Eduard Hitschmann, had a still different view of telepathy. In a paper titled "Telepathy and Psychoanalysis" he denied "the reality of telepathy in the occult sense," but attributed alleged instances of telepathic communication to projection of unconscious wishes, or as he put it (p. 117), telepathy is "based not on mystical or unknown physical forces, but on the psychology of the unconscious." This means that with reference to just the restricted topic of telepathy these three pioneer psychoanalysts, Freud, Jones, and Hitschmann, had three differing views of the unconscious.

Furthermore, with reference to other topics both they and their successors did not always see eye to eye. In other words, all who call themselves psychoanalysts endorse the concept of mind as unconscious, but differ among themselves in what they attribute to the unconscious. For some the death instinct is fact, for others it is fiction. Nor do they agree on what is to be ascribed to the infant's unconscious or to that of the adult in terms of the libido theory. In addition, as just shown, even with respect to the nature of insight both they as well as the sponsors of other schools of psychotherapy disagree, with the patients of each school tending to reflect insights consistent with its school's distinctive tenets.[16]

As a result, a Jungian's unconscious differs from that of a Horneyite and that of the latter from the unconscious of an Adlerian. It seems safe to say that there are as many different kinds of unconscious as there are such distinctive schools of psychotherapy. For this reason, to revert to a statement made in Chapter 1, it is impossible to formulate a comprehensive definition of the word *unconscious* broad enough to do justice to what the word has come to mean to these rival schools, each member of which is persuaded of the truth of what is revealed by *his* insight into what he takes to be the unconscious. Thus, by way of example, the psychoanalyst Erich Fromm prefaced an account of the unconscious from *his* viewpoint by disassociating himself both from the Freudian and the Jungian unconscious. He was careful to point out that for him the unconscious "is neither Jung's mythical realm of racially inherited experience nor Freud's seat of irrational libidinal forces" (p. 29).

Nevertheless, despite such differences in viewpoint and interpretation, it may be possible to refer to unconscious ideas and impulses in a way that will be acceptable to adherents of all schools and also to those who are not affiliated with any school or not even concerned with psychotherapy. This will be possible provided there is recognition of the unconscious factors implicit in the concept of non-sensory ideation.

IN CONCLUSION

By way of introduction to these concluding paragraphs it is pertinent to recall the fact that although Freud made thinking the sole justification for belief in the existence of unconscious *psychical* processes, he did not introduce an analysis of thinking per se. This was first undertaken by the Würzburg psychologists. Their discovery of conscious attitudes, determining tendencies, and other imageless components of thinking was tantamount to discovery of *unconscious* components. These components were unconscious in the sense of having eluded prior observation and they were imageless because, as Woodworth put it, they contained elements "wholly irreducible to sensory terms"; hence their non-sensory characterization. Additional evidence in support of this distinction between thoughts and images or, as figuratively expressed, between naked thoughts and their imaginal dress was supplied by Würzburg reaction time studies of meaning. In these studies, upon presentation of a

[16] A clarifying exposition of such adherence to the distinctive tenets of given therapeutic schools is to be found in the recent (1975) volume edited by C. A. Loew and associates. Entitled *Three Psychotherapies*, it has representatives of psychoanalysis, Gestalt therapy, and behavior therapy discuss their respective therapeutic approaches by confronting each of them with the same set of clinical problems. For each case or problem they were requested to analyze the patient's difficulty, their particular therapeutic objective, and their means of reaching this objective.

word the subjects reacted as soon as they were aware of the word's meaning in one series of presentations and as soon as they were aware of the word's imaginal representation in another series. It was found that it takes longer for arousal of associated imagery than for apprehension of meaning. In other words, awareness of a word's meaning precedes its imaginal representation. This finding is related to studies of determining tendencies, when it was found that initiation of a given determining tendency preceded execution of specific acts or arousal of particular thoughts.

Now conscious attitudes and determining tendencies as psychological processes were taking place long before the Würzburg psychologists called attention to their existence by giving them distinctive names. As occurrences they failed to become objects of awareness and thus were *unconscious* concomitants of ideation. This made them *implicit* non-sensory concomitants, but once observed and described they were rendered conscious and *explicit.* In this way they serve as a paradigm for equating the unconscious with implicit non-sensory ideation.

The word *unconscious* in this paradigm does not refer to a separate autonomous mental agency in the form of an unconscious mind—as if man is endowed with two minds, one conscious and the other unconscious. In this respect it differs from the way Freud employed the word *unconscious* when contrasting the conscious with the unconscious. As explained in Chapter 4, Freud stressed this conscious-unconscious dichotomy in the *Traumdeutung* (pp. 612–613) by first identifying consciousness with sensory processes and then, by way of contrast, identifying all other mental processes with the unconscious. It was with reference to these other processes that he wrote, "the most rational thought-processes . . . can occur without exciting the subject's consciousness." These thoughts were also presumed to occur without revealing their "existence in any way to consciousness." He declared the unconscious to be "the true psychical reality" and that it "must be assumed to be the general basis of psychical life." Just why such an assumption is required was not explained. Neither was any evidence introduced in support of the dogmatic assertion describing the unconscious as "the larger sphere, which includes within it the smaller sphere of the conscious." In the same context the "innermost nature" of this larger sphere was acknowledged to be "as much unknown to us as the reality of the external world." This came close to trying to account for the known in terms of the unknown. Sensation was identified with the conscious and intellect with the unconscious and the Freudian two-minds paradigm came into being. The one-mind paradigm entails fewer assumptions and tries to account for the unknown in terms of the known and thus might be said to come closer to "the true psychical reality."

As already mentioned, this one-mind paradigm recognizes the occurrence of unconscious mental processes and equates them with implicit non-sensory ideation. An example of such unconscious ideation was introduced in an earlier section in connection with the subject of social stereotypes. As there pointed out, people are unconscious of the bias and misperception reflected in their talk about the humorless British, immoral atheists, or effete intellectuals. Similarly, they may be unconscious of their superstitions as superstitions, of paranoid attitudes as paranoid, or of their arguments being evasive or fallacious or unconvincing.

It would be easy to continue with a long list of ways in which the stream of ordinary thinking is characterized by trends of which the thinker is unconscious. Thus most of us when engaged in casual reflection or in heated argument may not know whether we are thinking inductively or deductively, convergently or divergently, concretely or abstractly, subjectively or objectively, critically or dogmatically, intelligently or stupidly, superficially or profoundly, or flexibly or rigidly.

In fact, some of these alternatives are included in factor-analytic studies of intellect. Since there may be a reservoir of 120 or more such factors from which selection is made in the course of thinking, even the factor-analytic specialist is very likely unconscious of the ones operative in specific instances of his own thinking. Those of us who are not specialists, even as psychologists, may have trouble recalling more than a small number of these factors. To the extent that they have a bearing on the course of our thinking and elude our observation we are unconscious of them.

In their totality they constitute the structure of the intellect and when groups of them function in the thinking of individuals they constitute conscious attitudes. As long as the individual is ignorant or unconscious of harboring such attitudes they constitute implicit non-sensory thoughts. To repeat: from this viewpoint they are unconscious concomitants of the stream of ideation and as concomitants they are events or happenings and not things or entities. Not being things or entities they have no habitat. Consequently, *it would be fatuous and meaningless to say that these implicit non-sensory thoughts are* in *the unconscious.* The one-mind paradigm does not provide for a separate mental realm called The Unconscious.

The foregoing denial of the existence of the unconscious when viewed in historical perspective becomes the counterpart of denial of the existence of consciousness as a distinct entity. Many decades ago William James raised this issue in an essay in which he asked, "Does Consciousness Exist?" and concluded that it does not exist. Anticipating the shock such a conclusion might occasion he introduced the following shock-absorbing explanation very early in the essay (pp. 3-4):

> To deny plumply that 'consciousness' exists seems so absurd on the face of it—for undeniably 'thoughts' do exist—that I fear some readers will follow me no farther. Let me then immediately explain that I mean only to deny that the word stands for an entity, but to insist most emphatically that it does stand for a function. There is, I mean, no aboriginal stuff or quality of being, contrasted with that of which material objects are made, out of which our thoughts are made; but there is a function in experience which thoughts perform, and for the performance of which this quality of being is involved. That function is *knowing*.

The importance of the function of *knowing* was also recognized by Freud when he described psychotherapy as being an educational experience for the patient. As is common knowledge, a chief objective for Freud as therapist was to help his patient gain *insight* and this means help in gaining more revealing self-knowledge. After all, he did expect his patients to heed the voice of intellect and thus learn to distinguish wishful thinking from realistic thinking, the irrational from the rational, the infantile from the mature or the regressive from the progressive.

In this connection it is well to recall that it was Freud who first called our attention to such self-deceiving maneuvers as projection, displacement, denial, and reaction formation. He perceived them as militating against honest thinking and as tending to result in ego-defensive misperceptions of self and others. Furthermore, viewed as hindrances to valid thinking, they constitute a psychoanalytic counterpart to the traditional fallacies listed in textbooks of logic; hence, more than he realized, Freud had heightened the eminence of the intellect's primacy.

Those who have recourse to such ego-defensive maneuvers are usually not aware of doing so. They are unconscious of projecting or rationalizing just as the illogical thinker is unconscious of his reliance on the *post hoc* or some other fallacy. As unnoticed concomitants of an ongoing pattern of thinking these maneuvers exemplify implicit non-sensory thoughts. Not until they are rendered explicit can their misleading and distorting effects be corrected.

This involves more than just being told about them as impersonal ideas in the way one may be told about the meaning of a new word. Instead, as Freud saw, the patient must come to appreciate them as directly related to personal difficulties. Acquisition of this kind of appreciation is not easy. Blinded by long established ego defenses the patient fails to see himself as his therapist sees him and being supplied with a description of the nature of these defenses will not bring about their recognition and elimination. In fact, as Freud found, the patient is likely to resist the suggestion that self-deception is taking place. Not until such resistance is overcome will there be appreciation of the distorting effects of given ego defenses. That of which he had been unconscious he will now be conscious. To this extent he will have achieved insight and it is in this regard that Freud came to think of psychotherapy as an educational experience. As the therapist Frieda Fromm-Reichmann once put it: "The patient needs an *experience* not an explanation." Whether experience in the form of psychotherapy is the only way for troubled people to be helped is another question; but to consider it would lead us too far afield.[17]

---

[17]This question is important for at least two reasons: (*a*) there are too few psychotherapists in relation to the number needing help and (*b*) the cost of psychotherapy renders it beyond the means of families of modest income. Consequently, it would be a decided boon to the troubled were they able to find less costly help–especially help that is immediately available. In a contemporary (1973) article Leona A. Tyler has called attention to the way some of the troubled are helping themselves. In fact, she describes this development as a "shift . . . away from reliance on psychotherapy as the solution to

A more immediately relevant question that might be raised concerns the relation of dreams to implicit non-sensory ideation. For Freud dreams constituted the royal road to the unconscious, and thus it might be asked, "Do they also constitute the same kind of road to implicit non-sensory ideation?" An affirmative answer is to be expected to the extent that the latter kind of ideation is equated with the unconscious. At least it can be presumed to hold true for dreams regarded as expressions of wish-fulfillment. This proviso is necessary because not all wishes give rise to dreams nor are all dreams instigated by wishes. A trivial wish like the wish for a good hand at bridge is not as likely to find expression in a dream as is a serious wish like the wish for the recovery of a very ill child. Freud's "model dream" mentioned earlier in this chapter comes to mind in this connection. In that dream, as interpreted by Freud, the grieving father was wishing that his dead child were still alive.

---

human problems." Among her observations concerning the nature of this shift the following ones are of particular significance and interest (p. 1022):

> For one thing, people who realize that they are in trouble and need help are increasingly turning to each other rather than to professional therapists for assistance. Alcoholics Anonymous was perhaps the first herald of this change in the manner in which psychological difficulties were to be dealt with. At first we did not sense how profound a change in orientation it represented. But we are being forced to pay attention to it now that the same process has repeated itself with many other kinds of people–weight watchers, heroin addicts, former mental patients, paraplegics–the list could be extended indefinitely. These people are convinced that they can get more help from others who are able to understand them because they have experienced the same difficulty than from professional "healers," however competent.

To this it is well to add that people report being helped by Yoga, by Zen, and by transcendental and other forms of meditation. Such presumed help is different from psychoanalytic, Adlerian, Jungian, Rogerian, or eclectic modes of psychotherapy. A well summarized description of each of these different meditational procedures is to be found in Ornstein's *The Psychology of Consciousness* (pp. 104–141). In addition, the latter descriptions ought to be supplemented by recent laboratory studies of ideational changes under conditions of relaxed wakefulness. For details and relevant references see the 1975 article by Foulkes and Fleisher.

Each of the preceding modes of psychotherapy and meditation has its coterie of supporters convinced of the effectiveness of a given mode and less convinced of the effectiveness of rival modes. However, these convictions are rarely if ever based upon carefully designed controlled investigations of results obtained in terms of therapeutic success or failure. Instead they tend to be based upon the therapist's personal impressions along with the testimony of grateful patients or clients. Like evidence cited in support of the efficacy of prayer, such evidence may be misleading.

Actually, subjecting any technique of psychotherapy to rigorous and valid determination of its effectiveness is a relatively formidable undertaking. The few attempts that have been made have failed to satisfy all critics–some of them are ready to argue that effectiveness of psychotherapy has yet to be demonstrated. An informative account of this issue is to be found in *The Effects of Psychotherapy,* a monograph by Hans J. Eysenck and some 17 discussants from this country and abroad and representative of the fields of psychiatry, psychoanalysis, and psychology. (The monograph is published by The International Science Press, Inc., 27 East 62nd Street, New York, N.Y. 10021.) As brought out by several of the discussants, the question involves so many variables as to preclude a categorical answer about the effectiveness of psychotherapy taken in the abstract. Recognizing and dealing with these variables, it was suggested, is a necessary prelude to sound investigation of such effectiveness in concrete instances. Only then will it be possible to dispose of the skepticism of those who have raised questions about cures attributed to psychotherapy.

This serves as a reminder of the fact that the Freudian wish has to do with balked desires. Gratified desires do not occasion dreams–only the frustrated ones do. Nor did Freud regard *all* dreams as products of frustrated instinctual desires. In the dream of the grieving father, for example, repressed erotic urges were not included in the interpretation. It would thus be well not to restrict Freud's dream theory to balked sexual desires.

Instead, as a theory it may be said to provide for any strong or persistent desire. Furthermore, recall that such abiding desires give rise to determining tendencies or perseverative trends. Once introduced they make us reaction sensitive to whatever might be related to them. Thus the conscientious physician worried about a patient suffering from a rare disease will be set to notice any reference to this disease as he chances to glance through a medical journal. Similarly, a determining tendency renders candidates for public office vigilant with reference to the moods, interests, and prejudices of voters. Those absorbed in scientific research–to cite another example–may find their dreams influenced by their preoccupation with laboratory problems.

There is a striking instance of such a dream reported by the famous German chemist F. A. Kekulé (1829-1896). As a result of his dream he was able to suggest a solution to the problem of accounting for the structure of the chemistry of carbon compounds. This made him one of the founding fathers of organic chemistry. His famous theory of the benzene ring with its chain of six carbon atoms came to him in a dream in 1865. At the time he was writing one of his chemistry textbooks; hence it seems safe to say that he was predisposed to think about chemical themes and, of course, such a predisposition is but another way of referring to a determining tendency. At all events, from his own account of circumstances leading to the dream in question it seems obvious that he was engrossed in something related to the subject of his textbook, because after noting the trouble he was having with his writing he had this to say (Hadfield, p. 113):

> I turned the chair to the fireplace and sank into a half sleep. The atoms flitted before my eyes . . . wriggling and turning like snakes. And see, what was that? One of the snakes seized its own tail and the image whirled scornfully before my eyes. As though from a flash of lightning I awoke. I occupied the rest of the night in working out the consequence of the hypothesis.

The meaning of the dream with its momentous implications for chemical theory was immediately evident to Kekulé. For him there was no need to be concerned about the dream's latent content or to treat the snakes in the dream as phallic symbols. An active determining tendency had initiated a train of ideas in line with his frustrated wish to solve the mystery of carbon compounds. The resulting emergence of the picture of the benzene ring came from a mind prepared. Another way to put this is to say it came from a constellation of related unconscious ideas or related implicit non-sensory ideas.

The Kekulé dream is reminiscent of a dream once reported by a psychologist who had been confronted with this question: "What in your opinion was Freud's most outstanding achievement?" For some days he had been preoccupied with the question without a satisfactory answer coming to mind. Seemingly, the preoccupation in itself was indicative of an activated determining tendency, and for a few nights sleep was troubled by this vain quest for an answer to what had become an important question. Then, on one of these nights there was a vivid dream in which a picture of Freud appeared. In the picture Freud was sitting in a comfortable chair gazing up at a bust of Lincoln with admiring eyes and Lincoln was glancing down at Freud with affectionate approval. At the bottom of the picture there was this title: *Two Great Emancipators.*

REFERENCES

Adorno, T. W., Frenkel, E., Levenson, D. J., and Sanford, R. N. 1951. *The Authoritarian Personality.* New York: Harper & Brothers.

Boring, E. G. 1950. *A History of Experimental Psychology.* New York: Appleton-Century-Crofts, Inc.

Bühler, K. 1929. *Die Krise der Psychologie,* Zweite Auflage. Jena: Gustav Fischer.

——. 1951. "On Thought Connections." In *Organization and Pathology of Thought–Selected Sources,* translation and commentary by David Rapaport. New York: Columbia University Press.

Foulkes, D., and Fleisher, S. 1975. "Mental Activity in Relaxed Wakefulness." *Journal of Abnormal Psychology* 84: 66–75.

Freud, E. L., ed. 1961. *Letters of Sigmund Freud-1873-1939.* Translated by Tania and James Stern. London: The Hogarth Press.

Freud, S. *The Interpretation of Dreams.* Translated by James Strachey. New York: Basic Books, Inc.

——. 1915. "The Unconscious." In *The Standard Edition of the Complete Psychological Works of Sigmund Freud,* translated by James Strachey, Vol. XIV, pp. 159–215. London: The Hogarth Press.

——. 1922. *Die Traumdeutung.* Leipzig und Wien: Franz Deuticke.

——. 1934. *The Future of an Illusion.* London: The Hogarth Press.

——. 1938. *A General Introduction to Psycho-Analysis.* Translated by Joan Riviere. New York: Garden City Publishing Company, Inc.

——. 1938. "Some Elementary Lessons in Psycho-Analysis." In *The Standard Edition of Sigmund Freud,* Vol. XXIII, pp. 279–286. London: The Hogarth Press.

——. 1950. "On Psychotherapy." In *Collected Papers,* Vol. I, pp. 249–263. London: The Hogarth Press. (First published in 1904.)

Fromm, E. 1951. *The Forgotten Language–An Introduction to the Understanding of Dreams, Fairy Tales, and Myths.* New York: Rinehart & Co. Inc.

Guilford, J. P. 1956. "The Structure of Intellect." *Psychological Bulletin* 53: 267–293.

——. 1972. "Executive Functions and a Model of Behavior." *The Journal of General Psychology* 86: 279–287.

——. 1973. "Theoretical Issues and Operational-Informational Psychology." In *Contributions of Multivariate Analysis to Psychological Theory,* edited by J. R. Royce. London: Academic Press.

Hadfield, J. A. 1954. *Dreams and Nightmares.* Harmondsworth, England: Penguin Books, Ltd.

Hitschmann, E. 1973. "Telepathy and Psychoanalysis." In *The First Freudians,* edited by H. M. Ruitenbeck, pp. 101 120. New York: Jason Aronson, Inc.

Hollingworth, H. L. 1926. *The Psychology of Thought–Approached through Studies of Sleeping and Dreaming.* New York: D. Appleton and Company.

James, W. 1938. "Does Consciousness Exist?" In *Essays in Radical Empiricism,* pp. 1–38. New York: Longmans, Green and Co. (First published in 1912.)

Jones, E. 1953, 1955, 1957. *The Life and Work of Sigmund Freud,* Vol. I, Vol. II, and Vol. III (respectively). New York: Basic Books, Inc.

Lippmann, W. 1922. *Public Opinion.* New York: The Macmillan Company.

Locke, J. 1956. *An Essay Concerning Human Understanding.* Henry Regnery Company.

Loew, C. A., Grayson, H., and Loew, G. H., eds. 1975. *Three Psychotherapies–A Clinical Comparison.* New York: Bruner-Mazel.

Marmor, J. 1974. *Psychiatry in Transition.* New York: Bruner-Mazel.

McKeon, R., ed. 1947. *Introduction to Aristotle.* New York: Random House, The Modern Library.

Ornstein, R. E. 1972. *The Psychology of Consciousness.* San Francisco: W. H. Freeman and Company.

Rancurello, A. C. 1968. *A Study of Franz Brentano–His Psychological Standpoint and His Significance in the History of Psychology.* New York: Academic Press.

Rapaport, D. 1951. *Organization and Pathology of Thought-Selected Sources.* New York: Columbia University Press.

Royce, J. R. 1963. "Factors as Theoretical Constructs." *American Psychologist* 18: 522–528.

Titchener, E. B. 1929. *Systematic Psychology: Prolegomena.* New York: The Macmillan Company.

Tyler, L. A. 1973. "Design for a Hopeful Psychology." *American Psychologist* 28: 1021–1029.

Whyte, L. L. 1960. *The Unconscious before Freud.* New York: Basic Books, Inc.

Woodworth, R. S. 1939. "Imageless Thought." In *Psychological Issues–Selected Papers of Robert S. Woodworth.* New York: Columbia University Press. (First published in 1906.)

Index